JUSTIFIABLY PARANOID
Resisting Intrusive and Malicious Influences

Dr. Peter J. McCusker

INTRODUCTION 1

CHAPTER 1: Battlefields & Combatants..............................13

CHAPTER 2: Becoming Justifiably Paranoid......................21

CHAPTER 3: Influencers' Plans of Attack 35

CHAPTER 4: Thoughts & Feelings Make Us Vulnerable 55

CHAPTER 5: Mindsets Make Us Vulnerable 65

CHAPTER 6: Marketing Influence to Aspiring Influencers 79

CHAPTER 7: Values & Vulnerability....................................103

CHAPTER 8: Expert Intimidation..113

CHAPTER 9: What Influencers Usually Want 123

CHAPTER 10: "Good" & "Bad" Influencers........................139

CHAPTER 11: Politicians & Other Government Officials 157

CHAPTER 12: Media Controllers 171

CHAPTER 13: Celebrities 181

CHAPTER 14: Salespersons & Advertisers 197

CHAPTER 15: Educators 217

CHAPTER 16: Scientists 231

CHAPTER 17: Control & Choices 245

CHAPTER 18: More Than Mere Talk....................................255

CHAPTER 19: Conversation Under the Influence..............269

CHAPTER 20: You as Resistance Warrior 279

CHAPTER 21: Time Bandits' Assaults on Health................291

CHAPTER 22: The Future of Influence Has Arrived 301

CHAPTER 23: Brain Dissection & Re-programming............313

CHAPTER 24: You Ultimately Determine Your Influences 325

POST SCRIPT 345

REFERENCES 353

INTRODUCTION

There's a laser beam tracking the movements of the mind within your head, and someone is taking aim. The camouflaged sniper has positioned himself on a lofty perch, looking down on you. He thinks you are a soft target. Schooled in influence, he will do all he can to penetrate your brain, swaying your thoughts, feelings, and behaviors in ways that promote his personal goals.

The sniper analogy is apt. Many contemporary marketers hunt consumers whom they call "targets." One of the two most influential marketing books of all time is subtitled "The Battle for Your Mind" (Ries & Trout, 1981) and the first chapter of the other is entitled "Weapons of Influence" (Cialdini, 1984). Moreover, since targets require targeting, state of the art practice is called "targeted marketing."

Although targeting is not particularly new, many of the soldiers, weapons, and battlefields are. In the not-too-distant past, the assault troops' operations were low-tech—limited to unreliable pencil-paper calculations, direct experience, and intuition. Marketing soldiers of yesteryear were relatively naïve. Today's influencers have smart weapons in the form of supercomputers analyzing precise personalized data, and battalions of communications experts instructing them to choose every influence venue, parse every word they speak, and rehearse every action they take.

Democrats will tell you that Hillary Clinton lost the presidential election because of fake news, and Republicans will say that Donald Trump won despite fake news. In truth, most news is, and always has been, fake to some extent. Although I unwittingly might be lying myself, Napoleon allegedly said, "History is a set of lies agreed upon," and either Winston Churchill, or Hermann Göring, depending on whom you read, supposedly said, "History is written by the victors." Since history is old news, the comments about history are relevant and belong in the same category as "fake news" that, itself, is ancient. For instance, the Greek academic, Theophrastus, (287 B.C.) reputedly complained about fake news (Jones, 2017). Similar to what I said above regarding influence in general, what is new mostly is that fake news and lies of history now can be promulgated widely by virtually anyone with a computer. This variety of negative influences is so rampant that Kathleen Hall Jamieson (The Annenberg Public Policy Center of the University of Pennsylvania, 2017) coined a term to describe it: "viral deception." Harmful influences are harmful whether they are framed as history or news.

You undoubtedly know something about influencers. I suggest, however, that you need to know much more. And my job is to help you reach that higher level of awareness and combat readiness. As they say, "War is hell." You are at war, even when you are oblivious of that fact. To succeed in the influence war, you must know yourself as well as your adversaries do. Many of those who wish to exert control—from the Pentagon, to Madison Avenue, to Wall Street—have studied the *Art of War,* a 5th century B.C. treatise by the legendary Chinese military tactician, Sun Tzu. Among his most salient bits of advice was "If you know the enemy and know yourself, you need not fear the result of a hundred battles. If you know yourself but not the enemy, for every victory gained you will also suffer a defeat. If you know neither the enemy nor yourself, you will succumb in every battle." Influencers, especially malevolent ones, do their best to know you; you must know them, too.

Of course, not all aspiring influencers are your enemies. Some are well-meaning supporters, such as parents, teachers, and doctors who know you intimately and who truly have your best interests at heart. You accept that these "true-gooders" are being straightforward, authentic, and honest in their influence attempts. Other people are not so well-intentioned. The worst are unabashed psychopaths who frequently lie, threaten, or intimidate, and who would drain your last drop of blood without a second thought. These "exploiters" also comprise a small minority. Most aspiring influencers are neither true-gooders nor outright exploiters, but garden variety "manipulators." Your best interests are not primary for them, but they generally would prefer to avoid harming you. The manipulators often rationalize to themselves that they have something worthwhile to offer.

Manipulators want to know enough about you to facilitate their ends—nothing more. And they may be willing to give you a little to get a lot. Some manipulators pretend to be, or even regard themselves as, authentic true-gooders. This often is the case for politicians and others in similar power positions who self-righteously believe that they know just what is best for everyone. Sometimes the powerful overtly deceive or coerce their targets into behaving according to their standards, and sometimes they surreptitiously, proscriptively "nudge" them in that direction. Government officials are especially fond of more or less opaque nudges to "promote the general welfare." However, if general welfare truly is their end, they would do well to minimize nudges and maximize what Ralph Hertwig and Till Grüne-Yanoff (2017) refer to as "boosts" which are transparent, prescriptive influences, oriented toward improving the competence of targeted individuals.

Please note that I am not condemning all possible influencers or all possible influences. Influence is inevitable and essential. Humans never would have survived and thrived if they had been unable to influence each other by exchanging life-enhancing information. My gripe only is with destructive, intrusive influencers and influences. Ideally, one should be aware of influencers' efforts, and afforded the opportunity to decide which influences to follow and which to ignore. We all seek influencers from time to time, but the influence ideally is self-controlled and elicited, not external and imposed.

Imposed and intrusive communications can arise at any time. In fact, as I now am writing this book using Microsoft Word, the document, itself, is being hacked. Although I have not activated Facebook, and very rarely do, at the bottom right-hand corner of this document has appeared the following pop-ups: "Peter, you have 8 new notifications, 2 friend requests, and 5 messages. You have more Facebook friends than you know. Jenny Jones commented on Betty Brown's photo of you. Sara Smith is waiting for you to see what she posted on your timeline. Sara Smith has 228 friends." The pop-ups present me with a choice: ignore them, or respond to them. To respond means I need to disrupt my ongoing activity. To ignore means I risk having the intrusive messaging continue. To respond also requires me to google how to disable the messages, and then to do the disabling. I am right now choosing the disabling option to provide a real-time example of how I prefer to resist intrusive and malicious influences.

Now that I have disabled the Facebook pop-ups, it is time to resume where we left off. For purposes of communication let's agree on three terms, two of which are neologisms that I introduce here. "Influence" will be our common parlance word to describe all influences, irrespective of their value. By contrast, the newly coined terms "posfluence" and "negfluence" will designate helpful and harmful influences, respectively. Ultimately, a posfluence or negfluence is determined by outcome. For instance, if a true-gooder, such as a parent, influences you to buy a particular house, believing that you would get a great deal, you act on the advice and have a good outcome, a posfluence resulted, and if you accede and have a poor outcome, it was a negfluence. Conversely, if an exploiter advises you to buy the same house, believing that you would be paying far more than it is worth, a posfluence or negfluence also would result according to the purchase outcome, regardless of the exploiter's nefarious intention. The implication is clear: we cannot know if an influence will be positive or negative at the time that it is delivered. However, we can do our best to know who is attempting to influence us benevolently or malevolently, and respond to their efforts accordingly. To put meat on the bones of these ideas, let's think about a widely publicized influencer.

He Seemed Like Such a Nice Guy

The amiable, silver-haired 65 year-old gazed down from the New York City Lipstick building's 19th floor at 53rd and 3rd, watching people streaming below. His financial investment business was steady. He took pride in his many notable clients, including the Hong Kong and Shanghai Banking Corporation (HSBC), the Royal Bank of Scotland, Steven Spielberg, and Kevin Bacon. He considered his affiliations with a host of Jewish educational and philanthropic organizations especially satisfying. He had come a long way.

From lowly initial jobs as a lifeguard and sprinkler system installer, he had risen to become one of New York's most successful stockbrokers, the leader of a multibillion-dollar investment firm responsible for managing nearly five percent of the city's trading volume. Investors flocked to his door to reap a reliable ten percent or more annualized return. This was a man who knew how to stay ahead of the curve, implementing computerized trading practices soon after the technology became available. His impeccable reputation propelled him to the prestigious post of NASDAQ stock exchange chairman for three one-year terms.

On March 12, 2009, the man who had presided over the NASDAQ, Bernie Madoff, confessed to having lost at least fifty billion dollars of investor funds. He subsequently was convicted of investment, securities, and mail fraud, money laundering, false filings, and perjury, and on June 29, 2009 sentenced to 150 years in prison. One year later Madoff's son, Mark, committed suicide by hanging himself, and a little less than four years thereafter, a second son, Andrew, died from cancer.

Bernie Madoff possessed many of the most essential qualities of an influencer that we will discuss. Among other things, he was very likeable, authoritative, and well-connected. He used his affiliations to target and exploit those most vulnerable. Harold A. Pollack (2016) agreed, writing that "Madoff's victims were not a random assortment of the well-off; he decimated a segment of the wealthy Jewish community and several Jewish charitable organizations" and that "Such crimes would not have been possible without the cultural ease and social entre Madoff enjoyed in the Jewish community" which was facilitated by Madoff's himself being Jewish. Like most influence predators then, amiable Bernie knew his targets and their weaknesses, and he did not hesitate to exploit them. They, unfortunately, neither knew the real Bernie, nor his methods.

Justifiably Paranoid exposes the motives, tactics, and techniques of influence snipers and influence storm troopers of all types, and advises how to handle them. You will better understand influencers, their communications/messages, proffered objects, you as target, and less obvious features of influencing contexts. Because influence research and practices can be rather abstract and obtuse, I will provide concrete, practical examples to make information relevant and useable. As a psychologist, I know that applying bookish ideas to daily life—a notion subsumed under the scientific term "transfer of learning"—can be very challenging. Waging war requires real action in the real world; it is not an academic exercise.

Warriors, Prisoners of War (POW) and Defectors

To prevail in the battle for your mind, you must remain an alert, active warrior. Influencers often conduct surveillance and guerilla campaigns. You never can be sure where they will be, or what they will do. That is why you need to maintain a cautious, questioning, and skeptical attitude whenever someone offers items, advice, or direction. A warrior defends her/his independence relentlessly.

You must strenuously avoid becoming a POW. That sad outcome can result after you have fought the proverbial "good fight" against negfluence and were defeated, nevertheless. As disheartening as that might be, however, you would deserve credit for resisting, minimizing your loss, or, at least, gaining time. When the enemy does prevail, you might spend your POW internment planning to escape, and mobilizing resources against the oppressor. An example of POW negfluence victimhood could be your impulsively signing a manipulative contract, realizing your mistake, and struggling unsuccessfully to void the agreement. You were able to recognize your attacker, but too late in the manipulation sequence.

When the going gets too rough, rather than risk becoming a POW, some choose instead to defect to the opposition. The defection could be because you erroneously believe that the enemy is in the right. Or, you simply do not have reliable, valid information with which to counter his propaganda. The negfluencer could be a high-profile professional who readily overwhelms your opposition with a weltering barrage of "facts" for which you have no counter-information. Or, the defection could be because you fear the enemy's might, and try to defend yourself against being crushed by "identifying with the aggressor." That means your defense amounts to imitating or otherwise assuming the ideas and/or attributes of the threatening entity. Whether through lack of counter-information or by fear, as a defector you try to convince yourself that, given the circumstances, capitulation is the best course of action. Defection, for instance, might take the form of compromising your belief in compassionate mentorship after a powerful authority asserts that you are "too soft" with your subordinates, and commands you to pressure them to produce more on the job.

The prisoner of war versus defector distinction is one implied by Neil Postman in *Amusing Ourselves to Death*, published in 1985. In that work, he contrasted lessons present within two dystopian classics: George Orwell's 1984, and Aldous Huxley's *Brave New World*. Postman's Forward encapsulates the essence of his insight:

> Huxley and Orwell did not prophesy the same thing. Orwell warns that we will be overcome by an externally imposed oppression. But in Huxley's vision, no Big Brother is required to deprive people of their autonomy, maturity and history. As he saw it, people will come to love their oppression, to adore the technologies that undo their capacities to think.

> What Orwell feared were those who would ban books. What Huxley feared was that there would be no reason to ban a book, for there would be no one who wanted to read one. Orwell feared those who would deprive us of information. Huxley feared those who would give us so much that we would be reduced to passivity and egoism …This book is about the possibility that Huxley, not Orwell, was right.

If you agree with Postman, you might choose to maintain a warrior stance. And if, as we all do from time to time, you become a POW, you continually will resist, until eventually escaping your influence confinement. Hopefully, you will not adopt the role of defector who embraces what the influencer advises simply because it is the most expeditious and/or the most popular course of action.

I hope this book will be a catalyst that incites in you a "crystallization of discontent" (Baumeister, 1994) wherein unsolicited influences are concerned. That means that you, first, learn to recognize formerly non-obvious links between your unsatisfying thoughts, feelings, and behaviors and the negfluences that have been directed toward you, and then act to overcome those negfluences. To do so, you need to become acutely, consciously, and emotionally aware of the costs attributable to unsolicited, negative influences. And that connection sometimes is difficult to discern. For instance, imagine, Harry, an introvert who regards himself as an outsider at work and who relates positively with only one co-worker, Joe. That gregarious colleague repeatedly urges Harry to join him for a drink after work on the pretense of having an opportunity to meet "good people" there. So, Harry falls into a habit of accompanying Joe to Happy Hour at Washington, D.C.'s Bar Charley (5 p.m. to 12:30 a.m. on Mondays) where the cocktails are $6.00. Given Harry's penchant for alcohol abuse, however, his Tuesday work productivity soon deteriorates. And, because of his natural defensiveness, Harry clashes with his boss, Miriam, whenever she expresses dissatisfaction with his recent lackadaisical performance.

One Tuesday morning, after months of Happy Hours, Harry and Joe coincidentally meet on the elevator, ascending together to their office. For all to hear and laughing uproariously, Joe describes Harry's wild antics the previous night. Harry not only is embarrassed, but also is alarmed not to remember half of his reported foolishness. Entering the office, he passes Miriam who seems to have a severe expression on her face. Harry heads straight to the bathroom and vomits. He experiences a crystallization of discontent in which he realizes, literally on a gut level, that by accepting Joe's negfluence, he has paid a too-heavy price in health and job security. He, therefore, resolves to cross Happy Hours off his to-do list.

Making Influence and Time Work for You

Something always to keep in mind: whenever you are conscious of a potential influence, consider its possible implications over time. If you do accept the idea being promoted, or intend to buy the product being sold, how will that affect you both in the short- and the long-term? It could be a benefit in one time frame, and a detriment in the other. recognize that time frames have greater nuanced significance than merely short- versus long-term.

Carlo Rovelli (2017), an Italian theoretical physicist, teaches that time comprises five distinct but linked features. And those five can be critical for the ways in which time contributes to influences that impact you. First, the influence might exert its power by determining the **succession of events**, as when an earlier influence leads you to make a later negative decision. Second, the influence might affect the **interval between experiences,** as when an earlier influence causes you to delay and miss an opportunity for a subsequent related positive decision. Third, an influence might be central in determining the **duration** of a given decision's affect, as when an influence would have been helpful had you followed it for a week, but you continued following it for a year. Fourth, an influence might occur at a pivotal decision **moment,** as when you fail to seize a once in a lifetime opportunity that briefly presents itself. And fifth, an influence might serve as your **measuring device that defines duration** of a decision's effect, as when you realize that a person who faithfully telephoned you weekly for years begins calling only bimonthly.

Although any or all features of time can be important in any given situation, and sometimes the distinction among features is debatable, let's separate the five to consider the following concrete examples:

Succession of events—A colleague at your place of employment encourages you to skip a mandatory work training program to play golf with him. You do so, are not caught playing hooky, and suffer no immediate detrimental consequences. However, two months later, you unwittingly conduct business in a way specifically and explicitly forbidden during the training program. You cause a major loss for your company. You are chastised by your boss, become progressively surly, and within two months you are fired.

Interval between experiences—You always had run a virus scan on your computer every day. Your brother, a self-professed computer sophisticate, says that you do not need to scan more than once per month. You abide and, within a week, your computer is full of viruses.

Duration—You intuitively had concluded that it is best to soak your garden for 20 minutes before leaving home for a long summer weekend. The next door neighbor, who spent college vacations working for a landscaper, assures you that a 10 minute sprinkling is sufficient to produce optimal results. Arriving home on Sunday night, you find a garden of withered plants.

Moment—You had been waiting for months to buy a particular car, and remained intent on continuing to wait for the absolute best time. The automobile salesperson with whom you deal calls you on a Friday, saying that he heard a rumor that the car's price will be raised tomorrow. You are a bit strapped for money, but buy immediately to avoid the increased cost. Months later, the price still has not moved.

Measuring device that defines duration—How to determine whether you have exercised enough, that had been your concern. You would like maximal results, with minimal effort. The gym's personal trainer shows you a high intensity workout that he guarantees will enable you to reach your goal, if you do it for 10 minutes per day. Half a year later, a physical assessment reveals that you are less fit than you had been prior to starting the high intensity regimen.

In addition to Rovelli's five distinct, linked features of time, there is another potential time-oriented factor to consider—something I call the "cascade of unintended and/or unanticipated negative consequences." Everyone acknowledges the possibility of future unintended negfluences. Such unintended negfluences often are recognized in advance as possible negative future outcomes that one can take steps to avoid. By contrast, unanticipated negfluences simply cannot be known in advance. Worst still are cascades in which one unintended and/or unanticipated negfluence leads to another that leads to another, and so on. The more time that elapses between the original negfluence and subsequent vulnerable conditions, the greater the chance that the next related downward negfluence will not be recognized as having been enabled by a previous negfluence.

Regardless of time dimension or cascade risk, reading *Justifiably Paranoid* will equip you to understand and resist intrusive and malicious negfluences in their myriad forms. Camouflaged influence snipers and conservatively-outfitted storm troopers no longer will be able to penetrate your brain. Rather, you will be fortified to mindfully avoid, or rationally to accept, overtly or covertly proffered thoughts, ideas, and actions on your own terms. Posfluences will predominate, because, by the conclusion of *Justifiably Paranoid*, you will be praemonitus, praemunitus— forewarned and forearmed.

CHAPTER 1: Battlefields & Combatants

Your conscious brain is an organ designed by evolution to resolve conflictual situations. In the absence of conflict, like the brain of any other animal, it primarily operates via a series of automatic modules, independent of conscious control. To resist automatic unwanted influences, then, you must learn to introduce mild, tolerable **conflict** into influence situations, because conflict short-circuits the natural default of cognitive automaticity. Conflict virtually forces you to be mindful and deliberative, offering the opportunity to make informed, beneficial choices. Always, then, adopt a challenging attitude to any perceived influencer, whether animate or inanimate. That does not mean that you should be hostile or otherwise confrontational, but merely cautious and questioning. If the word "conflict" rubs you the wrong way, think in terms of "skepticism," a notion pioneered by the ancient Greeks. "Skepsis" means to investigate, and skepticism has at its core the conviction that we must suspend judgment, maintain criteria of truth, and question superficial appearances. Your readiness for conflict and/or skepticism massively reduces your vulnerability to unwanted influence. There is a well-accepted corpus of psychological research to support the idea that a person who is experiencing negative emotion makes more consciously thoughtful decisions than does one who is in a positive frame of mind (e.g., Chinander & Schweitzer, 2003).

Since human influencers usually know what you want, the greatest dangers are presented by ideas toward which you naturally are inclined. Resist that receptive proclivity: don't blithely, mindlessly accept from them what you would **like** to accept. Create a personal default tendency that seeks information or conclusions contradictory to what is being presented, especially when the information or conclusions seem obviously correct and consistent with your usual beliefs and orientations. Employ your best inquiring attitude and rational resources before you accept that which the influencer has presented. To become effective in that endeavor you must understand influence more thoroughly than the prospective influencer does. So let's get started in developing the necessary competences.

Influence Is Everywhere
As implied in the Introduction, influence is a regular feature of daily life; we are both influenced by others and we influence them. We know, too, that influence can have positive (posfluence), negative (negfluence), deliberate, or unintended consequences, and that persuasion is a special form of influence that also can have positive (prosuasion) or negative (negsuasion) consequences. In all cases, persuasion implies a deliberate process. Moreover, persuasion usually is executed verbally with the goal of encouraging a particular outcome. If the persuasion goal is to discourage a particular outcome, the conventional term "dissuasion" of course applies. Because I classified people who deliberately try to influence us as true-gooders, exploiters, or manipulators, when we attempt to influence others those terms describe us as well.

Although you can be an influencer, we primarily focus in this book on you as a target of influence and persuasion in all their myriad forms. True-gooders provide the least challenge. Although you might not always want what they are attempting to promote, true-gooders typically are persons whose influence is well-meant, and with whom you can communicate comfortably. You know them and their values. Such is not the case for exploiters and manipulators. You typically are unaware of their true, self-serving intentions, and uncertain how best to respond to their overtures. The situation is further complicated because both exploiters and manipulators usually are expert influencers with very definite self-serving goals. They have acquired the experience and have mastered the methods that enable them to get at least some of what they want from you.

Although anyone is a potential influencer, professionals warrant our closest attention. They are persons literally schooled in influence peddling. In alphabetical order, some of the most common are: Advertisers, Ambassadors & Diplomats, Authors, Behavioral Economics Specialists, Broadcast Managers & Staff, Campaign Directors, Celebrities, Communications Specialists, Copy Writers, Corporate Training Specialists, Creative Directors, Cultural Advisers & Liaisons, Customer Service Managers & Staff, Debate Coaches & Staff, Disc Jockeys, Radio, & Television Hosts, Human Recourses Managers & Staff, Journalists, Labor Relations Managers & Staff, Language Specialists, Lawyers, Legislative Managers & Staff, Lobbyists, Managers of All Types, Market Researchers of All Types, Marketing Managers & Specialists, Media Analysts, Media Planners & Buyers, Mediation & Negotiation Managers & Staff, Newscasters, Personnel Recruiters, Politicians and Staff, Producers and Directors of All Types, Psychologists, Public Information Managers & Staff, Public Relations Managers & Staff, Publicity Managers, Reporters & Correspondents, Religious Leaders, Salespersons, Social Workers, and Teachers of All Types. Seems only the butcher, baker, and candlestick maker are missing, and that merely underscores the ubiquity of professional influencers.

Even a quick browse of the list, however, suggests that some of the professions are more likely to attract exploiters or manipulators whose influence readily can inflict significant harm. Although I certainly am not saying that nefarious motives deliberately are promoted by any given training regimen, most Americans are especially wary of Behavioral Economics Specialists, Broadcast Managers & Staff, Campaign Directors, Celebrities, Communications Specialists, Copy Writers, Corporate Training Specialists, Customer Service Managers & Staff, Disc Jockeys, Radio & Television Hosts, Journalists, Labor Relations Managers & Staff, Lawyers, Legislative Managers & Staff, Lobbyists, Market Researchers of All Types, Marketing

Managers & Specialists, Media Analysts, Newscasters, Politicians and Staff, Public Information Managers & Staff, Public Relations Managers & Staff, Publicity Managers, Reporters & Correspondents, Religious Leaders, and Salespersons.

Everyone included on this abbreviated list is expected to and/or rewarded for changing the thoughts and/or feelings and/or actions of their targets. And the rewards to them commonly are money, power, prestige, and position—all highly prized within our contemporary culture. Moreover, for the most part, the aforementioned abbreviated-list professionals are the very ones who have the sophisticated computer systems and battalions of communications experts, mentioned earlier, that enable them masterfully to parse their words and execute their actions.

Since sometimes you are an influencer, presumably you want to use your influence for good. In fact, Dale Carnegie, a founding father of influence strategies in America, in 1936 released the first edition of *How to Win Friends and Influence People* to encourage everyday people to pursue prosocial goals. The book has been in continuous publication since its release and, according to Wikipedia, has sold a minimum of 30 million copies. The very first page of its 1981 edition advises:

> Eight things this book will help you achieve
>
> 1. Get out of a mental rut, think new thoughts, acquire new visions, discover new ambitions.
> 2. Make friends quickly and easily.
> 3. Increase your popularity.
> 4. Win people to your way of thinking.
> 5. Increase your influence, your prestige, your ability to get things done.
> 6. Handle complaints, avoid arguments, keep your human contacts smooth and pleasant.

7. Become a better speaker, a more entertaining conversationalist.
8. Arouse enthusiasm among your associates.

Whether one is an everyday person or a professional influencer, Carnegie's advice is worth heeding. As explained from the outset, influence is inevitable and can be an essential force for good. When it is applied properly, individuals and societies thrive. But influencers often have their own best interests at heart, not ours. When you are targeted in the battle for your mind, think Aristotle: "We make war that we may live in peace." (brainyquote.com)

In the Crosshairs
What causes anyone to be targeted by an influencer? There's no simple answer to that complicated question. Some factors reside within the self, a result of how an individual target thinks, feels, and acts. Volitional behavior is never due to a single factor, but, rather, is multiply determined. If I were to ask you why you go to work, you might reply, "To make money." But there are many other reasons as well. You may go because it is expected of you, it would be boring to stay home, you enjoy your coworkers, you are fascinated by the tasks that you confront each day, and so forth. Thus, when we attempt to explain behavior we must be mindful that we are choosing to focus only on what we believe to be one or more primary causes; we are not exhaustively describing all the contributing causes, and some of the non-primary factors may be important in their own rights.

Our explanations for behavior also vary in precision, from very global to very specific. If I observe a person who shouts "Not again!" and who simultaneously slams his fist against the table, some within-the-self explanations, ranging from global to specific, might be: He's in a negative emotional state, He's angry, He's angry because his current expectations have been thwarted, He's angry because he failed to perform in an area integral to his self-esteem, and He's angry because he has not resolved his sibling rivalry. Global explanations of behavior are likely to be more accurate and more reliable in cross-situation or cross-person comparisons. The challenge for global explanations, however, is to show that they can offer insights that are more than obvious. Although much more useful, specific explanations of any given person's behavior can only be rendered by someone who has intimate knowledge of the individual under consideration. Accordingly, presuming adequate introspection, you ideally are suited to decide what you have contributed to allowing yourself to be influenced. Of course, from the point of view of the target, some factors outside-the-self are central. Foremost are the influencer's reasons for choosing one particular person rather than someone else. His reasons, like within-self reasons, are multiply determined, and range from general to specific, as well. Similarly, if introspective, he, too, could gain insight into his reasons.

Everything said so far about your being in the crosshairs is fairly obvious. You know that some of your personal qualities, and some of the influencer's personal qualities must be factors in your being targeted. However, there is another large factor: you are a target because of the ways that your characteristics and the influencer's characteristics interact. That interaction frequently is central to the outcome. If you are targeted initially because you appear weak in some way and later are found to be strong, the influencer will be stymied. If you cooperate with an influencer because you perceive him as weak and he turns out to be strong, you will be victimized.

So, your personal qualities and the personal qualities of the influencer interact and contribute to your becoming a target. However, as you soon will learn, the persons within an interaction, and any institution linking them, comprise only one conjoint element of four primary influence vehicles. In addition to person/institution, the other three are: the object/idea (concrete item or abstraction that is being promoted), the situation (environment where the influence is provided), and the process (the timing and sequencing of influence). All four primary vehicles contribute in some degree in determining who is targeted by whom, and in the influencer-target outcome. That outcome can be a relatively straightforward consequence of the deliberate actions and intentions of the principals. However, sometimes the outcome results more from an emergent process than from any single actor, meaning that the four primary influence vehicles combine in ways not under the direct control—perhaps not even within the conscious awareness—of either target or influencer. When the outcome is emergent, then, it may be one totally unanticipated by either participant. For instance, the target unwittingly might become the one who influences the influencer rather than vice versa, or the influencer might exert far more control over the target than he ever had intended. This book regularly addresses all of the four primary influence vehicles, and the dynamics of target, influencer, and emergence.

CHAPTER 2: Becoming Justifiably Paranoid

Nobody wants to be paranoid. That literally would be crazy, wouldn't it?

Pathological paranoia certainly is nothing to be coveted or cultivated. Paranoids, by definition, are suspicious in the extreme. They relentlessly scan the environment, hyper-attentive to relatively minor indications of potential threat. Because they selectively attend to dangers, they often deliberately or inadvertently ignore positive features of their surroundings. Their perceptual and cognitive styles contribute mightily to lifestyle dissatisfaction. The paranoid person regularly employs maladaptive personality defenses, especially projections—attributing his own unacceptable, unconscious feelings to others. A frequently projection subtype is "projective identification" in which the paranoid is conscious of his unacceptable feelings but does not take responsibility for them, instead blaming their occurrence on a person or thing outside himself.

Because paranoids are suspicious and globally unyielding in their beliefs, they presume that others are intent on taking advantage of them, and remain continually alert to that possibility. David Shapiro (1965) explains paranoid thought in detail. According to him, paranoids are especially hypervigilant and resistant to perceived threats regarding their autonomy. Therefore, they tend to be proactively defensive, always scanning the environment for any potential threat, no matter how remote.

Paranoids strive to maintain control. They immediately challenge external information that contradicts their essential personal beliefs. When confronted with such contradictions, they search for arguments to challenge vigorously that which they don't believe. They think deeply about proffered unpalatable information, attempting to negate, or at least to degrade, it.

"Normal" people perceive suspiciousness as a personality defect. Some psychologists, in fact, regard trust as the human default position. Roderick M. Kramer (2009), for instance, refers to "presumptive trust," rationalizing that "Things seldom go catastrophically wrong when we trust, so it's not entirely irrational that we have a bias toward trust." That presumption is fine if we merely are interested in averting catastrophe, but averting catastrophe is not an especially desirable condition. The spouse of an abusive person may feel that she averted catastrophe whenever she is verbally, but not physically, assaulted. Averting catastrophe is a poor excuse for mindless presumptive trust, and an unreliable strategy for resisting professional 21st century predators of all types. We typically need time, experience, and reflection in order to determine who or what is trustworthy. Better to be a little paranoid than naively trusting.

A paranoid attitude certainly is appropriate whenever you are being targeted. Although we frequently do not know when and by whom we are targeted, some common circumstances usually warrant our wariness. Although you know most of those circumstances, let's enumerate a few now, and comprehensively address coping later:

Whenever you make a single decision or enact a simple action for the first time
Whenever you make a single decision or enact a simple action that is made to appear familiar to you (even when it is not really familiar)
Whenever you purchase an item
Whenever you contract for services
Whenever you take a course
Whenever you watch television
Whenever you attend a movie
Whenever you attend a play
Whenever you attend a concert
Whenever you speak to a politician

Whenever you listen to a critic of any kind
Whenever you read a nonfiction book
Whenever you read a fiction book
Whenever you read a newspaper
Whenever you read a magazine
Whenever you attend a club
Whenever you attend a home owner's association meeting
Whenever you attend religious services
Whenever you turn on your computer
Whenever you move to a new website
Whenever a streaming ad or popup appears on your computer

Manipulators

All's fair in love and war. Accordingly, in their relentless battle to control your mind, some influencers are not above subterfuge and sabotage. The ones that we are most likely to encounter are everyday manipulators. Therefore, let's learn the specifics of what such manipulators believe and do, so that you can understand them and resist their negfluence.

All professional manipulators begin with a distinct advantage: a plan that they have rehearsed and have previously implemented. Part of their plan is to subvert your defenses. Just as no football coach would restrict his game plan to offense, no manipulator would limit himself to offense via persuasion; he also wants to understand your resistance resources, and to take surreptitious steps to neutralize them. The manipulator's subterfuge and sabotage begin during your very first encounter with him, and are enabled by his robust offensive and defensive strategies and maneuvers.

If, like most people, you tend toward Kramer's "presumptive trust," automatically treating the influencer like a normal individual and presuming that he is being honest and straightforward, you have committed your first huge mistake. In face-to-face communications, you need to separate the transactional element from the interpersonal element. When an interaction is limited to a single interaction, or to few interactions, rather than to an ongoing relationship, you are more susceptible to being deceived. Savvy marketers are keenly aware of the power of relationship. Some of the best and worst influencers try to develop a relationship with you to increase their effectiveness. Those who instruct influencers encourage them to operate via relationship, instead of transaction. Mark Sanborn (2018), for instance, teaches marketers by contrasting the less valued elements of transaction with the more valued elements of relationship, as follows:

Transactional	**Relational**
professional	friendly
self-interest	mutual interest
what you get	what you give
stay in touch	keep informed
understand the process	understand the person in the process
judge the results	evaluate the relationship
win conflicts	resolve conflicts
agree	accept
evaluate results	evaluate how the other feels about results

Regardless of whether you agree with Sanborn's analysis, the more you know about what he and other marketing teachers are recommending, the better. Without a doubt, the transaction-relationship parameter is important to them and, therefore, is high on their instructional agendas.

During interpersonal situations of influence, which might be almost any interpersonal situation, it is, of course, appropriate to be kind and respectful to the person with whom you interact. In truth, all communications, to some extent, include both overt and covert transactional and relationship elements. The difference is a matter of degree. You must remain attentive both to the transaction and to the person. Some seemingly very pleasant, even well-known, persons can engage in very unpleasant and nefarious transactions. If your counterpart is a saboteur, acutely aware of your defenses and vulnerabilities, he will attempt to minimize the former and exploit the latter. How?

The manipulator tests you continually. Do you appear taken by him as a person? If so, he'll slather on the charm. If, on the other hand, you seem wary of his person, he will shift to being a purveyor of cold, hard convincing facts. Should you eventually lower your interpersonal guard, he subsequently might return to his charming persona. Reading you in real time, he quickly and seamlessly can shift focus between the interpersonal to the transactional, exploiting the more advantageous extant route.

Subterfuge

Trusting persons, of course, are perfect targets for subterfuge whose cardinal feature is covert, deliberate deception. There is subterfuge by commission in which the manipulator deliberately presents inaccurate information that prevents you from undermining her nefarious goal. And there is subterfuge by omission in which the manipulator deliberately refrains from revealing known information that would undermine her nefarious goal. Consider that subterfuge by commission occurs when a bogus for-profit training program promises you a "good paying job" immediately upon graduation, despite knowing full well that you will be lucky to find a minimum wage position. Think, too, that subterfuge by omission occurs when a salesperson gives you a teaser rate, but does not reveal that it applies only to the first year of a three year contract.

Sabotage

Whereas subterfuge primarily is covert, deliberate deception, sabotage is deliberate covert or overt obstruction or destruction.

Let's continue with themes presented within the two aforementioned examples: A saboteur would advise you to quit your current acceptable job in order to enlist you into an expensive, dead-end training program. Or, a saboteur would advise you into a high interest contract with a deeply hidden no-termination clause, cognizant that eventually you will be bankrupted. In either case, succumb to his influence and you end-up a very big loser.

Uncovering Your Defenses

How do people intent on subterfuge, sabotage, and other manipulation learn your particular weaknesses? In our Internet age, general information about psychological defense mechanisms is a mouse click away for anyone remotely interested. I googled "determining a person's psychological defense mechanisms" and in .57 seconds retrieved 4,430,000 results. Surprisingly, however, by adding the word "research" to the beginning of that very same search phrase, in .95 seconds I found 17,600,000. Those paid to advise professional influencers go beyond general Internet searches to learn and teach defense deciphering methods as an essential component of their profession.

Imagine that you hear from someone—anyone—that the stock market is on the verge of collapse. If you google "stock market collapse" you are sure to find someone sometime recently that predicted just such an event. Thereafter, whenever you check your electronic device, you will find some intruding information consistent with an imminent collapse. The shear relentlessness of the messages might spook you into selling your stocks prematurely. On the other hand, had your initial google been "stock market is ready to surge," your Internet experience would have been consistent with that perspective, perhaps prompting you to buy at the most inopportune time. The messages are proof that the creators of a google algorithm have targeted you for manipulation.

A Manipulator Guidebook

Manipulators have a plan that helps them anticipate how they and you will act. At minimum, that plan is guided by their direct past experiences and by well-practiced strategies. In full control of themselves, manipulators prefer to implement well-rehearsed scripts that they have debugged over time. One essential component is that they have learned how they usually are perceived by targets. Accordingly, they are prepared to implement past successful maneuvers and avoid past mistakes in order to counter any of your suspicions. However, the most effective manipulators also know how to improvise at a moment's notice, having learned the battle wisdom attributed to Field Marshall Helmuth Karl Bernhard Graf von Moltke (1800): "No plan of operations extends with any certainty beyond the first contact with the main hostile force."

The 48 Laws of Power by Robert Greene (2000) is a prime candidate for a manipulator's guidebook. Amazon.com characterizes the book as "Amoral, cunning, ruthless, and instructive, this New York Times bestseller is the definitive manual for anyone interested in gaining, observing, or defending against ultimate control." The strategies presented are ones that allegedly have been advocated by the most "successful" Machiavellians of all time. Since no one adequately can distill Greene's entire forty-eight laws in a few pages, below I merely categorize and explain them in ways relevant to our purposes here. The distillation is far from perfect, but its loose categorizations enable you to understand the 48 sufficiently. To make the actual laws crystal clear, they are italicized. For effect, I have retained the wording of the more ancient laws. Because the advice comes from multiple sources across multiple times, some laws superficially contradict other ones.

BEARING AND DEPORTMENT: Be *formless* so that you can morph into whatever you need to be in any given circumstance. R*e-create yourself* to fit. Construct your persona to satisfy *other people's fantasies*. Sometimes it is best *not to be perfect,* so as to present a common touch. Other times, *behave like a king* to inspire awe. In all cases, it is critical that you *cultivate a positive reputation*. Carefully *hide your misbehavior*.

ATTENTION: *Capture attention*. Sometimes you should *create spectacles*. Often it is best that the spectacles are ones that greatly *stir-up* the emotions of onlookers. *Ignore what you cannot have or achieve*.

CONTROL: *Timing* is paramount. Always engage at the right moment. For instance, you might employ *absence,* in an absence makes the heart grow fonder type strategy. Be *unpredictable,* particularly in an intimidating manner. The more you can cause others to *respond to your conditions* rather than to their own, the better. Finally, control your collaborative relationships by having helpers believe that *you do not really need them*, but rather that doing what you want is in their own *self-interest*.

DOMINANCE: *Act, don't just talk*. Present yourself as *performing effortlessly*. *Be bold* when possible. However, know when it is best to make *changes incrementally*. Become so prominent that *people follow you cult-like*. Because it usually is best *not offend a great man* or woman, consider becoming their *esteemed courtier*. On the other hand, if you can successfully *strike the shepherd, the sheep will flee*. And, when advantageous, consider *completely crushing the enemy. Concentrate your power* to maximize your ability to act quickly and efficiently.

PASSIVITY: N*ever outperform* the most powerful. In some situations, you might want to surrender, if that enables you later to *parlay the weakness into strength. Interpersonal mirroring* is another useful form of passivity by which you mimic a strong competitor to eventually outmaneuver him.

UNDERSTANDING: First *learn and then exploit the emotional and cognitive limitations of competitors*. Achieve advantage by *addressing the specific and special vulnerabilities* of each person. *Plan to the end point.* Know how to *quit when you are ahead.* Think for yourself, but *do not reveal your unpopular thoughts.*

CONVERSATION: Since knowledge is power, *the less you tell other people, the better*. Selectively *play dumb*. Most important, *conceal your true intentions*, and use conversations to say what you believe listeners want to hear from you. Use *others to complete important work, then explicitly and verbally take credit* for their accomplishments.

RELATIONSHIPS: *Do not isolate yourself. Keep people dependent;* induce them to *come to you* rather than vice versa. Know who is *happy and lucky*, and associate only with such persons. Still, you should *refrain from relying too much on friends*. Take advantage by *posing as a friend while working as a spy*. And be sure to *manipulate enemies to your advantage. Never make a firm commitment* to anyone. *Only accept from others that which you have earned.* On the other hand, *be generous and forthright* only when that approach facilitates your own goals.

Personal Insight

The 48 laws certainly do not explain all the methods employed by manipulators. Moreover, any influencer can use them, not just manipulators. Knowing the laws is useful if, and only if, you have a resistance strategy to follow. So, let's go there now by considering one approach, while limiting ourselves to the aforementioned manipulator categories of bearing and deportment, attention, control, dominance, passivity, understanding, conversation, and relationships.

Perceive

Resistance or compliance depends in part on perception. All sensory data must be interpreted, and interpretation means almost everything. You need to be acutely aware of what you are perceiving, a sometimes formidable task. Take in the influence scene in as much of its sensory complexity as possible. That means you must be fully alert and attentive. Be open to seeing, smelling, tasting, touching, and hearing to your maximal limits. If you cannot be fully "with it," then you should not subject yourself to an influence circumstance relevant to an important choice or decision. When you are tired, stressed, or otherwise sensory-compromised, you are extremely vulnerable to misperceptions.

Interpret

Presuming that you are able to take in the sensory information relatively correctly, you must interpret it. The interpretation will be specific to you. You must consider the meanings you attribute to each feature of the entire sensory experience. What aspects are important to you? Do you care mostly about the look, the smell, the taste, the touch, the sound, or, more likely, some combination of the five?

Integrate

The information not only is integrated in terms of the senses, but also in accordance with multiple aspects of your thought, emotion, and action tendencies. Accordingly, the idiosyncrasies of your thought, emotion, and action tendencies are as essential as your perceptions and interpretations. You might be one who relies more on thinking, or emotion, or action in making your choices and decisions. Moreover, that prepotent tendency to be guided more by thought, emotion, or action could be general, or merely specific to a particular extant choice or decision. You must "know thyself" not piecemeal, but in terms of integrated information accessible to you.

Deliberate, Remember, Act

Presuming that you do your best to accurately perceive, interpret, and integrate the raw sensory information, your choice or decision will depend on deliberation, memory, and action. Sometimes your choice or decision will be immediate, with no conscious deliberation or reference to a past memory. But, more often, you will have at least a dim, conscious awareness of a previous relevant choice and/or what determined it. Your level of impulsivity-reflection, a dimension of temperament, is an issue. As the words suggest, a reflective person is predisposed to careful deliberation whereas an impulsive one is quick to act. [You no doubt are aware that many merchants position products to encourage impulse buying.] However, anyone can behave like a "cognitive miser" who defaults to thinking that requires the least intellectual effort; it is not a matter of intellectual incapacity, but rather a propensity toward not thinking deeply enough (Toplak, et al., 2011). Moreover, regardless of your cognitive style, if you consciously reflect at all, retrieved memories can sway you in one or other direction. Because action is what ultimately matters in our decisions, I will be a little more detailed in this deliberation, memory, and action subsection than I had been for the above perception, interpretation, and integration subsection.

Deliberation requires data. So, what you get and where you get it are pivotal. Are you fully or partly dependent on the influencer for information, or do you have more objective, valid, reliable sources? Once you have quality data, what premises do they imply, and what conclusions seem warranted? Even when the accurate data, premises, and conclusions are available to you, they must be accessed at the time that the choice or decision is made. Because thoughts and feelings spin incessantly through your mind, you must stop the mental carousel at the proper locations. Moreover, unless the data, premises, and conclusions are fresh, their retrieval is only as good as your memory of them.

Psychologists refer to "prospective memory," meaning that you consciously intend to perform a mental and/or physical action in the future. The more prospective memory control you have, the better. Think, for instance, that you know you have a supervisor who regularly pressures you to perform a task that is not in your job description. Intending to resist his influence, you create a foolproof, elaborate story that you are sure will render his pressure useless. Research (Sellen, et al., 1997) suggests that, all else being equal, we tend prospectively to remember better when the setting for the action is more primary than is the time to execute the action. Our prospective memory also is usually better when the stimulus that triggers the relevant recollection is located closer in time to the situation that requires the intended action rather than further in time from it. So, you are more likely to remember your supervisor-resistant story when you practice remembering it in the room wherein you and he will meet and, ideally, at a time reasonably close to the time during which reciting the story will benefit you. In the best of all worlds, your prospective memory practices and implementations eventually will result in your developing an unconscious habit that makes it unnecessary for you to think prospectively in every relevant situation. Instead, the influence resistance will become automatic and less setting- and time-dependent.

As we all know, memory—prospective or otherwise— is often incomplete, flawed, and unreliable. Even under ideal circumstances, the more time that passes between your accurate processing experiences, the more prone you are to errors associated with your imperfect memory. But, as was true for misperceptions, your memory is worse when you are fatigued, stressed, or depleted. And, of course, stressed perception and memory problems comprise your decision making. Moreover, the type of stress and the type of decision determine the extent of your compromise. For instance, Nowacki and colleagues (2018) found that when stressed, men made riskier decisions than women did.

Suppose that your perception, interpretation, and integration of the raw sensory information and your deliberation and memory have been just right. You still need to act, and that means that the action has a temporal component. It is possible to act too soon or too late. Even if you address the current "pulling the trigger" issue, such as by having an effective prospective memory strategy, another time-relevant issue is worth your consideration: you need to think beyond the present, however that is defined. Will the choice or decision that you make at point X cause major problems or benefits at point Y?

Making good choices and decisions sounds complicated because it is. Of course, when choices and decisions pertain to trivial matters, you need not be concerned. On the other hand, it is the important choices and decisions that attract influencers because influencing those yield the highest returns.

If the influencing agent is a true-gooder, such as your parent, that's fine. When the agent is a manipulator, such as the proverbial corrupt used car salesman, you can be in real trouble. Moreover, the most pernicious influencers know how to manipulate your own personal choice and decision making. They initially accept your reasoning, and then work you back from it so that your conclusion becomes consistent with their goals,—a perverted process termed "motivated reasoning." To minimize that and other sorry circumstances, we next decipher tactics used by intrusive and malicious influencers

CHAPTER 3: Influencers' Plans of Attack

Executing Power and Applying Influence

To everyday people, influence connotes "gentle," and power connotes 'strong." That popularly held distinction is not lost on most manipulators who prefer to cloak their surreptitious tough power plays in the garb of what seems to be soft influences. Since to be seen as exerting power is to invite counter-power, power struggles, or retaliation, they much prefer being regarded as using influence, rather than wielding power. If you doubt for one minute the value that professionals place on knowing how to parse power and influence, you need only attend to the language that the Harvard Business School uses to describe their Course Number 2056:

> In this module, we will also consider how to leverage personal, positional, and relational power bases through influence tactics that fit individual and situational needs. We will learn how to understand our **"influence targets,"** [emphasis added] so as to tailor our approach accordingly. What motivates people to respond to influence attempts? How can you cater your influence approach to the different needs and preferences of those around you? How can you recognize when your influence attempts are not working, and how do you change approaches when this happens?

The eighty-eight words in Harvard's Course Number 2056 module description succinctly summarize the mission statement of virtually all those who teach professional influence tactics to persons aspiring to become professional influencers, or to professional influencers seeking to hone their skills. You need to be mindful of that mission statement whenever you are in the presence of professional people intent on swaying you in their direction. How are they trying to leverage their personal, relational, and power bases, and tailoring their presentation to make the leveraged power of their bases relevant to you? How do the professional influencers change their tactics when they are not working? Every one of their tactics—every manipulative statement and action—will be expressed overtly, at some point, in their strategies. That means that you have opportunities to recognize, and to evaluate, every one of their manipulative statements and actions. The tactics that professional influencers employ against you reveal something important about them, and about how they perceive you, themselves, and the relationship between you and them. If you can decipher their strategies quickly enough, you can defuse the intended influence, and maintain your autonomy.

The possibilities for being influenced are limitless, since vulnerability is determined by each target's unique qualities. For instance, our personality dynamics predispose some of us to be suckers for flattery and some to sell their souls for a buck. The influence professionals have conducted thousands of research studies, focus groups, and surveys to determine the best ways to influence the most targets. Dr. Robert Cialdini, Professor Emeritus of Psychology and Marketing at Arizona State University and founder of Influence at Work (IAW®) subtitled "Proven Science for Business Success," arguably is the contemporary world's most famous and most respected influence authority. His www.influenceatwork.com business website explains that in addition to providing keynote presentations at prestigious sites, he and his employees also educate Cialdini Method Certified Trainers who instruct companies involved with finance, pharmaceuticals, healthcare, national associations, government, law, information technology, consumer objects, media, and telecommunications.

Robert Cialdini rose to fame after the publication of *Influence: The New Psychology of Modern Persuasion* in 1984 whose fifth edition was released in 2008. Over the years, it truly has become the influence bible, largely because in writing it Cialdini methodically and comprehensively reviewed relevant research, distilled its essence, and presented it in plain English. In that seminal book, Cialdini explained that influence can be asserted by leveraging six major factors: liking, authority, reciprocity, social consensus, commitment, and scarcity. He consistently encouraged ethical application of his advice; however, as one would expect, that admonition probably has been embraced most by aspiring influencers who already are ethically-oriented. Over the years, many marketing-hungry professionals had encouraged Cialdini to update his book. Finally, in 2016, he completed *Pre-suasion: A Revolutionary Way to Influence and Persuade* that primarily emphasized the importance of establishing the pre-conditions that enable one to exert maximal influence. What Cialdini did not say is that despite his catchy neologism, variants of pre-suasion have been regular features of human influence since antiquity. For instance, teachers have used advance organizers before introducing a lesson to their students, salespersons have used prospecting and preparing before attempting to hook their customers, and prospective lovers have used flirting and courting before initiating moves toward the ultimate intimacy. Regarding the *Pre-suasion* book, the only truly noteworthy element that Robert Cialdini added to his original formulation was a seventh influence factor—Unity/Identity.

We regularly are reminded of the power of unity/identity as expressed in such popular notions as "identity politics" by which people lobby and vote according to their self-perceived identities, rather than according to objective realities. Not surprisingly then, the Washington Post (2018) employs Eugene Scott, an "identity" reporter who, in that capacity, pursues news from identity to issue rather than vice versa. On the one hand, Cialdini's original six factors had accounted for almost all that unity/identity explains. For instance, if you identify with someone or something, you probably like her/him/it (likeability), are committed to her/him/it (commitment), and look to her/him/it for feedback (social consensus). Despite some implicit redundancy, however, unity/identity is a factor so ubiquitous and culturally salient to warrant being addressed here as thoroughly as the other six factors.

The concept of unity/identity, like virtually any psychological concept, can be applied variably, depending on context. The elements that comprise your identity neither carry consistent relevance, nor equal weight. You can perceive yourself as a man/woman, husband/wife, son/daughter, father/mother, Democrat/Republican, American/Pennsylvanian, Christian/Jew/Muslim/atheist, athlete/scholar, friend/acquaintance, and so forth. The list, of course, is virtually endless. Some of those identity components always are more important to you, and some components are more important in certain contexts. Component features of your personal identity render you more susceptible to some influences than to others. The more you understand and deal with that, the better. For instance, if being a parent is central to your identity, you might readily be swayed to grossly overpay for an item that you believe will give your child an advantage, whereas you never would overpay like that for yourself.

Four Primary Influence Vehicles

So, your personal qualities and the personal qualities of the influencer interact and contribute to your becoming a target. However, as you soon will learn, the persons within an interaction and any institution linking them comprise only one conjoint element of four primary influence vehicles

Although the seven Cialdini factors can be packaged and delivered in many forms, we do well to consider them in terms of the four primary influence vehicles introduced earlier. You will recall that the first are **people and their institutions** ("human" influencer), the latter being a kind of personification of the people who populate them. Some persons and some institutions are very attractive and/or compelling to us and, therefore, quite likely to elicit our compliance. We are more inclined to accede to the wishes of a high status than a low status person. Likewise, we tend to accept medical advice written below a Mayo Clinic letterhead than from one written below a small, rural community hospital letterhead.

Objects and ideas (concrete item or abstraction that is being promoted) are the second primary vehicle. We often are impressed by an item that is shiny, sleek, and sturdy, whether or not those characteristics make a difference to decisions involving that object's essential function. Although the attitude is not always wise, people generally are more impressed by claims associated with a Mercedes Maybach S600 than with a Kia Soul Base, even if they have no clue as to their prices or qualities. Certain ideas also tend to be very appealing. If one is told that eating avocados reduces the likelihood of needing cholesterol-lowering medication, most people would give that idea careful consideration.

The aphorism "There is a time and a place for everything" succinctly summarizes the third primary vehicle: situation. For our purpose, think of **situation** (the environment where the influence is provided) as a gestalt or unified whole that uniquely involves particulars of the environment, influencer, and the target of influence. Consider the following situation: You not only need a new car, but you desperately need one. Your automobile precipitously "died" yesterday, and you have a series of critically important short trips that must be completed within the next week. You inadvertently disclose your desperation to the car salesperson who informs you that he has just the car you need, but its special sale ends tomorrow. "Coincidentally," the salesperson has a close relationship with a local car financing company. He can get you into that sales car within 24 hours, if you sign a contract today. So, in our example, the situation is ideal for the salesperson and inimical for the customer.

A given **process** (the timing and sequencing of influence elements) is the fourth, and final, primary vehicle. Sometimes the steps taken by an influencer are pivotal for his/her achieving their desired outcome. The process, for instance, might revolve around the timing of steps, or the dosing of that which is presented. Whether delivering a joke or a threat, the timing and sequencing of their communications can cause a would-be influencer to be applauded or assaulted.

As will be obvious, the Cialdini seven and the four primary influence vehicles can be combined explicitly, implicitly, consciously, or unconsciously. What follows are explicit examples of common ways that they are combined in our day-to-day lives.

How Influencers Combine the Cialdini Seven and the Four Primary Influence Vehicles

Liking

> Luscious, that's what she was. Walking along the
> beach, I saw nothing else. Uncharacteristically
> bold enough to speak I was. And amazingly, it
> worked. When she said she was hungry, I jumped
> at the chance to take her to lunch. Also unlike me,
> I chose the swankiest place in Malibu, and happily
> spent $170 to for food, drinks, and tip. When she
> realized the time, the lady explained that she had
> an important meeting and must leave pronto. We

walked to her car, a sparkling, new, red Porsche 911 Carrera S. After sliding into the driver's seat, she popped open the glove compartment, looked inside in horror, and said that her wallet was missing. Frantic, she added that her gas tank was virtually empty. I replied, "No problem" and offered her $50. Thanking me profusely, she jotted down her email address, handed it over, and asked that I contact her later that day. That was three weeks ago. I have tried emailing her five times. No reply!

Person/Institution

Influencers, especially during the introductory period, attempt to endear themselves to you. They present as attractively as possible. That includes efforts to be physically and interpersonally pleasing and likeable. Some even try to be coquettish and "cute," especially those of the gender opposite to yours. They are likely to be lighthearted and even joking.

Object/Idea

The object or idea promoted is presented as the best, the shiniest, the most durable, et cetera. Every effort is made to cause you to attend to the dimensions that the influencer accentuates, and to have you avoid thinking about aspects of the item or idea that cannot be hyped readily.

Situation

Environmental cues are carefully considered by the influencers. They are intent on putting you in the place that makes their object or idea most attractive. Sometimes they want you to be in your house, sometimes in their office, and sometimes in a posh resort.

Process

All professional influencers have a well-honed routine that enhances the likeability of their object or idea. For instance, they might try to control the sequence or timing of their interactions with you. After the smiles and jokes, they try to find some pleasant common link with you that they can use as a springboard to more self-serving discussions. Now that you are in a good mood and feel good about them, they attempt to transfer the good feelings to the object or idea that they are trying to "sell" you.

Social Consensus

> I don't know. I'm on the fence about where we should have the party. I don't want to spend too much, but I do want somewhere nice. I have these five brochures. Some of the places look real good. And two are pretty affordable. Where did you say the Campbells had their party? Actually, I did see that brochure too, but I put it aside. Much too expensive. The Schaefer's had their party there, too? Oh, alright, but we won't be able to afford to go out to dinner for several weeks.

Person/Institution

We all have been told, "Don't toot your own horn," so influencers know that they must be clever when they boast how important or popular they are. Many circumvent the challenge by having someone else inform you of how esteemed they are. When you are scheduling an appointment, for instance, the telephone receptionists might comment how "everyone in the neighborhood loves Bill." The influencer also could post a photo or article from the local paper in his office that shows him surrounded by smiling people similar to you.

Object/Idea

Of course, sometimes social consensus is object/idea, rather than person, focused. Influencers can provide free objects/ideas to trend setters whom they believe you prefer to emulate. A most well publicized, extreme version of this tactic is the decades' long tradition for fashion designers to gift or loan to actors clothing worth thousands, believing that the publicity is well worth the cost. Allegedly, the opposite even has occurred, such that "undesirable" people on television shows were paid to desist from wearing an object that they had been wearing previously.

Situation

Persons who share with you a common desirable characteristic have congregated in a space devoted to the influencer's object/idea. They are conversing in words and styles familiar to you, and they are buying what the influencer is selling. The place and ambiance is attractive and consistent with that which is important to you. You feel at home and inclined to do what others are doing in that space.

Process

The influencer ensures that you first are acclimated to the socially comfortable situation, feeling that you are among people like yourself. Next, he promotes his likeability and that of his object/idea. Perhaps you subsequently are provided some very palatable trinket or concept to get you into a receptive frame of mind. Only after all the other elements are in place are you subjected to the sales pitch that your compatriots also receive.

Unity/Identity

I don't really enjoy sports. I'm rather awkward, I think. It's not that I haven't tried. I just lack coordination. So I am not sure that I want to go to this weekend's family reunion. Everybody will be playing softball. Everybody always plays softball at our reunions. My people are sports nuts. Maybe I should stay home. You've known my family forever, Emma, what do you think? Should I go or sit this one out? I guess you're right; if I don't play, they'll mock me and make me feel like an outcast. You also are right about the fact that if I'm a Simmons, I gotta play softball at family reunions. That's just how it is.

Person/Institution

Influencers would like you to believe that you and they are kindred spirits. Much effort is directed toward driving that notion home. The influencer might announce that you and they are from the same home town, enjoy the same sports, or drive the same car.

Object/Idea

Whatever an influencer is trying to promote often is framed to be consistent with what he knows about your sense of self. If you are fitness-oriented, the object/idea is healthful. If you are religious, the object/idea is morally appropriate.

Situation

Some situations provide just the right ambience that aligns with you and your identity. If an influencer can locate you in the right situation, she can exert maximal impact. For instance, by accessing you at your workplace, the influencer can discover important features of your status there, how you perceive yourself, and how others perceive you. She then can use that information to customize an identity-consonant way to deliver whatever object/idea that she is trying to "sell" you.

Process

Like most influence techniques, identity/unity is most effective when it is incorporated into a comprehensive process. The more that elements of person, object/idea, and situation can be combined, the more effective the influence. If the influencer can encourage you to believe that you, he, his object/idea, and your situations are similar, your defenses will be lowered and you will be much more welcoming to that which is offered subsequently.

Authority

> Hey George, great to see you. Last week I mailed my fourth big check to Dr. Harry Lewis, an independent financial planner in New York City. I told you about him, a very impressive Wharton graduate and former consultant to the state employees union. You remember that he had been e-mailing me with leads for almost a year. Well, I finally found something appealing. This company, Synergistext, had an initial public offering at $15 a share that closed the first day at $21. Although he couldn't get me in from the start, I bought it on day five at $28 and by the end of the week it was $30. The stock has been going straight up. Last week I sent a check for 500 shares at $33 each. You should jump in while you can afford it. What? What Wall Street Journal article are you

talking about? The Synergistext stock just did
what this morning? I'm screwed!

Person/Institution

Influencers want you to regard them as experts. Toward that end, they often tactfully cite their education, experience, and success. You can be sure that they will try to mention their association with some highly esteemed person or organization. In addition to overt authority-relevant credentials, they might employ more subtle signs, such as exhibiting some item that includes a logo from a prestigious institution.

Object/Idea

In addition to or in lieu of authority-relevant credentials related to their person, the influencers might present such authority signs that pertain to the object/idea that they are recommending. Thus, they could say, "This is the very same computer software used by most Ivy League schools."

Situation

Also pivotal is the environment wherein the object/idea is embedded. Realtors prefer to meet you at the house that they are brokering so that they can underscore and elaborate its valued features. Travel advisors like you to come to their office where they immerse you in a dazzling world of travel posters and exotic souvenirs suitable for aristocrats.

Process

Although the influencing process almost always is critically important to the aspiring influencer, sometimes it is difficult for you to discern. An exception is the approach by most sellers of home improvements. First they insist that you and your spouse must be present for the session. And then they methodically proceed page by page through their propaganda material, dissuading your questions until they have concluded their entire pitch. Insurance agents characteristically follow the same rigid sequence.

Reciprocity

> You surprised me by volunteering on a Saturday
> to help me paint the garage. I know how much you
> like to golf on Saturdays and the weather is
> beautiful today. But I've prepped the garage well,
> and this only should take us about an hour or less.
> Let's start with the ceiling. I'll grab a couple
> extension poles so we don't have to strain our
> backs. As you can see, I never bothered to paint it,
> so I figured that it's about time. Yours isn't
> painted either is it? That's what I thought. I
> certainly would be glad to help you do it if you
> want to paint your place. Oh, you would prefer
> that I help you build a wraparound deck on the
> back of your house . . . . I guess I could.

Person/Institution

In everyday parlance, reciprocity is straight forward: You scratch my back and I'll scratch yours. If you mow my lawn this week, I'll mow yours next. But who goes first? Who initiates the reciprocal process?

Influencers know how to play the game. They know that reciprocity most often occurs without any pre-discussion, even without any conscious awareness. They know that if they do the good deed first, you will be beholding to their later request. Therefore, the influencer always goes first so that his is the one in control. You then are expected to treat the "nice" influencer nicely, acceding to what he wants, even if it exceeds what he had done for you.

Object/Idea

Similarly, most manipulators understand that reciprocation, especially an unconsciously determined reciprocation, need not be strictly equivalent in value. A smiling car salesman might give you a free tinted windshield upgrade, and later expect you to overpay for the brand's most expensive tires, hubcaps, and interior accessories. Of course, it is noteworthy to add here that the free strategy derives its power from more than reciprocation. All salespeople know that most consumers are drawn to "free' no less ravenously than Great White Sharks are drawn to blood. Case in point are today's omnipresent "free" apps. You can be sure that those apps exact their own costs, however, mostly in the form of mining your personal information. Thus, the admonition, attributed to Tim O'Reilly (quoteinvestigator.com), stands: "If you are not paying for it, you're not the customer; you're the product being sold."

Situation

Did you ever receive an invitation to a free buffet where you will be educated about something or other? This is a favorite venue for some financial advisors. They require you to complete a number of questionnaires, schedule a "complimentary" follow-up one-on-one interview to review of your finances, and then provide a decent meal. How could you resist your host's "simple" requests, when you, figuratively speaking, are in his kitchen waiting to be served?

Process

Reciprocity proceeds in a sequence. Already noted is that the influencer strives to give first so that the target will feel compelled to give later. The person who goes first determines the timeline and sets the standards. Continuing with the buffet example, the influencer gave you his time and he spent his money on your behalf. If you subsequently resist his proffered meeting or other simple requests, he is "entitled" to continue to press you to comply. He might "justifiably" ask for your phone number so that that he can call later to offer an appointment time more acceptable to you

Scarcity

> If you hold on just a minute, I will get that silver Bluetooth speaker you want . . . Uh oh, there are none on the shelf down here below the counter. I'll have to go into the rear storeroom. What? Yeah, I'm sure there's a silver one back there . . . . Sorry you had to wait so long. I looked all over and there's no silver one. In fact, all the speakers are gone. I can't believe it. We had a bunch yesterday. The next shipment probably will arrive in about 10 days. Sure, I'll see if I can get one at our other store . . . . So, I called. It's their last one and it is the premium model. If you want it, it will be almost double the price of the one that you asked about. It's up to you.

Person/Institution

As noted earlier, the influencer wants you to see her as an authority. That exalted status is only enhanced if you believe that she will not always be available to you. Therefore, don't be surprised if you are told that the influencer has a limited time window. Similarly, you might be advised that she is in such heavy demand that you must make a commitment today in order to be entered into her schedule. To soften the interpersonal challenge, the influencer could say that it is not she, but her team or boss who is responsible for her relative unavailability.

Object/Idea

Accessibility to objects/ideas also is manipulated by influencers. Most of us have experienced that object/idea scarcity maneuver firsthand. All sales are time-limited by definition. We regularly see a "while they last" sale sign next to an item promoted as a big bargain. When an idea, rather than a concrete object, is the sought after item, the influencer might present it as privileged information whose value is contingent on your quickly acting upon it. The "hot tip," for example, could be related to a stock purchase, home sale, or dramatic impending change in the law that soon will limit you future opportunity.

Situation

Where you are influenced can highlight your perception of scarcity. Suppose you want to buy new hardwood flooring and need guidance. You call your favorite home store to determine what would be best. Imagine that the salesperson asks you to visit so that he can present a wide range of options. Further suppose that he schedules your visit during his busiest time to impress upon you how popular his objects are. Having seen what is available, you equivocate about making the purchase. In the situation of a crowed showroom, the salesperson can credibly say or imply that the material might not be available if you do not seal the deal today.

Process

Manipulators can increase scarcity via the process by which an object/idea is presented. The old "bait and switch" is one such strategy. You have been searching for a particular popular, yet affordable, car model and finally have found an advertisement for just that car. When you arrive at the dealer, however, you are told that they sold the last one an hour ago, and they have no idea when another will arrive. The salesperson adds that they only had two cars at the advertised price and don't anticipate being able to duplicate it in the future. When you express your disappointment, he agrees to call other dealers but, of course, only finds a "slightly more expensive" version of your coveted car. He then adds that the car is the "last one" so you must buy it quickly or risk missing out again.

Commitment

> You know that I am in total support of getting the legislation passed. I already have donated to fund its lobbying effort, and that should count for something. I don't know about working at the campaign office Wednesday, Thursday, and Friday night. I have to check to see whether I can change a couple things before I give a definite answer. Are you kidding? Bill promised that he would cover this week. How could he back out at the last minute? Alright, you can count on me for Wednesday and Thursday, at least. But I just can't say about Friday until I look at my current schedule.

Person/Institution

Later we will discuss in greater detail the "foot in the door phenomenon," meaning that influencers who convince you to permit them a brief initial entrée are more likely to get you to give them more later. "I only need a minute of your time" is a typical request. Then the minute turns into an hour. Please realize that you usually expend much less energy short-circuiting the beginning an unwanted engagement than terminating an interaction already in progress.

Object/Idea

Instead of creating a new commitment, an influencer might prefer to take advantage of your extant commitments. The more they know about you and your preferences, the better they can manipulate them. The influencer wants you to believe that her object/idea is perfectly continuous with your other objects and ideas in order to appeal to your desire for consistency. If what they are peddling is not obviously like what you prefer, they are adept at finding some shred of similarity upon which to build. For instance, if you always have bought a Ford, the Chevy salesperson could frame his Chevy as "a U.S. company, just like Ford. When you buy a Chevy, you still are buying American, like you always do."

Situation

If you want to encourage people to donate money for children's sports, hold a fund raiser on a dilapidated basketball court where you ask for a "small donation" sufficient to replace its two poles, hoops, and nets. After that is completed, re-contact the contributors, thank them for their participation, and request that they assemble to observe the improved court. At the assembly, ask for additional money to resurface the court's blacktop. Those who had given initially almost certainly will want to maintain their participation in order to see the project completed.

Process

The above example shows the value of locating donors and prospective donors at the site of their good works to influence them to commit. However, it also illustrates the benefit of process for commitment. After donating once, the attendees are more inclined to donate again. Professional influencers know that every donation primes a subsequent one, and having you onsite further increases the likelihood of your making another donation.

Conclusions

So there you have it: the bedrock seven Cialdini principles of marketing combined with the four primary influence vehicles. Knowing them makes you a most formidable warrior in the battle against influencers. The seven undoubtedly are the most widely taught, studied, and applied. And the four are present, to some degree, in virtually every influencer scenario. However, the Cialdini principles in no way exhaust all possible influence strategies. We will address a host of other factors offered by first tier theorists and researchers other than Cialdini that are used to persuade and to otherwise influence. Because expert influencers' advice overlaps in places, when I introduce a given expert's ideas, absent any compelling reason to do otherwise, I will not dwell on what I already have attributed to someone else.

CHAPTER 4: Thoughts & Feelings Make Us Vulnerable

The power of influence largely derives from the ways that it appeals to our cognitions and emotions. Professional influencers have clear, specific goals that they hope to achieve. They first strive to seize your attention. Then they seek to prepare you cognitively and emotionally to receive their message before they begin to deliver it. Once that is attained, they want to ensure that your frame of mind continues to remain as fully consistent with their goals as possible. In the language of psychology, that means the influencer offers "advance organizers" intended to create in you an enduring "mental set" that renders you continually susceptible to them. Further, because the influencer knows that his likelihood of success depends on how you align with him, he wants to make you feel that he values you. To do so, he might appeal to any of your thoughts and/or emotions. In the present chapter, we look at your mental functions that can be manipulated by those who want to exert their control, and how they might do so.

Attention
Most of our mental functions are steered by attention—attention that can be deliberate or incidental. "Attention capture" is a marketer's first objective. They understand our primitive orienting response by which we turn our attention to a sudden and/or distinctive environmental stimulus. For instance, in the recent past, we all noticed that television commercials typically had broadcasted louder than the shows that they accompanied. After a citizen revolt, the United States government passed the Commercial Advertisement Loudness Mitigation (CALM) Act. However, on their website, (https://www.fcc.gov/consumers/guides/loud-commercials-tv), the current Federal Communications Commission (FCC) rationalizes that "Some commercials with louder and quieter moments may still seem 'too loud' to some viewers, but are still in compliance because average volume is the rule. The FCC does

not monitor programming for loud commercials. We rely on people like you to let us know if they think there's a problem. If you have experienced what you believe is a violation of the rules regarding the loudness of commercial TV ads, you may file a complaint with the FCC at no cost." Whether watching television or strolling the avenue then, we ultimately are responsible for deciding how we direct our deliberate attention. That is a first step in maintaining control of our decision making. Individuals who deliberately attend to every new stimulus, fad, or circulating meme will find plenty of reasons to be influenced. Incidental attention, obviously, is less amenable to conscious control, but not totally intractable; we manage it by confining ourselves, as much as possible, to non-coercive places, people, and information. The more we position ourselves in open settings populated by open people, the more we can maintain and express our own opinions, and rationally evaluate the external influences exerted upon us. When we are in closed settings populated by chauvinistic people, we are less prepared and less inclined to resist their influences.

Framing
This concerns the parameters that we place around the influences to which we are subjected. For instance, if we frame meeting an individual of a higher status as an opportunity to emulate them, we may devalue aspects of our own uniqueness. On the other hand, if we frame the meeting as a narrow opportunity to achieve some specific, previously identified outcome, we both can accept our own overall value, and the value of the high status person that motivated our meeting with them. In all cases, your susceptibility to influence is contingent upon the frame with which you perceive the potential influencer.

Familiarity
Does familiarity increase or decrease the influence that others exert upon you? An old adage advising that "familiarity breeds contempt" finds some support in research by Michel I. Norton

and his associates (2013). After exploring the issue, they conclude that it not uncommon for increased familiarity to cause less liking. That conclusion can be explained at least in part by recalling and extrapolating from Roderick M. Kramer's belief that trust is the human default position.

Let's assume that you meet someone for the first time. In that situation, you and he presumably would engage in courteous, pleasant interaction—a default both of trust and conviviality. You are looking for reasons to "like" him, and are inclined to focus on your compatibilities. Non-compatibilities probably would be avoided and/or minimized. This scenario is common in many influence situations; influencers know and exploit it. Often they only need to relate to you for a brief time to get you to sign on the dotted line—literally or figuratively—and thus achieve their purpose.

With repeated exposure, however, perceived differences accumulate. The more differences that you know, the more potential for moving from extant trust and conviviality to disagreement and disliking. That, of course, does not mean that you no longer "like" the person, but perhaps that you like him "a little less" than previously.

My recommendation from the start of this book has been that you enter into new or otherwise vulnerable influence situations with an attitude of mild, tolerable conflict, or at least skepticism, in order to short-circuit the trust default. Trust clearly is a laudable goal. However, we must make a conscious effort to reign in trust, so that automatic liking does not prevent us from critically evaluating what is and is not right for us as unique individuals. Better to pause and take time to evaluate an influencer than to quickly capitulate to their implicit or explicit requests.

Cognitive Dissonance

If, like Norton, you believe that trust is the proper default when dealing with people, you might be reluctant to accept my advice to introject mild, tolerable conflict and/or delay into your influence situations. In psychological jargon, presumably that means that you are experiencing cognitive dissonance between how to handle interpersonal trust versus mistrust. That is precisely what influencers hope. They want you to be in the automatic acceptance mode, not the automatic skeptical mode. Whatever a communicator or communication can do to get you into trust default makes their influence task immensely easier.

Any conflict between what is and what we thought can occur for better or worse, as when we are pleasantly surprised or sadly mistaken. Therefore conflict need not always be a bad thing. You learn important information about yourself and your sources of influence by carefully processing both positive and negative dissonant events as learning opportunities. When the surprise is that the influence turns out to be "better" than we thought, we need to have the integrity to revise our expectations of it. And when the surprise turns out to be worse than we thought, we need to have the courage to revise our expectations of that as well.

Hedonic Treadmill

Since influencers are in the business of changing your thoughts and behaviors, if you are content with the status quo, you usually are less susceptible to them. Many professional influencers know about the crystallization of discontent, discussed earlier, and will use it against you if they can. Marketers and salespersons, for instance, want you to believe that your clothes are out of fashion, your car is technologically limited, and your house is too dated. Prospective influencers might create a vivid story, animating the limitations of your status quo. Then, having incited discontent within you, they propose their tried and true solutions, promising to provide for you what you "truly" need to be satisfied.

The influencers exploit our common human tendency to become disenchanted over time with the way things are. All people tend to run on a hedonic treadmill in that we readily acclimate to our current circumstances and possessions; what had pleased us formerly soon becomes uninspiring. Failing to appreciate what we have, we focus instead on that which we lack. We itch for some sort of significant change. Counting our blessings is a proven remedy to the hedonic treadmill. Let's stop running to nowhere. Instead, start counting blessings, and keep counting.

Bad Is Stronger Than Good
Interference from our hedonic treadmill tendencies is merely one feature of a more pervasive human propensity that interferes with our ability to resist influencers. Roy Baumeister and his colleagues (2001) illuminated one of these cognitive predilections: the unfortunate truth that, in general, "bad is stronger than good." According to them,

> the greater power of bad events over good ones is found in everyday events, major life events (e.g., trauma), close relationship outcomes, social network patterns, interpersonal interactions, and learning processes. Bad emotions, bad parents, and bad feedback have more impact than good ones, and bad information is processed more thoroughly than good. We are more motivated to avoid bad self-definitions than to pursue good ones. Bad impressions and bad stereotypes are quicker to form and more resistant to disconfirmation than good ones. Various explanations such as diagnosticity and salience help explain some findings, but the greater power of bad events is still found when such variables are controlled. Hardly any exceptions (indicating greater power of good) can be found.

Evolution theorists believe that the natural human tendency toward pessimism kept our ancestors alert to potential dangers and, therefore, promoted their survival. So, we descendants of survivors all inherited that pessimistic mindset. As the old saying goes, "Better safe than sorry."

Taken together, these findings do support "bad is stronger than good" as a general principle across a broad range of psychological phenomena. In influence situations, fear of the bad often trumps striving for the good. Some people fail to resist voluble persuaders because they are so intimidated by the prospect of saying the wrong thing, looking foolish, or being considered behind the times. In other cases, the fear is not related so much to the persuaders, but to their anxiety-arousing messages. For instance, soon after I enrolled into a Mutual of Omaha medical insurance program, I received a solicitation encouraging me also to apply for separate cancer insurance, and another solicitation for life insurance that advised in bold print: **"This is your Last Chance, Peter McCusker, Don't lose this opportunity to take good care of your loved ones."**

So, we cannot just blame influencers, including the media, for the fact that counting our current blessings is easier said than done. We must work explicitly to combat the "natural" pessimism that lurks within us. Just as social support makes smoking cessation or alcohol cessation more achievable, success in maintaining one's personal preferences will be more achievable if we do two things: First, we need to engage with like-minded others who are determined to maintain their own opinions regardless of external influences, including fear-mongering influences, and, second, we must accept that maintaining an internal locus of control requires sustained effort. Locus of control will be elaborated and emphasized later, as it arguably is the single most important personality trait that determines own vulnerability to influence. For now, be aware that locus of control refers to self-directedness, and that those with a strong internal locus of control tend to be conscientious and independent, while those with a strong external locus of control tend to be anxious and dependent (De Fruyt et al., 2000). Many important behavioral consequences have been linked to locus of control. For example, research (Lachmann, et al., 2017) suggests that persons addicted to the smartphone and/or the Internet evidence low self-directedness; that is, they have a strong external locus of control.

Broaden and Build versus Narrow and Destroy
Although bad might be stronger than good, positive definitely is better than negative regarding health and interpersonal satisfaction. No one has explained this any better than the "good" not "bad" psychologist, Barbara Fredrickson. According to her University of North Carolina Positive Emotions and Psychophysiology Lab web page:

> Central to many existing theories of emotion is the
> concept of specific-action tendencies – the idea
> that emotions prepare the body both physically
> and psychologically to act in particular ways. For
> example, anger creates the urge to attack, fear
> causes an urge to escape and disgust leads to the
> urge to expel. From this framework, positive
> emotions posed a puzzle. Emotions like joy,
> serenity and gratitude don't seem as useful as fear,
> anger or disgust. The bodily changes, urges to act
> and the facial expressions produced by positive
> emotions are not as specific or as obviously
> relevant to survival as those sparked by negative
> emotions. If positive emotions didn't promote our
> ancestors' survival in life-threatening situations,
> then what good were they? How did they survive
> evolutionary pressures? Did they have any
> adaptive value at all?

Barbara Fredrickson developed the Broaden-and-Build Theory of Positive Emotions to explain the mechanics of how positive emotions are fundamental for survival. According to the theory, positive emotions expand cognition and behavioral tendencies. Taking issue with the view that all emotions lead to specific action tendencies, the theory argues that positive emotions increase the number of potential behavioral options. Emotions should be cast as leading to changes in "momentary thought-action repertoires" —a range of potential actions that the body and mind are prepared to take.

When applied to decision making, the expanded cognitive flexibility evident during positive emotional states results in resource building that becomes increasingly useful over time. Even though a positive emotional state is only momentary, the benefits last in the form of traits, social bonds, and abilities that endure into the future. The implication of this work is that positive emotions have inherent value to support your self-determination and, therefore, your decision making.

Frederickson's theory and research prepare us for the distinct likelihood that honest dialogue with an influencer will not necessarily cause them to relent in the short-term, since compromise and seeing another's point of view usually is not what they are after. In fact, honest discourse might even cause a brief period of increased tension with a persuader who has no intention of permitting you to resist his views. But, I agree with Barbara Fredrickson that, in the long run, positive emotions win out by enabling you to counter the opposition that often arises when you maintain a justifiably paranoid stance vis a vis persuaders. You can demonstrate that your "paranoia" is benign, if you present your skepticism and defensiveness with a positive demeanor.

Suppose that you are being pressured to buy a more expensive, higher end item, when you had intended to get a lesser, more affordable one. Empowered by your calm, confident positive state, without arguing, apologizing, or dwelling on the issue, you can acknowledge the admirable features of the expensive one, and then briefly and firmly reiterate your decision, permitting no room for further discussion. Case closed.

Leveling-Sharpening
Consider this a kind of arithmetical-geometrical understanding of influence elements. Leveling is a process by which we look at two disparate things, focus on their commonalities, and decide that they basically are similar. Depending on our framing, we can level virtually any two items: A whale is like a shark: both are sea creatures. A Mercedes is like a Ford. Both are cars. Sharpening is the inverse of leveling: A whale is nothing like a shark. A whale is a mammal and a shark is a fish. A Mercedes is nothing like a Ford. A Mercedes is luxury, comfort, and performance. A Ford merely is basic transportation.

Influence peddlers and their propaganda regularly employ leveling-sharpening toward their narrow self-serving ends. When they discover our preference, they attempt to link their message to it, leveling the two. And when they realize that we associate their position with something toward which we are averse, they try to disassociate from it, sharpening the distinction between the two.

The plane geometry of leveling-sharpening is plainly true: When in the presence of influencers, we sometimes need to level differences that they try to sharpen, and sharpen differences that they try to level. More often than not, the leveling-sharpening distinction is a matter of opinion and preference. Your opinions and your preferences need to be primary, not those of the influencer.

CHAPTER 5: Mindsets Make Us Vulnerable

We all have our own characteristic styles of interpreting the world. Those styles predispose us to some influence strengths and some influence weaknesses. The following three interpretation styles are especially important and common, and deserve your consideration.

Self-serving Bias

Self-serving bias is pervasive and critical in our lives. In short, self-serving bias refers to our inclination to recognize, remember, and act upon that which we already believe. To elaborate, I begin mostly by paraphrasing the report of Thomas Shelley Duval and Paul J. Silvia in the Journal of Personality and Social Psychology, January 2002. Contained within their work, but not specifically mentioned by them, is the locus of control concept that I introduced earlier.

Duval and Silvia suggest that our self-serving explanations typically involve internal attributions for success, and external ones for failure. However, while psychological studies consistently show the expected internal attribution for success, some research finds internal attribution for failure as well. The manner in which the self-serving bias plays out certainly has major consequences for decision making.

In essence, Duval and Sylvia assert that the self-serving bias is modulated by two psychological mechanisms—a system that sets personal standards and a system that evaluates personal responsibility. The more we focus on ourselves as the responsible agent, the more we are inclined to claim credit for success—an internal locus of control. A self-focus coupled with an accompanying ability to improve, prompts us to acknowledge our role in our failures—also an internal locus of control. In contrast, when self-focus is high but we believe that we cannot improve, we project blame for failure to something outside ourselves—an external locus of control.

The self-serving bias can render us vulnerable to influencers. Confirmatory bias, for instance, is a subtype of self-serving bias by which we look to confirm what we already believe. Consistent with that bias, research suggests that prior to making a decision we often seek information for and against a position. But after deciding, we ignore contradictory information that we encounter, looking only for that which supports the decision that we had already made (Plous, 1993).

When they know our bias, influencers can manipulate their information to be consistent with it. As I have written previously, this telling us what we want to believe is especially pernicious, slowly and subtly eroding our resistance to whatever is being presented. The influencers hope to learn both your personal standards and your personal responsibility. Once they do, they have the capacity to alternate back and forth from your standards to your responsibilities, finding the points of least resistance and capitalizing on them. They then try to convince you to reason backward from their conclusions to your preexisting premises— "motivated reasoning" based on your emotion rather than on hard empirical data.

Take, for example, an individual who prides herself on keeping physically fit. Her standards are to exercise for 30 minutes a day, 3 days per week, and her personal responsibility is to ensure that she schedules her work and home chores to make the exercise happen. If her local gym gets paid by the day, and they know the lady's standards and personal responsibility, they can target them in a way that moves her self-serving bias in their direction. For instance, they might tell her that new research advises that one should exercise a minimum of 4 days per week.

Mindlessness

Although the self-serving bias and, essentially, all the cognitive-emotional mechanisms that we have considered above, can operate as the result of deliberate or inadvertent effort, the inadvertent is particularly important, since one cannot correct decision errors that he does not recognize. Ellen Langer refers to inadvertent thinking as "mindless." Writing in the May, 2010 Psychology of Aesthetics, Creativity, and the Arts journal, she, Michael Pirson, and Laura Delizonna explain mindless as they see it. Namely, mindlessness is depicted as automatic, ubiquitous, and at the heart of the how people determine "the merit of achievements, expectations of ability, and mood" in social situations.

Locus of control is implicated in the work of Langer and her associates, as well. Insights from locus of control and context-dependent studies play a prominent role in their conclusions. They underscore inimical effects on one's self concept, adaptive skills, and social relationships when global-stable locus of control (GSLOC) attributions, rooted in other times and other places, are inappropriately applied to current situations. For us, their essential conclusions are: When mindfully engaging in decision making, one should not deny the relevance of categories derived from past experience, provided that they are experienced as flexible and permeable enough to be susceptible to change in response to newly relevant information. Mindless choice comparisons, on the other hand, over-utilize categorizations made in the past, adhering to them a rigid and impermeable fashion that obscures newly emergent contextual information. Mindfulness, by definition, promotes the experience of self as a continually changing subject, whereas mindlessness promotes the experience of self as a passive, stable, and reactive object.

Mindlessness is a friend to influencers. Influence propaganda works best with passive, compliant persons. Especially troubling is that once we have received it, propaganda resists extinction. For instance, when corrective information later is accessed, persons over age 65, and those of all ages who have not affirmed the corrective information, tend to remember the propaganda better than the correction (Swire, et al., 2017). So, the more mindful we are initially, the more here-and-now and contextualized our thoughts and feelings are, the more autonomous and rational we will be. Earlier I wrote that you would do well to introject mild, tolerable conflict and/or delay into your influence situations; I did so to encourage you to be mindful in the presence of influencers and propaganda. Mindful people are more capable of realistically and reasonably understanding human nature and their own nature—both critical for resisting manipulation.

Miscalculation

Miscalculation is the ubiquitous human tendency by which we mistakenly believe that we have weighed every gram, and counted every bean in arriving at our "objective" conclusion about an issue—in our case, an influence issue. You certainly may miscalculate when you decide a leveling-sharpening issue, or any other matter. If so, you can revise your decision, provided you can access truly objective, substantive proof. Never forget that even a well-intended influencer can make an honest calculation error that causes problems for you. Remain vigilant about their potential for miscalculations, and for your own miscalculations. There are many, many relevant varieties of miscalculation. I, however, will present just a few of the more important ones.

Pseudocertainty Effect

This principle suggests that we are inclined to make a risky choice when we confidently calculate that an outcome will be positive. Imagine that you are on a team supporting your local Senator and receive the following email from her:

> I was thinking last night that if I support bill HR 323, I stand immediately to gain 200 new female voters and lose about 215 male voters from my usual male constituency. I say I should support the bill, anyway. I need to maximize gains into the female community. When the final tally is made, women's votes will decide the election.

At the same time, pseudocertainty might encourage someone else to avoid the very same risky choice if she calculated that the outcome would be negative:

> I was thinking last night that if I support bill HR 323, I stand immediately to gain 200 new female voters and lose about 215 male voters from my usual male constituency. I say I should oppose the bill. I need to hang on to my male voters. When the final tally is made, men's votes will decide the election.

In both cases, the senator's decision is gender-based. She either dichotomously believes that she either needs to fortify her female base, even if it means netting less males votes than she usually gets, or that she must retain her male base, even if it means limiting the growth of her female support. But this is pseudocertainty thinking because the senator assumes, without data, that gender differences will determine her re-election; it is merely her supposition—not an objectively calculated fact.

Many of our decisions are similar to that of the Senator. We feel certain that we will gain by following the advice of an influencer, but typically we have no objective evidence that that will be the case. It would be far better to resist influence, at least temporarily, using the additional time to gather and evaluate as much factual information as possible before reaching a decision.

Failure to Consider Base Rate

A base rate is simply the true frequency of a phenomenon in the real world, whether the number of people in a population or the average number of hairs on a human head. Obviously, knowing the base rate is not easy for an everyday person in an everyday situation, and people rarely consider base rates when making interpersonal decisions. What happens instead is that we only have gross impressions about relevant frequencies.

In our supply and demand culture, base rates can make the difference between a wise and foolish decision. This is especially obvious and important when we want to buy a house. If the neighborhood is "hot" with bids coming fast and furious and we really want the house, should you bid more than the asking price? You can't know, but you trust that your realtor has accurate base rates about bids, numbers of bidders, and so forth. Although some of that information might be available online, you mostly are at the mercy of the realtor's privileged information. You clearly are in a one-down position. The realtor can persuade you to overpay to jack-up his commission. In order to resist manipulation, it is well worth the effort to accumulate maximal, valid, preliminary base rate information before entering into any important influence situation.

Forward Projection

The habit of forward projection is in force when we smugly, authoritatively apply old, outdated data to new situations. This is a frequent source of decision errors, as when we rely on information from our remote past to justify our current decision calculus. Perhaps for ten years you have gone to a particular garage for advice about your automotive needs. In the earlier months and years, you carefully reviewed every bill and found the garage's prices to be reasonable and fair. However, as the years rolled by, you stopped checking. Despite the fact that the garage's policies and ownership changed, you never again investigated their significantly increasing charges. Because the fees and advice always had seemed helpful, you continued to patronize the business, and that turned out to be a costly decision error. It would have been far better to refrain from forward project, reasonably checking their current prices versus current prices of their competitors.

Prospective Forecasting

Regardless of your current health, wealth, or intelligence, you will die. Not a particularly pleasant or reassuring thought, but one that incontestably is true. However, dwelling about one's mortality is enough to drive anybody insane. The tendency to anticipate our own demise is merely one example of what psychologists call prospective forecasting. That is, our natural human tendency to imagine what the future has in store for us. Prospective forecasting can lead to miscalculations that we can make with or without conscious attention to numbers. Prospective forecasting, also, is the proverbial double-edged sword—great when it predicts the positive, and dreadful when it does the opposite.

Even when imagining circumstances far less dire than death, negative prospective forecasting poisons our current experiences and aspirations. We all fall victim to negative prospective forecasting at times. While awaiting the results of a medical blood workup, most people recall some recently experienced minor or major ailment, wondering whether the tests will imply an impending medical crisis. Similarly, after submitting the competed exam for a professional license, we remember all the "tough questions" that we fear we answered incorrectly, and forget all the ones we answered confidently.

Whether positive or negative, prospective forecasting powerfully influences our decision making. Research (Burns, et al., 2018) suggests that, compared to our perception of the past, we regard the future as more valuable, closer in time, and more emotion-laden, and that orientation begins in childhood. The prospective forecasting bias frequently results in our making more urgent, more emotional decisions that ignores, or undervalues, past lessons, especially ones learned through painful, personal experience.

A negative prospective forecasting bias is burdensome enough. Unfortunately, it is made more onerous due to counterfactual reasoning, another common thinking style. This is the "what if" aspect of reflection. After receiving upsetting news regarding your blood work or licensing exam, you ruminate about what you could have done differently to avoid the outcome you just experienced. Had you eaten more sensibly or studied more diligently, you reason, you would not be in your current predicament.

Sometimes counterfactual reasoning causes us to dwell obsessively on unproductive features of our past that cannot benefit the present. And sometimes prospective forecasting causes us to dwell obsessively on unproductive features of the future that never will come to pass. Whether of positive or negative emotional valence then, we must ensure that unproductive counterfactual reasoning and unproductive prospective forecasting do not impinge on our abilities to deal with the present, since it is only in the present that we can make wise decisions.

Think again about "mindfulness" as being a mental state in which we focus on the present to the exclusion of all else. You know now that mindfulness typically promotes relaxation and clarity of thought. When you are mindful—present—you will be much better able to resist unwanted influence.

What decision-oriented insights can we glean by integrating the notions of prospective forecasting, counterfactual reasoning, and mindfulness? First, be aware that your mind frequently is pulled by one or more of the three. Second, consider whether you are more vulnerable to one or another of the three. Prospective forecasting, counterfactual reasoning, and mindfulness can have helpful or detrimental effects, depending on how and how often they are employed. Because the future is extraordinarily difficult to predict and the past cannot be changed, too much prospective forecasting and too much counterfactual reasoning usually predisposes us to problems.

Concorde Effect

Another miscalculation concerns the Concorde Effect—named for the super-polluting "supersonic" passenger jet jointly built by the British and French that first operated in 1969 and last flew in 2003. The two countries lost tons of money on this transatlantic speed demon, but they felt compelled to fly it anyway because they had "sunk" so much money into its development. Accordingly, the Concorde Effect also is called the "sunk-cost" effect.

The Concorde Effect encourages decision makers to stick with decisions in which they have invested substantial resources. And the resources could be of any type, such as money, time, or prestige. Once you calculate that you have substantial chips in the game, you might feel compelled to continue to maintain your position in the hope of eventually producing the outcome you originally desired, even when faced with mounting losses.

Accordingly, influencers not only try to get you to commit to their view, they also encourage you grow your investments with them to the maximum extent possible. One obvious example can be found in the electronics industry. Think about Apple Computer. Having created a proprietary operating system, they have launched product after product tightly or exclusively tied to that system. Because the company's items smoothly integrate with each other, they know that the more of their products you purchase, the more you will want because of their compatibility. You have sunk your money into their system, and with each purchase you are increasingly invested in it.

Although you might be more than willing to become hooked into a good line of products or ideas, be aware that influencers deliberately and progressively are attempting to minimize your capacity to resist them. Don't let them sink you.

Availability Heuristic

The final miscalculation is mathematical in a statistical sense, and one of the most important heuristics for most people most often. The availability heuristic refers to a common human information processing strategy for accessing from memory data believed to be relevant to the issue at hand. The strategy is statistical in that more numerically abundant and recent information intrudes most readily into our consciousness. Having accessed the information so easily, people often presume that it must be true. Moreover, the easily available information typically is accompanied by a collection of thoughts

supporting it. One commonly cited example is the
most frequent answer to the question, "Which is a
more likely reason for death in America, murder
or suicide?" Most respondents incorrectly reply,
"murder." That erroneous answer mostly is given
because murder receives pervasive media
attention, and suicide tends to be hushed. Incidents
of murder, therefore, come to mind far more
quickly than do those of suicide Having retrieved
so much supportive information so effortlessly,
the respondent cannot be blamed for assuming that
murder must be the more common. Challenging
such "obvious," albeit incorrect, presumptions
would require individuals to put forth more energy
than they usually would be willing to expend.
Ease of information access too often is the default
for most people, and for their miscalculations.

Caution: Human Vulnerability at Work

The last two chapters explaining cognitive-emotional
mechanisms have not been presented in the belief that either you
or I can overcome them readily or totally. In fact, David Buss
(2010), specialist in Individual Differences and Evolutionary
Psychology at the University of Texas, admits that he still
struggles to overcome those cognitive-emotional obstacles. In his
words, "One nagging thing that I still don't understand about
myself is why I often succumb to well-documented psychological
biases, even though I'm acutely aware of these biases."

Buss's comment indirectly relates to the psychological notion of
"working through," a term used to explain the difference between
knowing something intellectually, and acting upon it
behaviorally. We "know" much about what is right and right for
us: "I should exercise more, eat more healthfully, stop smoking,
save for retirement, speak respectfully to my spouse, and treat all

people the way I want to be treated." But knowing is not doing. To do things differently requires us to be vigilant, to sacrifice, and to persist. It is not so simple to move from talk to action. In order to implement significant, enduring changes in our behavior, we must work them into our lives, over time and over contexts. Working through is not easy, most often requiring a "corrective emotional experience" or two. At one time or another almost everyone has had such a corrective emotional experience that transforms superficial, intellectual understanding into gut level, authentic awareness and action. Imagine that your mother forever admonished that, "You don't care about anyone but yourself," and you always had responded mentally to her with a "Yeah—blah, blah, blah" self-statement. Mother's advice remained little more than background noise in your mind. Then, at age thirty-seven, you land a coveted job, the job you have pursued for a decade, the job that you just love. As with many jobs, you have been on a probationary period, and the moment of truth has come. The boss starts the review complimentarily, reciting all your technical skills, but ends with, "Unfortunately, we must let you go. You do not fit in socially with us. This is a business built on relationships and, I hate to say it, but several people have told me that you only care about yourself. Sorry that the job didn't work out for you."

We all must work through our influence-resisting skills. We need corrective emotional experiences that motivate our everyday actions. And we must understand biases that undermine our decision-making styles. Ryan Hamilton (2018) recommends that we can compensate for common, psychological biases if we attend to four dimensions:

Reasons—find logical, relevant reasons to reach your conclusions.
Resources—ensure that you have the raw data and requisite energy to process correctly.

Reference Points—use central, quantifiable comparison information rather comparison information that is peripheral and vague.
Replacement—do not substitute a convenient data set for better data that is harder to obtain. Do not make an easy, inconsequential decision to avoid making a more difficult, important one.

Influence resistance and decision-making, then, are neither intuitive nor painless. Whether or not you employ experts to assist, in the end, you need to maintain what I call a DECA strategy: Decide Each Choice Autonomously. If you sincerely aspire to being an independent rational thinker, be prepared for a relentless, life-long struggle of working through. Although you will not always succeed, you gradually will build your influence-resisting and decision-making muscles.

CHAPTER 6: Marketing Influence to Aspiring Influencers

Early on I emphasized the extreme overlap common in marketing strategies, and that most strategies are minor variations on Cialdini's seven. I said that I prefer to avoid repeating strategies common among the influencer theorists and consultants. In this section, however, I deviate slightly from that preference. I do so because the following marketing experts are second only to Cialdini in their impacts on the field. You will see that, despite significant overlapping in places, each expert emphasizes a factor or factors that you can use to resist negfluences. True influence professionals employ influence tactics consistent with the following approaches that exploit, respectively, the roles of memory, interpersonal relationships, and technology.

Emphasis on Memory

Remembering

Memory can be enemy or friend to decision making, either undermining or facilitating our rational thoughts and personal choices. To date, professional persuaders have held the upper hand in that they have the have had smart weapons in the form of their supercomputers that analyze precise personalized data, and battalions of communications experts who instruct them to choose every influence venue, parse every word they speak, and rehearse every action they take. The professionals use their smart weapons to manipulate us by controlling such institutions as advertising, news, entertainment, politics, and government. In so doing, they not only implant their ideas into our minds, they also do their best to keep them there. For instance, in their 2007 book *Made to Stick*, brothers Chip and Dan Heath explicitly guide influencers to make their ideas unforgettable. To make their own persuasion advice unforgettable, they employ the acronym "SUCCES" (simple, unexpected, concrete, credible, emotional). So let's deconstruct the acronym-summarized Heath method by imagining an influencer who wants to sell a new edge trimmer called "Weed Lopper."

The brothers enjoin potential influencers to keep their messages SIMPLE. They first advocate speaking in terms of a core idea that is embedded into a memorable frame. In our example, the hypothetical Weed Lopper is described as "the cutter that never needs sharpening." And the memorable advertising frame could be a catchy rhyme, "The Weed Lopper is a never stopper. It's ready to cut when you're ready to cut." Second, the Heaths want your message to be UNEXPECTED." For instance, a video clip might show the Lopper leveling a field of sky-high corn stalks. Third, they want it to be CONCRETE. The Lopper is not an alternating, reciprocating landscaping device; it is a "cutter." Fourth, the message must be CREDIBLE. The ad should provide some reasonable justification for believing it, such as explaining the edge-retaining power of the superior metal used in fabricating the blades. Fifth, since affect guides attention and action, the Lopper message needs to be EMOTIONAL. That could be achieved by suggesting that Zika mosquitoes breed in weedy environments, and elaborating the unhealthful consequences of that disease. And, finally, the Heaths encourage encapsulating the entire message in a STORY. The razed section could be memorialized as a tale about how a former corn field was leveled to make space for a playground to entertain institutionalized children.

Chip and Dan Heath clearly believe that they understand how to manipulate you memory. They want to elicit your past personal memories favorable to their products. And they want to implant into your mind new memories favorable to them, as well. Therefore, you must be aware of the memories that any influencer brings to your consciousness, and be equally aware of the memories that the influencer is trying to establish in you. Moreover, since memory is person-specific, aspects of memory that affect one person need not affect anther. The more you know your personal vulnerabilities, the more you can resist memory's unwanted influences.

Emphasis on Interpersonal Relationships

Social Contagion

Just as memory can be enemy or friend to decision making, so, too, can relationships. Before you can remember a message, you must receive it, and all professional influencers agree that social contagion—circulating messages throughout a group—is one of the best vehicles, if not the best. Although presented via the theme of social contagion, Jonah Berger's ideas (2013) are consistent with those of the Heath brothers. He advises influencers to control the ways by which targets are exposed to the promoted products and ideas, to control how targets perceive them, and to control how targets remember them. Similar to the Heaths, Berger summarizes his advice to professional influencers with a six-letter acronym. His is "STEPPS" (social currency, triggers, emotions, public, practical value, stories). You immediately notice that the Berger dimensions include two of the Heath dimensions—story and emotion— but please note that Berger emphasizes their social contagion value, whereas the Heaths emphasize their memorial value. Each STEPPS component relies on its social power.

Social currency for Berger is the extent to which an interpersonal communication enhances the speaker's self- confidence and self-esteem. In our example, the Lopper tactfully might be framed as SOCIAL CURRENCY in that that it is presented as a premium product that only a wealthy or savvy person would own. A trigger refers to the fact that people talk about items associated with ideas and activities in their lives whenever they're reminded of those ideas and activities. A TRIGGER for purchasing the Lopper could a flyer strategically placed on a section of the homeowners' lawns by a local high school student during the summer. Emotion is central because people share that which generates their high-arousal. If the Lopper truly works within any given community, its effectiveness will generate EMOTION within that community. By definition, anything public is available to be perceived, and people frequently will do what other people are doing. The Lopper is PUBLIC in its operation, no less than in its results. When people realize practical value, they often share the source of that value. Anyone who has struggled to trim a lawn realizes that Lopper clearly has PRACTICAL VALUE. Finally, since people are hard-wired for story-telling, when the aforementioned four STEPPS components are present, people are likely to share STORIES about the Lopper over the backyard fence. Positive stories should facilitate its sales, but, of course, negative stories probably would undermine sales.

Externally Generated Stories

The Heath brothers, Jonah Berger, and a host of others emphasize the influence power of stories. They advise the influencer to relate a compelling narrative rather than to deliver a sterile lecture. The advice has a strong psycholinguistic rationale that centers upon the importance of a storyteller creating in her listener a deictic shift, meaning a transition from the present reality to an immersion within the story's world (Hamby, et al., 2018). That immersion is achieved by skillfully-crafted story elements, such as ones that facilitate engagement and identification. The story deliverer seeks to cause the story receiver to lose himself by fully embracing the scenarios and messages presented. Following that deictic shift, the listener almost automatically is swept along by a well-crafted story. A proficient storyteller, therefore, becomes a potent influencer when she is able to embed her suggestions within an absorbing narrative.

Despite endorsing the power of stories, almost none of the influencer gurus sufficiently explain what they mean by "stories." There are two noteworthy exceptions. Writing in the Harvard Business Review, Carolyn O'Hara (2014) proffered a little insight into stories suitable for delivery by professional influencers. Given what you just have read, nothing she suggested will surprise you, but it is instructive for us to look behind the corporate curtain to understand their methods of story persuasion. In brief, O'Hara recommended that influencers should rehearse how best to deliver a simple, moving message based on their own experience. Persuasive stories, she felt, were most effective when they involved some significant struggle, but one in which the influencer played a supporting, or otherwise minimal, role. Donald Miller's *Building a StoryBrand* (2017) eclipsed O'Hara's article by providing detailed advice on how to use stories as the central core from which to promote an idea or product. Miller encouraged marketing with messages framed to create a kind of adventure story, starring a client surrogate. He specified a story hero besieged by a problem with whom the client could identify. The hero then would be assisted by a guide—a metaphorical embodiment of the marketed idea or product—who calls the hero into action that enables her/him to avoid a crisis, and whose struggle culminates with victory. Moreover, Miller coached marketers to craft a story whose problem is primarily personal and internal, but that includes some external, and, perhaps, philosophical aspects. Citing often quoted research that people are more motivated by the likelihood of loss than by the likelihood of gain, Miller also instructed his acolytes to incite client fear, and then to explain how the proposed idea or product would extinguish their fear. In other words, he promoted StoryBrand as a marketing method primarily implemented via highly personalized stories that appeal to a target's primitive emotions.

Both Carolyn O'Hara and Donald Miller, then, teach marketing professionals to craft stories that covertly or overtly appeal to your emotions in ways that further their ends. So, you need to be able to recognize their stories, dissect them rationally, and separate hype from sober reality. By thinking a little more fully about stories, you empower yourself to recognize and respond on your own terms, rather than to be manipulated by influencer tales.

Your empowerment begins by understanding the structure of the stories presented. One excellent way to do that is to separate story genera via the classification system of Eggins and Slade (1997). According to them, story genera can be divided into four types. The fullest story form is the conventional narrative that begins with an orientation, and then moves to a complication, evaluation, and resolution. In a narrative, movement toward resolution is key. An anecdote is sparser. Here the orientation merely is followed by a remarkable event and then a reaction, not a true resolution. By contrast, an exemplum proceeds from orientation to incident to interpretation; it tells how things should or shouldn't be, often with moral implications. Last is a recount, in which an initial orientation is explained by a record of specific events, and then by a reorientation. Central to a recount is the storyteller's appraisal of reconstructed events in which their sequential flow is emphasized. Eggins and Slade explain that all story genres are maintained and contextualized by the evaluations implicit or explicit within them. So, to experience someone's story is to be exposed to their evaluation/interpretation of its elements. Influencers want you to accept the self-serving evaluations embedded within the stories that they tell.

Any of the four genera can be employed to exert emotional influence, such as by inspiring, cajoling, or frightening us. A gripping narrative requires time to develop, but not too much time: think short stories, such as *The Gift of the Magi* and *The Lottery*. Although any situation could be structured to permit a brief narrative, narratives are especially suitable for an extended presentation, as occurs in a lecture or formal business meeting. On the other hand, any competent influencer is able to deliver a quick, engrossing anecdote, exemplum, or recount in any imaginable setting.

Narrative

Short narratives regularly are employed by university commencement influencers. And, when it comes to narratives, none are better than the three that Steve Jobs delivered at the June 12, 2005 Stanford University commencement. He needed only fifteen minutes to relate all of them. But we merely will address the last—the one that he introduced with the statement, *"My third story is about death."*

Jobs oriented the Stanford audience by emphasizing how ephemeral life is. The complication occurred when he revealed that one year earlier he had been diagnosed with a malignant pancreatic tumor. The narrative was elaborated to explain that his doctors regarded him as terminal—within six months. According to him, "My doctor advised me to go home and get my affairs in order, which is doctor's code for prepare to die." The narrative resolution consisted of his subsequent claim that, "It turned out to be a very rare form of pancreatic cancer that is curable with surgery. I had the surgery and I'm fine now." Steve Jobs' evaluations were deliberately transparent, advising the graduates to make the most of their time, and to follow their hearts and intuitions.

A sad postscript is that Steve Jobs died of his cancer on October 5, 2011. According to Alice G. Walton (2011), Jobs had delayed his surgery for nine months after his initial diagnosis in order to try alternative medicine, such as one involving diet change. More tragic, given his Stanford speech that encouraged "intuition," the Apple founder was said to have relied too much on his own intuition in making his medical decisions, rather than following his surgeon's early recommendation for a quick surgery. Thus, as moving and appealing as his influence story was, like all advice, the receiver always must accept personal responsibility for deciding when to accept or reject influence, especially when it is dispensed by someone who is, or who should be, a true-gooder.

Anecdote

Our anecdote is delivered by a salesperson, Jennifer, during a pitch. Asked why you should buy the toaster oven being offered, she began by telling how she, herself, never used one very often until last year. She said after receiving what for her was an astronomical electric bill—$370— she sought an explanation. Jennifer then realized that her husband just had begun baking virtually every carbohydrate that he ate, from toast to left-over potatoes, oblivious to the cost of preheating and of using a full oven for each morsel of food. He had read something about baked goods being healthful, and, besides, he enjoyed the crunchy consistency of overbaked food. After a brief spat about the bill, she and he agreed to purchase a toaster oven to determine its value. Jennifer exclaimed that the smaller appliance reduced her bill by three-quarters, and from that point forward, it has become her default cooker: "The most economical purchase I ever made."

Exemplum

A thirty-something traveling evangelist knocks on your door, and delivers an exemplum. He hopes you will be able to contribute something to help further the philanthropic work of his civic-minded group. The young man speaks at length about how his sect began in the rural south, started by a former "dirt-poor" social worker. Then he tells just what he managed to do last week at minimal financial expense. What follows then is a detailed recitation of the particular needs of a given family whose breadwinner recently lost his job. The evangelist asserts his belief that "a few contributions right now should help this family manage until their unemployment insurance begins." He adds, "Do you think that this is a cause worthy of your support?"

Recount

You meet with a local builder to ask him about constructing a small cabin on your vacation property in the mountains. He says he would proceed as he did for a previous job, and recounts that as follows: "What I did was get a surveyor out there. Then I had to fell a couple trees. I tested for and sunk a well, and a septic system. I had the foundation laid in about two weeks. After that, it was just, I'll say, about another month until the entire project was complete. Of course, the last step was to have the county inspection." You ask if he anticipates doing anything different for you, and he recounts the same basic plan again, substituting elements specific to your job. He requests, and you produce, half his fee upfront, and he agrees to start within three weeks.

Internally Generated Stories

Everyone of course has their own story preferences, ranging from long, intricate narratives to brief, crisp anecdotes. And those preferences tend to vary by topic. Some relish a detailed narrative about cars, but tolerate only anecdotal stories about politics. Every story you hear is subjected to your cognitive and emotional filters. What is externally delivered is not necessarily what is internally received. You are re-creating the stories you hear in real time. The external story becomes your internal story. Everything that had been suggested is edited by you. The resulting images and ideas are ones that make "most sense" to you in terms of your personality and experiences. The edited images and ideas usually are consistent with images and ideas that comprise your pre-existing personal, internal stories. Those internal stories provide a baseline from which all else is compared and evaluated

The fact that you compare external stories with internal ones means that the more you understand your internal stories, the more adaptively you can handle the external. Your values, opinions, and behaviors are determined by your ego strength—the unique "you" that is a result of interactions among your history, temperament, personality, and environments. Accordingly, ego strength is both your master internal story creator, and your external story editor and evaluator, as well. We will discuss ego strength in great detail shortly.

When you hear Steve Job's narrative about his illness and the importance of following your heart and intuitions, you automatically and unconsciously compare it with the experience-based internal narratives that you had already created about illness, following your heart, and intuitions. You take from his story those elements that fit your narratives, and dismiss those that do not. Job's narrative would have negfluential consequences if you interpreted it, like he once had, as trusting intuition about malignant pancreatic tumors. Jennifer's toaster anecdote pitch must also be assessed via your ego strength. You might be able to use a toaster oven, but not necessarily the one she that is promoting. Your history, temperament, personality, and environments could combine to make you very susceptible to the evangelist's exemplum appeal to assist "a family whose breadwinner recently lost his job." But perhaps you should inquire about the percentage of your requested monetary contribution that the family will receive. Finally, an ego strength-based evaluation needs to be employed in judging the local builder's recount. His step-by-step explanation of the previous construction project might or might not apply to yours. For instance, how many trees need to be felled on your property, how deep does your well need to be, and what kind of septic system is most suitable for you? How firm is the price that he quoted you?

Understand the Memeing of Influence

Most stories are created expressly for transmission. That certainly
is true regarding the stories that influencers create. And, from the
influencer's point of view, the best stories are ones that spread far
and wide—to as many potential targets in as many places as
possible. The most successful stories, however, are not
necessarily the ones most repeated by any given influencer.
Rather, the most successful stories are the ones that are so
compelling that they are remembered and volitionally
disseminated by the people who hear them. Influencers strive to
insert their stories into the ears of "hub persons" who are
interpersonally connected with many persons within many
interpersonal clusters, and who can serve as a link to reach even
more remote interpersonal clusters. In the next section, the
critical importance of hub persons and interpersonal clusters also
will be explained at length.

For now, to understand the transmission of stories, and of all
forms of influence, we apply concepts popularized by Richard
Dawkins, an Oxford University Professor of evolutionary
biology. At the conclusion of his world renown *The Selfish Gene*,
[chosen by *Time* magazine as one of the 100 best most influential
nonfiction books written in English since 1923 (Morrison, 2011]
Dawkins (1976) introduces the concept "meme" to describe a
gene-like unit of cultural, rather than biological, transmission.
Like genes, memes self-replicate in a single-mindedly selfish
manner and, like genes, they do so with fidelity, fecundity, and
longevity. By that we mean that behaviors or ideas qualify as
memes when they faithfully, widely, and lastingly spread through
a culture or subculture. Memes include phenomena as diverse as
individual words, the handshake, the "Happy Birthday" song, and
the notion of god.

To understand Richard Dawkins' hypothesis, we first need a very
brief review of a few elementary biological facts. Please recall

that the genetic code that is passed from parent to offspring is the genotype. The actual physical characteristic that the genotype delivers is the genetic phenotype. For example, a male with blood type A and genotype AI i can father a child with any blood type—A, B, AB, or O—depending on the genotype of the female with whom he mates. The nature of the receiving individual organism is critical in determining the phenotypic expression of the genotype offered. Just because one has a gene does not mean that it will be expressed. Geneticists are acutely interested in determining the internal and external factors that cause genotypes to become expressed as phenotypes. In fact, a relatively recent field of biology, called epigenetics, primarily seeks to determine the external and/or environmental factors that facilitate the genotype to phenotype transition.

Analogously, we can think of the memetic code that is transmitted from one individual to the next as the memeotype, and the information that endures in the receiving individual as the memetic phenotype. Memes are real, and probably have existed as long as humankind, itself. But, like a gene circulating through your body that never becomes expressed as your phenotype, a meme circulating through society need not be expressed as your memetic phenotype. The physiologic information encoded in a gene or the mental information encoded in a meme is processed by a whole, finely-articulated individual organism that has its own preexisting physiology and mind. It is this preexisting complex that determines whether the gene or meme can be incorporated at all, and the extent and quality of the incorporation. In short, the fidelity of a gene or meme requires communion of sender and receiver. Fidelity presumes an intra-individual readiness, and inter-individual match, if the phenotype is to be a faithful copy of the original. So, a meme, ipso facto, needs to be consistently and specifically appropriate to its target—a necessary memeotype-memeohost compatibility—to yield a memetic phenotypic expression.

To relate memetics to our discussion, then, we understand that stories or other social influences that affect us are ones that we permit to pass through our cognitive and emotional filters. The images, ideas, and stories that stick with us do so because the memeotype offered is epigenetically suitable—memeotype-memeohost compatible—to become our memetic phenotype. A memeotype derives its power from the way it aligns with our ego strength. The memeotype could become your memetic phenotype either because your ego strength is such that you are voluntarily receptive to the proffered message, or because you are "too weak to resist" it. One person hears a story and is driven to convulsive sobbing, while another person is totally unmoved—both occur as a result of memeotype-memeohost compatible or incompatibility rooted in ego strength.

The Special Power of Interpersonal Influence

Social Networks and Social Comparison

Most of us have heard of the Kevin Bacon-associated-game called "Six Degrees of Separation," positing that anyone on earth can reach anyone else through the intercessions of six or fewer interpersonal contacts. Actually, science partially supports that astounding generalization. For instance, Duncan J. Watts and Steven H. Strogatz (1998) have proposed a small-world networks theory, describing how easy it is for people to connect with unknown others. Their model graphs the interpersonal **distance** between individuals and the **clustering** among the members of a given network. The fewer the interpersonal contacts necessary for one person to communicate with another, the closer their interpersonal distance. And the less distance among the interpersonal contacts that they share, the tighter their cluster. Now is the time for us to elaborate on the idea of "hub persons," briefly introduced earlier. Hub persons" are the keystones of every cluster, because they connect many other cluster members. Practically speaking, their centrality means that they can spread messages more widely, quickly, and efficiently. Having a greater number of interpersonal contacts, hub people have the potential for greater influence than other cluster members do.

The Watts-Strogatz paradigm is precise and mathematical, but similar to other less rigorous ideas about interpersonal links. Gladwell (2000), for instance, offers nothing particularly new, but uses the term "connectors" to designate hub people whom he describes as those who can introduce an individual to a network previously unknown to them. He makes the further common sense suggestion that strong connectors are close acquaintances while weak connectors are minimally tied to you or to your network. Whether any given person is interpersonally distant from you, part of your tight cluster, or a strong or weak connector, hub persons are special targets for those seeking to exert influence. If you can recognize connectors of all types— hub and otherwise— you can better decide when to heed or ignore them.

How then do you make the most of your group affiliations? Because hub persons tend to be extraverted and/or very assertive, they often wield excessive influence, even though they might not be the most knowledgeable or brightest. Mariano Sigman and Dan Ariely (2017) have some suggestions. They find that group decisions are most valid and helpful when individual group members of diverse opinions deliberate. After deliberation runs its course, members usually should place their confidence in the opinions that are most widely shared and reject the outliers. The strategy presumes that you resist the most extraverted/assertive ones until you can determine the validity of what they and all others have to say. It also requires you to be self-assertive and energetic enough to implement Sigman and Ariely's ideas. Most times you are not sitting together with your most valued friends, discussing a decision conjointly. So, to make the most of your social network's wisdom, you need to solicit it from one or two persons at a time. Therefore, you first must ask yourself whether a given issue is worth the substantial investment of time and energy needed to make best use of the aforementioned strategy. Moreover, since you know more about the contextual factors most relevant to you than anyone else does, sometimes even after correctly assessing the group's opinion, you might choose correctly to ignore their advice. The group opinion simply might not fit your unique context, your ego strength.

Even if you are blasé about your own vulnerability to social influence, you might be concerned about the vulnerability of our children, since youngsters increasingly are targets of a marketing invasion that co-opts Cialdini's social consensus marketing principle. An unsolicited Walmart email sent to me, for instance, illustrates how businesses try to create and exploit child-friendly hub persons.

On December 15, 2018, I received the email entitled, "Which toys are a hit with influencers?" The page showed the names and photos of three children, each allegedly rating toys for their age group. There was Latisha for ages 1 to 2, Jaiden for 5 to 7, and Ava for 8 to 11. The email promised that "Our experts' best picks by age," and invited the reader to, "Meet our influencers. Learn more about our group of young social media gurus!" Clicking the link revealed a page with names and photos of 33 more children whose toy picking expertise was age-designated, from 6 months to 11 years. The photo of each of the email's 36 children served as a link to their Walmart page, and each page provided a short descriptive comment about her or him, and photos of the toys they were endorsing. By clicking on the product picture, the reader advanced to a page that fully described the item and enabled a quick purchase. Since children, no less than adults, look to each other for cues about what items are best, Walmart merely has attempted to exert control over what allegedly is peer-advocated, and has made it maximally easy to order the promoted toys. Because children possess minimal ego strength, absent adult intervention, they will are destined to be manipulated by aggressive influencers who exploit hub persons whom they create.

Emphasis on Technology

Memory is critical for influencers because memory is the most powerful internal mental variable that you always carry with you, and that always affects your decisions to one extent or another. Interpersonal relationships are critical for influencers because, like all people, whether you realized it or not, you are always comparing yourself to others to determine what is and is not desirable and effective. Acutely aware of the two aforementioned facts, influencers continually seek means by which to control your memory and the interpersonal memes that flow around you. And their favorite means of control increasingly has become 21st Century technology. In the final analysis, those who deliver technology exert the greatest influence on professional influencers and, by extension, on you, me, and everyone else in contemporary society. Since electronic technology now is pervasive, so, too, is electronically-enabled influence. To continue with our *Justifiably Paranoid* warfare metaphor, electronic influencers and their troops are forever trying to surround and to capture us,

Accordingly, Stanford University's Persuasive Tech Lab seeks to dominate the influence battlefield through the "Persuasive technology" and "captology" approach. To quote their website, captology.stanford.edu/about/what-is-captology.html:

> Captology is the study of computers as persuasive technologies. This includes the design, research, ethics and analysis of interactive computing products (computers, mobile phones, websites, wireless technologies, mobile applications, video games, etc.) created for the purpose of changing people's attitudes or behaviors. BJ Fogg derived

> the term captology in 1996 from an acronym:
> Computers As Persuasive Technologies = CAPT.

The Tech Lab and Fogg, its founding and current director, are deployed in numerous, diverse influence theaters of operation. For instance, they strive to influence the influencers by advising individuals, institutions, and businesses about the best ways to use technology to promote their goals. One of many Tech Lab methods involves delivering a two-week learning module, entitled, "What Makes a Website Credible?" To be credible is to be believable and/or convincing. And using technology to enhance credibility is an especially powerful way to spread your message effectively—to get others, literally and figuratively, to "buy into" what you are selling.

Knowing how to come across as credible, of course, is absolutely essential to the success of any influencer. It, arguably, is even more important at the level of website. The site initially is all that people see. Anyone arriving at a website can leave it with the instantaneous click of a mouse. Moreover, a website often is the keystone to all present day marketing. Many businesses are primarily, or exclusively, web-based. Only by having a credible website, do such businesses have any chance for viability and profitability. Credibility does not guarantee integrity. Whatever is learned at the Persuasive Technology Lab can be used for posfluence or negfluence. In that respect, the Lab is no different than any other institution in the education business. What sets Stanford Persuasive Technology Lab apart is its own ethical credibility, and its reach. That credibility is far greater than it is for a run-of-the-mill educational influence group. An idea promoted by Stanford is likely to be contagious, not only due to the esteem by which they are regarded, but also because the Stanford Lab is, itself, in the business of influencing. And it does so by making the most of technology that relentlessly can distribute its ideas and products across the world at virtual electron speed. A stellar reputation, interpersonal, institutional, and inter-continental connections, along with cutting-edge technology to deliver at will make the Stanford Persuasive Technology Lab a powerhouse that few institutions on earth can match.

Digital marketing also is advocated by another Stanford professor, Dr. Andreas Weigend, who describes himself as expert in big data, consumer behavior, and social-mobile technologies. Weigend (weigend.com) recommends the following critical guidelines for using big data (Columbus, 2012): If you are marketer, begin your strategy by focusing on the problem you seek to solve rather than on the data being collected. Next, collect as much relevant data as possible. Make sure that you do not impede your data-gathering efforts in any way for trivial reasons. The aggregated data subsequently should be assessed via metrics important to the customers. Consider providing some of your data to the customers, if that encourages them to divulge their own relevant data to you. Facilitate important interpersonal connections, contributions, and collaborations. Be as transparent as reasonable. Know and capitalize on computers wherever they are best, but also engage people in areas wherein they are best.

One presumes that Weigend's sage advice is being used by cable television providers, such as Netflix. That company has a treasure trove of information about you. They offer you log-in via Facebook, raising the opportunity for them to mine that incredibly rich source of information. You must click on an icon that identifies you as the household member presently on-line. Netflix relentlessly collects your viewing preferences. They present to you their viewing suggestions, based on the viewing data they have amassed from your past choices. Netflix asks you to rate programs that you have seen. Among other things, they tell you what is "popular" and "trending," potentially tempting you to follow a given reference group. Some Netflix suggestions are rationalized with the heading, "Because you watched…" After you leave their website, they regularly, and often quickly, email you, "[Your name], we just added a movie you might like," along with a marquee-like picture of the new show that you can click-on to either play it immediately or add it to your existing list. Absent big data, Netflix would be totally unable to implement virtually any of the aforementioned strategies.

Knowing everything described in the previous paragraph, some people readily accept Netflix's use of digital marketing as a reasonable cost of being their subscriber. After all, that entertainment company is providing a transparent, legitimate service that you can cancel at any time. But there is other big data tracking wherein the benefits are far from transparent and far from worthwhile. One involves the gambling business. Ian Leslie (2016) provides an illuminating summary of Natasha Dow Schüll's work (2012) regarding computer-assisted games of chance in Las Vegas. So, let's consider what she has described.

Schüll correctly explains the roots of gambling behavior in terms of Skinnerian operant conditioning. As you may know, B. F. Skinner was the premier 20th century psychologist who demonstrated that animals, such as rats and pigeons, could be conditioned to respond to a stimulus, even a meaningless one, if they are rewarded for doing so. Rats, for instance, could easily be taught to tap a small lever to receive a food pellet. For our purposes, the most relevant finding was Skinner's demonstrating that different schedules of reward (reinforcement) resulted in more or less resilient learning. And the most resilient learning occurred when the rat received the reward on a variable schedule. That is, it did not get the food pellet every time, but at unpredictable intervals. Because the animal never "knew" when the food pellet would be delivered, it persisted at the tapping behavior over long stretches of time, persevering despite the "frustration" of being fed sparingly. People, too, are most strongly conditioned by variable schedule rewards.

The Skinner experiments are relevant because they explain much of human gambling behavior. A casino's slot machines and money offer almost perfect analogies to a rat's levers and food pellets. Just like the rat, the gambler never knows when the slots will "feed" him. Some of what Schüll reveals about slot machine operations is well known. Most people realize that casinos try to keep gamblers on the machines by such tactics as having pleasant, attractive, scantily clad women deliver complimentary snacks and drinks to gamblers at the slots. There is nothing new about that gambling-as-conditioning aspect. Schüll's new contribution is the light she sheds on the extent of big data, machine-enabled customer manipulation. According to her, some algorithms can keep track of the player's wins and losses to customize the gambler conditioning. Thus, programs are able to estimate the player's loss tolerance so that a machine-cued intervention can be delivered to him at the most opportune time—for instance, delivering a free meal coupon when he becomes exasperated. Manipulations also include presenting near misses for some susceptible persons, and the potential for either big or more modest payouts—all based on insights derived from big data deemed most appropriate to a specific individual playing the slots in real time.

The casino industry is merely one of scores of businesses that have used strategies based on the Stanford Persuasive Tech Lab method and other big data methods. Another business is CXL that describes itself as "the world leader in optimization know-how" (conversionxl.com) that helps companies deliver "extra lucrative results." An advertised core service is their conversion marketing—the ability to facilitate customer "conversions," from browsing to a purchasing (Webopedia.com). With the alleged approval of Stanford, CXL provides an excellent summary of the core Persuasive Tech Lab concepts of customer-specific motivation, their ability to act as you wish, and the triggers that incite them to do so. Better still, it summarizes the concepts via a few general guidelines: First, understand and sculpt customer motivation, ability, and triggers to be consistent with your goals; second, proceed from their motivates to exploit their natural predilections by making it simple and easy for them to do your bidding; third, be able to deliver the triggers that impel them to immediate action, fourth, pay continual attention to the triggers in order to modify them, if necessary, and, finally, use digital technology to refine as many of the preceding steps as possible.

Conversion Uplift Ltd (https://www.conversion-uplift.co.uk/about-us/) is an example of a completely non-Stanford-affiliated entity that applies Persuasive Tech Lab and other digital marketing concepts to increase conversion rates. Uplift, for instance, emphasizes the importance of reducing customer "friction" by which it means to make the customer experience as effortless as possible. They specifically address a number of common website problems that confuse, frustrate, or irritate visitors. Focusing on business websites, they recommend that customers, and potential customers, "land" immediately on a registration page whose purpose is to persuade, inform, and recruit. The home screen should contain a welcoming message, and clearly and succinctly educate the customer about company essentials and its mission. Nothing should impede quick movement to a sign-up form; it is especially crucial to refrain from creating pop-ups. Conversion Uplift also dissuades any placement of captchas, those coded messages intended to differentiate visiting people from visiting computer interlopers. The website should provide sufficient time and enticements for potential customers to convert. It should emphasize the company's credentials and provide triggers in the form of at least two call to action cues. That is, at least two ways that the customer can sign-up or otherwise engage. Doing so conveys an impression of choice that appeals to most people and disarms them. Uplift decries using sliders and carousels—a gauntlet of images, texts, or buttons through which the customer must pass to be informed. In short, Conversion Uplift Ltd empowers companies to employ digital technology not only to reduce customer friction, and potential customer friction, but also to make them feel welcomed, engaged, understood, and appreciated.

Marketing to Marketers Memory Interpersonal and Technology

Take Away

Now that you know many more ways that the marketing elite advise the marketers with whom they consult, you should be able to use that knowledge to defend against their influence invasion. Be aware of how your memory is operating. Be on the look-out for messages that are simple, unexpected, concrete, credible, emotional, and delivered via stories, since they are likely to be maximally memorable. Be equally alert to interpersonal affects that employ social currency, trigger, and emotions, and that are public, practical, and, also, story-centered. Know that you, I, and everyone are especially vulnerable to messages that have assumed memetic status. Do your best to ensure that a popular meme does not automatically evolve into a cultural memeotype that you permit to become your personal memetic phenotype. You need to make a conscious, not unconscious, decision as to whether any circulating meme is or is not compatible with your needs and values. Be sure to think about your interpersonal relationship tendencies when thinking about influence. You almost certainly want to be accepted, to be in tune with your reference groups, and to give people the benefit of the doubt when issues are unclear. Those proclivities, however, can come back to bite you when you are dealing with individuals who dispense inaccurate misleading guidance, whether inadvertently or deliberately. Similarly, most of us want to be current, and it is impossible to be current if you are not technologically connected. You want the electronic gadgets and the Internet experiences that enable you to keep-up with the proverbial Joneses. But in your haste to do so, you easily can fall victim to technological spies, assassins, and invaders of all types. No one likes to experience customer friction. However, be wary of big data-enabled influence situations structured to make compliance too easy. For instance, companies love to give you a small discount for a product or service, provided you agree to automatic renewal of that product or service. They market automatic renewal as making your life easy—frictionless, to use their lingo. But, of course, the real intention is to make renewal frictionless and lucrative for them, more than for you.

CHAPTER 7: Values & Vulnerability

To resist unwanted influence, we must understand how we assign values to features contained within potential decisions. That is, we must know what is important to us in which contexts. Contextualized value is a very personal thing. For instance, a person might accept a particular social situation that radically limits her choices, but resist a different one. Perhaps she almost never would balk at going to a personally unappealing restaurant or movie, if her girlfriends had selected it. Another individual readily would resist the personally unappealing restaurant or movie, but be totally unwilling to wear a blouse out of fashion with her group. That is, the first lady assigned only the personally unappealing restaurant or movie decision to her "I must conform to this social norm" category, whereas the second assigned only the wearing a blouse out of fashion decision to the "I must conform to this social norm" category. The contextualized value concept is similar but not equivalent to Richard Thaler's thoroughly researched notion of "mental accounting" (Thaler, 2016). According to him, people make relativistic, uneconomical decisions based on how they categorize a choice. An oft-quoted example is of a person who, arriving at the theater and discovering that he has lost an already-purchased $100 ticket, goes home rather than purchasing another. However, that same person who arrives at the theater without a ticket does not hesitate to buy one, even after discovering that he just has lost $100 cash on the train. In the first case, the buyer's mental accounting indicates that he does not want to pay twice for a ticket, but in both cases, his trip to the theater costs him $200.

Our focus, however, is not limited to monetary decisions or to a particular influence. Any value can be pivotal in our decisions and in our susceptibility to influence. To comprehensively consider those possibilities, in a moment we will view the issue through the prism of the Shalom Schwartz (2012) basic human values theory, but first let us refer to what was said earlier about some common, primary motives. At that time, it was noted that:

Everyone wants to be physically **comfortable and safe.** Most seek both **beneficial social connections and autonomy.** We all sometimes look for **excitement and tranquility.** People try to attain **competencies, order, and stability.** Desire for **money, power, and sexual fulfillment** are common, as well. Finally, most of us have some "higher order" motivations, such as quests for **meaning, self-actualization, or transcendence.**

Motives often reflect our values, but not always. Everyone has occasions when they violate their values to expedite achieving a pressing motivation. In fact, conflicts between values and motives can be the single most important factor rendering us susceptible to untoward influences.

Although we already have identified some common, primary motives, we have not defined motivation which for our purposes will be considered to be the psychological energy that impels us to decide and to act. That leaves the task of defining values. For that, we will use the Parks-Leduc and Quay definition (2009) of values as principles that guide personal thoughts and behaviors. As thus defined, values are pivotal to our decisions and influences. Therefore, it is important to know your values. That task could be overwhelming, since anyone **could** value virtually anything, and values can conflict and shift.

In the psychological literature, there sometimes is a fuzzy boundary between what is called a primary motive and what is called a value. That is understandable, since we most often are motivated toward that which we value. You will notice, then, that a couple of the below-listed values also were mentioned as motives. Just think of the motive aspect as the energizer, and the values aspect as the guiding principle.

That said, what are some of the more common values within our culture that guide us? I believe we can agree for our purposes here that they are, in alphabetical order, the extent to which we place a premium upon: activities, experiences, health, ideas, material objects, money, nature, people, and status. As mentioned above, the priority that we assign to these and other values can shift and conflict. Influencers know that and use that knowledge to their advantage.

To deny influencers the advantage, understand how your values began and how you sustain them. The critical variable, once again, is your "ego strength"—history, temperament, personality, and environments. History is critical because, all else being equal, the history of your behavior is the best predictor of your future behavior. In fact, there is evidence that misinformation about your past behavior provided to you by others can influence your current behavior (Albarracín & Wyer, 2000). Temperament—the biological substrate of your behavioral repertoire, including such factors as your activity level and frustration tolerance—also is critical. For instance, if you are hyperactive, when someone is pressuring you toward their position you may be unwilling or unable adequately to delay and deliberate so as to make your own independent decision. Personality—relatively non-biological features of your self— often will skew you one way or another. If you are too strongly inclined to be agreeable, for example, you might eschew resisting influence so not to be perceived as unfriendly. Finally, your environments—both physical and social—tend to cue you in one direction or another. If you are in a place emblematic of harmony and cooperation, such as in a school, or are surrounded by friends, you could be less inclined to express disagreement with ideas being proposed by an influencer.

Knowing the elements of your ego strength enables you to know why you think, feel, and behave as you do, and it points to how you can resist manipulation. Consider how people make purchases. Some marketers presume that we mostly focus on an item's price, quality, availability, and whether our reference group makes a similar purchase (Berger, 2013). And those four factors certainly are important. However, ego strength considerations are even more central. To illustrate what I mean, let's elaborate the central role of ego strength by imaging that you are in the process of buying a car.

Your History

In the past, you have made thousands of purchases that constitute your history as a customer. Your current car-buying effort will share some features with earlier purchases and some features will be different. However, you have developed some consumer habits that will implicitly or explicitly affect what you do presently. You might be one who typically goes to several sites to find the best deal. Or you might be one who preferentially has gone to one spot that you regard as "the best." Perhaps you usually have bought a product of intermediate price, or have gotten the high-end one. In buying a car, you would do well to consider your consumer purchasing history, especially the aspects of that history that, as close as possible, match making an automobile purchase. Your past car-buying history of course is the most obvious match. Use whatever historical understanding you have to inform your efforts to resist unwanted influences from car salespersons and advertisements.

Your Temperament

Many dimensions of temperament could be involved, so let's just consider one: persistence. Again look to your past. Think about important purchases wherein you were especially persistent or impersistent. The examples of adequate persistence are particularly important, if you are a person inclined to readily withdraw from complex and/or challenging situations. We all know that the proverbial car salesperson is the archetypal maximally persistent influencer. Let lessons from your previous persistence experiences prepare you for the current endeavor.

Your Personality

Any aspect of your personality can be a factor in your purchase. How about the extent to which you are introverted versus extroverted? Once again, the prototypic car salesperson is an extravert par excellence. If you are introverted, you readily could be overwhelmed by the force of the salesperson's extraversion. If extroverted, you might get into a "let's have a good time buddy" mood that compromises your rationality. In either case, your personality will be an impediment to your dispassionately evaluating the pros and cons of the automobile purchase decision. And, due to your personality, you will have been unduly influenced by the interpersonal features of the transaction instead of the financial ones.

Your Environments

The most obvious car-purchase-relevant environment is the showroom with its glittering autos and smiling salespeople. But, for the sake of discussion, let's think outside the showroom box. Rather, consider other environments that might sway you. Other physical environments certainly can affect car buying. For one, on the highway you might notice cars zipping past your lumbering vehicle during the daily commute, or in the parking lot, you might compare your car with the others. Day after day you view the array of autos, from flashy to decrepit. Consciously or unconsciously, you have contrasted your vehicle with those you see. On the other hand, perhaps it is not the car comparison per se that would influence your new purchase. Maybe it's the social fact that when you and Waldo walk from the parking lot to the office together, you slink away from your old $18,000 Ford Focus while he gazes lovingly at his brand-spanking new $96,000 Mercedes S550 Sedan. If a salesperson either can tap into your automobile comparison or your social envy frames of mind, you might be willing to shell out $40,000 instead of the $30,000 that you would prefer to pay for a new car.

Contextual Symbiosis

When your ego strength is fully compatible with your values, current intention, and situation, you achieve contextual symbiosis. That is, the consistency of your history, temperament, personality, and environments predisposes you to understand what you want and don't want, and you are inclined to act accordingly. That of course is an ideal synchrony that usually does not fully obtain. Ego strength is more likely to be only partially compatible with your current intention. In that more common case, you must work to achieve a satisfactory compromise. You might value employment-related learning and truly intend to work toward honing a particular skill. You have a history of learning success, a temperament that enables you to endure the delayed gratification that comes with rigorous study, and a personality characterized by conscientiousness and a work ethic. However, your environments conspire against you. Perhaps your financial situation is such that you cannot afford the expensive learning program that you want, or maybe your spouse is antagonistic to the prospect of you diverting time and money away from him/her.

Whenever a constituent of your ego strength is incompatible with your values and current intentions, you are especially vulnerable to influence there, whether it be posfluence or negfluence. And whenever you can remedy that incompatibility on your own, the greater your resistance to influence, and the greater your autonomy will be. As is apparent, there is no context without you. You must be the glue that holds the constituents of your ego strength together, and that makes them work to your advantage. You are the agent who promotes or undermines contextual symbiosis. And contextual symbiosis is your key to success in any worthwhile endeavor.

So, you need proactively to manage your ego strength to improve contextual symbiosis. In influence situations always strive to achieve as much symbiosis as possible among your ego strength constituents. If, for instance, your history reveals that you have been manipulated by fast talkers, you should prime the resistance-enhancing features of your temperament, personality, and environments to compensate for your historic vulnerability. Perhaps you can imagine the manipulation beforehand, or literally rehearse with someone ways to hone temperament and personality defenses. To make those defenses even more effective, also use environments to your advantage. For instance, when anticipating a decision, do your best to could move its venue to a location in the physical environment, or next to a person in the interpersonal environment that creates a supportive feeling in you.

Rational Decisions?

From all that has been said thus far, you might be tempted to conclude that I am advocating a purely logical approach to decision making. But that is not at all true. I believe that much decision making is not at all rational. Most of what we have discussed so far supports that belief. And we will return again and again to recommendations that underline the critical importance of emotion. Later, for instance, we will elaborate the role of emotion-directed decisions as contained in Daniel Kahneman's System 1 theory, and Antonio Damasio's gut-level theory. Both of them, in fact, underscore that automatic and emotional processes typically are the default mechanisms that determine most of our choices. We overcome habitual, non-rational decision processes only by deliberate efforts to do so. Most often, we unconsciously and erroneously expect that the effort toward rationality is either unnecessary, or not worth the energy expenditure.

In the not-too-distant past, economists did believe that most of our choices are logical. That "rational choice theory" was replaced, however, by the now widely accepted notion of "bounded rationality"(Simon, 1991). The newer idea is that although we strive to be rational, there frequently are at least three formidable impediments to purely logical decisions. First, we incorrectly believe that we have **access** to the relevant, valid, and reliable information with which to decide. Second, we presume that we possess the intellectual and/or educational **skills** to use the relevant, valid, and reliable information that is available. And third, we think that we are willing and able to devote the necessary **time and effort** to use the relevant, valid, and reliable information to make our decisions.

Maybe you do realize that you lack information access, skills, or time and effort to make a good decision. In fact, that realistic realization might be the very reason that you turn to an influence provider. And if you do, looking to the influencer could be a very good option, or a very bad one. The influencer also is limited in their relevant, valid, and reliable information access, skills, and time. But unlike you, the influencer presents him/her-self as the expert whose worth is based on having solid, bounded rationality competencies. They may not really know as much as you or they think they do. They may not have the capabilities that you or they think they do. They may not devote the necessary time and effort that you presume they do. Even worse, they may deliberately deceive you about any or all of their limitations in order to exert their influence. So, before you turn to an expert influencer, educate yourself to the point that you have reasonable, informed expectations about the relevant, valid, and reliable state-of-the-art information available, and about the skills, time and effort required for an authentic professional to properly assist you.

One other related decision issue deserves your consideration. In the aggregate, influencers regularly present us with too many choices. And too many choices can be overwhelming to the extent that we become paralyzed, and refrain from choosing at all (Schwartz, 2005). Our quest for material goods, such as automobiles, is a case in point. The Ford or Chevy days are long gone. The following list of auto manufacturers is abstracted from globalbrands.com, and, of course, does not include the specific models from each company.

German— Mercedes-Benz, Audi, Volkswagen, BMW, Opel, and Porsche

Italian—Fiat, Lancia, Alfa Romeo, Lamborghini, Maserati, and Ferrari

French—Citroen, Renault, Bugatti, Alpine, and Peugeot

British—McLaren, Aston Martin, Vauxhall, Bentley, Rolls-Royce, Land Rover, and Mini

American—Chrysler, Dodge, Jeep, Chevrolet, Buick, GMC, Cadillac, Lincoln, and Ford

Japanese—Honda, Toyota, Suzuki, Lexus, Infiniti, Mazda, Mitsubishi, and Nissan

Korean—Hyundai, Kia, and Daewoo

Chinese—Geely, Chery, Hongqi, Brilliance, and BYD

Although not choosing is one way to deal with such a large array of choices, there is another common strategy decried by Mark Penn (2018). His focus is not so much with material choices, but with ideational and ideological ones. Penn believes that many people first confront a welter of choices, choose one option impulsively, and then never deviate from it. He mentions American cable news consumption as particularly destructive. Like many of us, he recognizes that viewers make a selection— such as Fox (conservative) versus MSNBC (liberal)—and become insulated from alternative ideas. In so doing, such viewers permit one influencer group to dominant their thinking, and foster an us-against-them mentality that weakens our democracy.

So, you might refrain from making proffered choices when too many are presented, or sample the field, find one, and never deviate from it. Both strategies restrict your access to potentially salutary change. However, whether you decide not to choose or to choose, please do not abrogate your responsibility continually to vet the information and advice that the influencer is providing before you reach your conclusion.

CHAPTER 8: Expert Intimidation

As repeatedly emphasized, influencers regularly attempt to convince us of their expertise; it is their touchstone. Both phony and true experts present information to sway us. In the first case, if we have the time and motivation, we have a fighting chance to discover the fraud, and resist the influence. The second case, however, poses a real challenge. Since even a true expert is only as good as her/his information, we must have the temerity to question the validity of what the "expert" tells us. Moreover, we need to ask whether the expert's general information is applicable within our unique context. Does the true expert really know us and our lifespace well enough to tell us what to do?

Phony experts are interested only in manipulating, not informing. Take, for example, a common practice called "paltering" in which an influencer actively delivers truthful information about one issue in order to deceive about another, more important one. That is, they do not lie and they do not omit relevant information about which you directly inquire, they merely try to distract us by introducing additional information that favors their position, even if it is trivial compared to the overwhelming information that they possess against their position. Malicious paltering includes, but is not limited to, subterfuge and sabotage. Todd Rogers and colleagues (2017) studied paltering in detail, finding it to be a common negotiation tactic. Not surprisingly, influencers considered their paltering more acceptable than outright lying, but their targets did not.

Now, let's think further about persons with authentic expert credentials who do not intend to palter or otherwise deceive. They certainly know much more about their area than you do, but they probably think they know infinitely more than they really know. Some experts have such an over-inflated sense of superiority that when provided a selection of information relevant to a given issue, they scrupulously avoid considering anything that seems counter to their pre-existing, entrenched beliefs (Hall & Raimi, 2018). More important is that many consumers of advice have an overly optimistic interpretation of experts' directives. Leong and & Zaki (2018) produced empirical results to that effect. In a series of three studies, they evaluated the performances of expert stock advisors and the reactions of their clients. Even when provided feedback about the limitations of their advisors, the clients tended to select the recommended stocks more often than the flawed advisor advice warranted. That is, the clients not only over-evaluated their expert initially, but also avoided changing those initial expectations after having information about the experts' limitations.

The power of experts is greatly enhanced by our "optimism bias" that is defined as our predilection to more readily accept personally favorable information than personally unfavorable information. Now, combine optimism bias with presumptive trust, that we discussed earlier, and what do we have? The obvious answer is that negfluencers profit from optimism bias by framing their interventions in ways that appear favorable to us. And negfluencers profit from presumptive trust merely by relating to you as a nice guy or gal, a regular Joe or Jane. When in the company of negfluencers, then, the more optimism bias and presumptive trust you evidence, the more likely you will be manipulated. Conversely, the more default skepticism you possess, the less likely you will be manipulated.

Of course, experts frequently cite convincing research to bolster their contentions. That certainly could increase client confidence in them. But perhaps, unbeknownst to the experts, the research that they cite can be so flawed that it is useless or harmful. Without dwelling excessively on the issue, a few facts are instructive.

Writing in the journal *Nature*, Monya Baker (2015) reported that only 39% of a group of prestigious psychology research projects could be replicated, and John Ioannidis of Stanford University was said to believe replication-failure could be at least double that rate. And, if you dismiss psychological research as too soft, Brian Nosek, a social psychologist from Charlottesville, Virginia, expressed the opinion that other professions rely on equally flawed data. For instance, he mentioned that a study of 53 high quality cancer papers found that only 6 of the outcomes could be adequately replicated. Even so-called "hard science" advocates questionable ideas from time to time. Take physics—perhaps the hardest of the hard sciences—in which the string theory controversy has raged for decades. In brief, proponents believe that "strings" are the fundamental force of nature and basically are the "stuff" that comprises even particles as elementary as neutrons and protons. A Massachusetts Institute of Technology website (http://web.mit.edu/demoscience/StringTheory/actors.html) lists 23 stand-out physicists who support the theory, but also 5 experts who vigorously oppose the idea. Among the latter are Nobel Prize winner Richard Feynman who called string theory research a "dead-end," and Peter Wolf who dismissed string theory as "untestable"—the kiss of death for a scientific theory of any type.

The obvious reason for addressing paltering and expert opinions is to caution you not to become enamored by either phony or authentic expert pronouncements. You need to adopt an internal locus of control that permits you automatically to resist any information, particularly any unsolicited information, long enough to assess it objectively and contextually. That takes resolve and effort that only comes with considerable practice and confidence.

I Understand What You Are Saying, But What Am I Seeing?

When advised to be vigilant toward unwanted influence, most people naturally focus on the explanations that an influencer articulates regarding any given issue. That is because we all have a natural tendency toward what psychologists call "theory of mind" (ToM), meaning that we regularly evaluate what we are thinking, what others are thinking, and the similarities and differences between the two. This bias toward language is both a strength and a weakness in that it sensitizes us to what is said, but distracts us from what is visually present. Think about the four primary influence vehicles—people and their institutions, objects and ideas, processes, and situations: all include visual components that persuaders can manipulate to their advantage. So you cannot merely be language-alert; you need to be visually alert as well. Marketers prioritize capturing your visual attention. Rik Pieters and Michel Wedel (2004), for instance, advise companies how to achieve "visual capture" in print advertisements via strategic use of three key components— presentation of the brand (as in the brand logo), pictures, and text. The three components are made distinctive and captivating by customizing their sizes, colors, contrasts, and placements in the ad.

You, in turn, can be more influence-resistant by understanding a few basic Gestalt principles (Wagemans, et al., 2012) that describe how we organize our perceptions [virtually any sensory perception]. By knowing the principles, you can carefully survey the environment to determine sensory elements that might be affecting you, either consciously or unconsciously. As examples, imagine some of the following Gestalt principles of organization being applied to advertising that attempts to bias you toward believing that items are meaningfully linked to each other.

Proximity: items placed near each other—an attractive person drinking a sponsor's beer.

Similarity: items superficially alike—a fancy home goods product placed in an expensive house.

Closure: items presented incompletely that highlight its best features and mask its worst—a shiny automobile shown at an angle favoring its expansive front end, not its stubby rear.

Parallelism: items presented with the same shape—two sales charts created with an identical slope, linking together information from two different, uncorrelated items.

Common Boundaries: items in a common enclosure—a line enclosing two items, such as a dish containing an unhealthful, greasy food product next to three broccoli stalks.

Common Fate: items shown moving in the same direction or at the same endpoint, suggesting a common result—a financial planning video that alternates between showing a young struggling couple camping and an older, established one sailing on a luxurious yacht.

Gorilla Basketball

Not all visual stimuli capture your conscious attention. We all occasionally fall victim to "inattentional blindness," failing to see that which is unambiguously present. The concept received nationwide popularity when Harvard's "gorilla study" received media coverage. For that research, Chabris and Simons (1999) recruited 192 subjects who were asked to observe 6 simultaneously-present young adults—3 wearing white shirts and 3 wearing black—during which time each color-coded group passed a basketball between members of their own group. Subjects were instructed to count the number of passes only of one color–coded group and to ignore the other one. While the action proceeded, a person in a gorilla costume walked in plain sight through the array of basketball-passing subjects. In fact, the gorilla even briefly paused, faced the camera videotaping the experiment, and pounded his chest. In a post-experiment interview, each subject was asked whether they had seen anything unusual while counting, and, amazingly, only about 50 percent had noticed the gorilla.

The usual interpretation of the study is that some subjects were so focused on counting that they were totally unaffected by the gorilla's presence. But Chabris and Simons are more cautious in their conclusions, writing that there might have been implicit affects that were not measured. That is, the supposedly unaffected subjects might have registered the gorilla's presence, but only unconsciously, and, perhaps, the unconscious affects would be demonstrable with proper testing. Such unconscious affects certainly would be consistent with all that we know about unconscious thinking. In any case, I mention the study primarily to underscore that we are not always aware of what is and is not in front of our faces. And that absence of attention renders us vulnerable to an influencer intent on manipulating our conscious and unconscious minds to his advantage.

The only way to resist influence is to expend deliberate, focused effort. You can't just want to resist unbidden influence, you must behave actively to resist it. Automatic, unconscious processing is the usual default mode and, in a propaganda context, automatic, unconscious processing can be insidiously harmful. However, there is real hope. Neurological research strongly indicates that your behavior determines and modifies your brain functioning. The more you practice an action, the greater and more robust the habit change. You need to do all that is necessary to develop an internal locus of control and self-determination as your personal influence default. Neuroscientist Lara Boyd (2015) puts it bluntly: "…you and your plastic [malleable] brain are constantly being shaped by the world around you. Understand that everything you do, everything you encounter, and everything you experience is changing your brain. And that can be for better, but it can also be for worse …" Make Gestalt principles, attention, mental processing, and overt action work for, not against, you and your malleable brain.

Self-Regulation

Making Gestalt principles work for you is one feature of self-regulation. In 1997, E. Tory Higgins wrote about an especially salient dimension of self-regulation/lifestyle change motivation that he termed "regulatory focus" by which he meant a person's conviction about making a desired change, and about how to make it. When regulatory focus and strategies for change match, the individual experiences an intuitive confidence about achieving his goals, and when regulatory focus and strategies conflict, the opposite occurs. Two primary dimensions comprise regulatory fit—prevention and promotion. A person adopts a prevention approach by framing a healthful change as being necessary to avoid an undesired outcome, such as seeking to become a vegetarian in order to avoid heart disease. By contrast, he employs a promotion strategy by framing a healthful change as being necessary to produce a desired outcome, such as seeking to become a vegetarian to enhance general health. To quote Higgins:

> A prevention focus emphasizes safety, responsibility, and security needs. Goals are viewed as oughts and there is a strategic concern with approaching non-losses (the absence of negatives) and avoiding losses (the presence of negatives). A promotion focus emphasizes hopes, accomplishments, and advancement needs. Goals are viewed as ideals, and there is a strategic concern with approaching gains (the presence of positives) and avoiding non-gains (the absence of positives).

Prevention, then, essentially is personal fear-oriented. So, like other fearsome situations, fear-based prevention should be most effective when several conditions obtain (Tannenbaum et al.,

2015). First, the fearsome message includes a high level of fear-arousing stimuli. Second, it suggests that the targeted person is particularly susceptible to the negative consequences. And, third, the presented information directs the targeted person toward strategies for avoiding the negative consequences that had been described. Promotion, on the other hand, is personal growth-oriented and, therefore, attractively resonant to virtually all people irrespective of conditions.

A prevention strategy encourages an individual to be 'vigilant" about negative outcomes while a promotion strategy encourages him to be "eager" about positive ones. Higgins posits that prevention and promotion either can be a "trait" or "state" characteristic, with trait meaning a relatively ingrained feature of personality, and state meaning a disposition that readily can change over times and situations. Moreover, prevention and promotion can be intrinsically or extrinsically motivated—tendencies, respectively, that mostly proceed from within oneself, or that mostly proceed from external cues.

You would do well, then, to consider whether a prevention or a promotion oreintaiton better enables you to resist any given unwanted influence. A resistant stance can begin with a thought or state of mind, but the stance also must include some action, such as movement away from the agent of influence. For that reason, the more directly and consciously you link a resistant thought or state of mind to an appropriate resistant action, the greater the likelihood that your resistance will become habitual.

Martiny-Huenger and colleagues (2017) provided empirical support for that advice. They showed that the more one verbally planned to execute a specific action, the more the action tendency became automatic. However, the tendency required an if-then intention action plan. For instance, experimental subjects who verbalized the goal of eating healthier and an intention to "grab" an apple were quicker to make that apple-grabbing movement not only in the session in which they articulated the intention, but also after the session had ended. The Martiny-Huenger group inferred that automaticity was achieved because the same brain structures were primed by the *thought* of grabbing the apple and by the *action* necessary to actually grab the apple.

For our discussion of influence, think about it this way: Whenever you are significantly influenced, you subsequently act differently. If, for example, a health provider delivers to you an inspiring talk about how to improve your eating habits, and you do not modify your eating in any way, you have not been influenced. Conversely, if after the talk you replace your cheeseburger lunches with salad lunches, that action provides health-inducing practice and the possibility for you to realize some concrete benefit, such as weight reduction or cholesterol lowering. The benefit, in turn, reinforces your tendency to think and act in other ways that are consistent with improved eating, and a virtuous cycle of healthful thoughts and healthful actions is set in motion.

You will remember that much earlier I suggested that almost any influence can have positive (posfluence), negative (negfluence), deliberate, or unintended consequences, and that persuasion is a special form of deliberate influence that also can have positive (posuasion) or negative (negsuasion) consequences. Those earlier suggestions must be integrated with our just-concluded discussion of regulatory focus, if we are to achieve a thorough, nuanced appreciation of influence. You certainly care whether the influence outcome is positive or negative, and you will view that outcome differently when you perceive the influencer as having deliberately tried to persuade you versus merely having offered you an unadorned genuine opinion.

Since no one is totally good or bad, we can identify some positive and some negative features of all but the most malevolent influencers. So, in the next two sections, we will focus on some potentially positive and some potentially negative features of several influencer types. But, because our focus primarily is on resisting intrusive and malicious influences, in the next two sections and all succeeding chapters we will devote most attention to negfluences.

CHAPTER 9: What Influencers Usually Want

As acknowledged from the start, attempts to influence are as old as humankind. However, concern about society-wide influence has tended to be epoch-specific. Potential dangers from institutional influencers became especially acute and recognized, for instance, during the 1960s after out-going president Dwight D. Eisenhower' s famous farewell speech. That televised address, broadcasted on January 17, 1961, became known as the Military-Industrial Complex Speech. In it, the 34th President of the United States warned about "grave consequences" that could result from "unwarranted influence, whether sought or unsought." Although mostly focusing on unwarranted influences coming from the military and from industrial companies that profit from it, Eisenhower strongly implied other, more extensive negfluences. He specifically said that "the very structure of our society" could be impacted deleteriously. Presciently, Ike cautioned that the scientific march of progress, itself, risked being hijacked by powerful influencers. In 21st century America, Eisenhower's admonition deserves to be quoted in its entirety, and its message must be understood implicitly:

> Today, the solitary inventor, tinkering in his shop,
> has been overshadowed by task forces of scientists
> in laboratories and testing fields. In the same
> fashion, the free university, historically the
> fountainhead of free ideas and scientific
> discoveries, has experienced a revolution in the
> conduct of research. Partly because of the huge
> costs involved, a government contract becomes
> virtually a substitute for intellectual curiosity. For
> every old blackboard there are now hundreds of
> new electronic computers.
>
> The prospect of domination of the nation's
> scholars by Federal employment, project

allocations, and the power of money is ever present and is gravely to be regarded. Yet, in holding scientific research and discovery in respect, as we should, we must also be alert to the equal and opposite danger that public policy could itself become the captive of a scientific technological elite.

Although prescient, President Eisenhower never could have imagined how 21st century technology, especially electronic technology, has developed so incredibly that it now is possible for virtually any powerful elite to exert society-wide influence. However, when apprised of the present culture, he, no doubt, would understand that today's influencers can be motivated by any number of posfluential or negfluential reasons. Some influencer motivations are no different than those held by most people across time and space. Psychologists have proposed lists of these common, general motivations. Although the composite list is quite long, several general motives are relevant for our purposes: Everyone surely wants to be **physically comfortable** and **safe**. Most seek both **beneficial social connections** and **autonomy**. We all sometimes look for **excitement** and sometimes for **tranquility**. People try to attain **competencies, order,** and **stability**. Desire for **money, power,** and **sexual fulfillment** are common, as well. Finally, most of us have some "higher order" motivations, such as quests for **meaning, self-actualization,** and **transcendence**. Although these primary motives certainly do not exhaust all the possibilities, they are sufficient for our purposes.

The key idea here is that both those who deliver influence and those who receive influence have their own highly personal motives for influencing and accepting influence, respectively. Sometimes the motivations are identical. For instance, an influencer might be motivated by a desire for power, and the person influenced accedes to the influencer in the hope of sharing in the influencer's power. Some motives tend to complement each other (e.g., money and power) and others often conflict (e.g., social connection and autonomy). When an individual attempts to influence another person, one or more of her/his motives will be in ascendance and others will be in abeyance.

Although general motives are common to most people, influence peddlers also tend to have specific profession-linked motives and desires. What follows is a kind of stereotyping of the influencer types that certainly does not hold for all those in any influencer category. However, the quasi tongue-in-cheek depictions that follow do offer some guidance about occupation-specific motivation.

Politicians and other government officials implicitly ask us to empower them to guide social policy and conduct. They use the social empowerment to enable them to legitimize their goals.

Media controllers implicitly ask us to respond to worlds that they fashion. When we do, it makes their worlds more real and worth their investments.

Celebrities implicitly ask us to look at them and to identify with the character that they portray. This satisfies their exhibitionistic and narcissistic desires.

Advertisers and salespersons implicitly ask us to desire the products that they promote. They want us to give them our money.

Educators implicitly ask us to learn and embrace the "established truths" that they disseminate They want to mold our susceptible minds.

Scientists implicitly ask us to embrace their novel, even revolutionary, machines and insights. They want to have their achievements recognized and actualized.

Influencer Stimuli and Target Receptivity

Since motives drive behavior, you can reduce your vulnerability to unwanted influencers by being especially attentive to any information that reveals their motivations. Determining basic motives is relatively simple in some contexts. A salesperson obviously has a money motivation. In other contexts, the determination is not so easy. For instance, you presume that a friend has your well-being at heart, but, in a particular situation, she actually might be competitive and attempting to sabotage you. Your own competitive feelings also can work against you. Persons who experience rivalry toward someone, some institution, or some idea, have been found to take greater risks when making decisions related to the object of their rivalry (Christopher To, et al., 2017).

Understanding the influencer's motivation usually requires considerable effort on your part. Awareness of others' motives is only one side of the influence-resistance coin, however. Never fail to consider your own motives as well. By becoming cognizant of them, you know where you are most open to being swayed. Your susceptibility and receptivity probably are greatest for any motive that has been over- or under-gratified in the past. For instance, if you have experienced much reward or much frustration regarding your physical appearance, you might be especially sensitive to any influence that proffers appearance-enhancing benefits. In the first case, you desire to maintain your appearance advantage, and in the second, to overcome your appearance disadvantage. Be aware, too, that any of the four primary influence vehicles— person/institution ("human" influencer), object/idea (concrete item or abstraction that is being promoted), situation (the environment where the influence is provided), or process (how the item or idea is packaged and presented) might be employed by an influencer to appeal to any of your motivation-related vulnerabilities.

When Deception Is Deliberate

Interpersonal Deception Theory (IDT)

We often speak of some people as "know it alls" whose self-esteem is dependent on demonstrating their superior knowledge—telling everyone what to do and how to do it. Such people often deceive us because we are taken-in by their domineering personalities. However, there are other persons who mislead us explicitly for personal utilitarian gain more palpable than ego enhancement, such as to reap financial rewards. It is obvious that we need to be on the look-out for these two, and for all other exploiter types. The question follows then: How do we understand manipulative personalities and their exploitive tactics?

David B. Buller and Judee K. Burgoon (1996) provided a well-respected set of 18 principles, contained within their Interpersonal Deception Theory (IDT), that empower us to resist manipulation. The comprehensive system that they created addresses relevant situations, deceivers, targets of deception, and the interactions between deceivers and their targets. In the discussion that follows, rather than enumerate the 18 individually, I will aggregate them to make IDT concrete and practical.

The situation almost always is pivotal for deception. Some situations encourage fluid back and forth interaction, and some are more one-sided. The latter, for instance, is likely to obtain when the deceiver is in a power position, either due to her personal qualities, due to being in a power-enhancing environment, or both. Think, for instance of an esteemed doctor interacting with a client who has no knowledge related to the doctor's specialty. The situation timeline also is a factor in deception, since interactions often evolve. In the aforementioned doctor-client scenario, the relationship of the two principals might become more or less formal over the short- or long-term, depending on their personalities and objectives. The history of the deceiver with the target exerts a strong affect, too. When they know each other, they have established mutual expectations, positive and negative. Those expectations can be recruited by either member to decode the nature of their ongoing transactions, and to use that knowledge strategically.

Both deceivers and targets evidence "leakage," meaning verbal and/or non-verbal behaviors that reveal their covert beliefs that conflict with their overtly expressed ones. Either person then may engage in "strategic behaviors" intended to cope with the situation as they truly perceive it. Therefore, the more accurately the deceiver or target interprets leakage and responds strategically, the more likely they will take control of the situation. Each of the interactors unwittingly reveals their level of suspicion in their leakage and strategies, and these can be interpreted and used to advantage by their interacting counterpart. The target is particularly vulnerable to the extent that he is passive, predisposed to default presumptive trust, and when dealing with a well-practiced deceiver. Moreover, those with strong default presumptive trust frequently also tend to relate more warmly and more inactively with their deceiver, increasing their vulnerability. The target is more inclined to correctly detect a deception when she is a careful listener, familiar with the deceiver, recognizes when the deceiver alters his demeanor or behavior in a self-serving or ingratiating manner, and when she is interpersonally wary. Conversely, the deceiver is more successful when he can distract his target, ensure that changes in his demeanor or behavior are subtle, or explicitly rationalize his personality change to the target.

Earlier we discussed "theory of mind" (ToM) by which we all regularly evaluate what we are thinking, what others are thinking, and the similarities and differences between the two. Our capacity for suspicion is one consequence of ToM. Both deceivers and targets can become suspicious of the other's intentions, especially in influence situations. And, to speak recursively, when the deceiver is suspicious that the target is suspicious, both are likely to increase the intensity of their strategic behaviors. And when the deceiver increases his strategic behavior the target also has a greater opportunity to notice the intensification and any leakage coincident with it. A vigilant, informed target, then, can counter any most intended deceptions.

The conclusion of a conversation is particularly important for the participants' evaluations of success and for their future expectations of the partner. Both deceiver and target look at their own final reaction and that of their counterpart. Each participant, therefore, has a greater chance of achieving their goals and of maintaining credibility, earned or unearned, when they continue to employ strong listening skills until the very end of the conversation. It is important, for instance, that each scrutinizes any of the other's final strategic moves and any leakage. With each successive encounter, of course, familiarity increases. One would expect familiarity to be particularly advantageous to a serial deceiver, and that often is true. However, the target also is becoming more familiar with the deceiver's personality and with his communicative style. When the deceiver perceives that the target is becoming increasingly suspicious, he might respond by becoming more fearful that his lies will be detected. If so, the fear could cause him unwittingly to increase the frequency and intensity of his strategic moves, causing a corresponding increase in his leakage. The target then has more data from which to deduce the deceiver's manipulation style.

Information Manipulation Theory 2 (IMT2)

Deception clearly has a negative connotation. Even those who truly want to deceive you "for your own good" can be criticized for their paternalism, and lack of faith in you. On the other hand, information manipulation has a less nefarious, even neutral, connotation. Under the best circumstances, information manipulation merely could involve a good faith distilling of a welter of facts and figures to make them comprehensible to others. Under the worst circumstances, information is manipulated to deceive or to harm, perhaps providing the deceiver personal gain at the target's expense.

Steven A. McCornack and his colleagues (2014) examine the deceptive side of information manipulation in a manner consistent with the focus of this book [and broadly similar to Interpersonal Deception Theory (IDT)]. The McCornack group primarily structures their work around the classic, highly-respected communication principles of Herbert Paul Grice (1989) that will be discussed again later. For now, you merely need to know that Grice's four principles are: the Maxim of quality—We seek correct information; Maxim of quantity—We seek just enough information, no more and no less; Maxim of relation—We seek the most relevant information; and Maxim of manner—We seek information that is expressed as clearly and coherently as possible. The McCornack Information Manipulation Theory 2 (IMT2) elaborates Grice's principles by presenting one central proposition that, for our purposes, essentially is defined by its eleven subsidiary premises, all of which are measurable. The subsidiary premises are grouped into 2 pertaining to intentional states (IS), 3 pertaining to cognitive load (CL), and 6 pertaining to information manipulation (IM) per se. IS concerns the timing and expected value of deception during speech production. CL is the amount of energy required to communicate an idea. And IF is the condition or conditions most likely to favor information honesty vs. information manipulation.

IMT2 suggests that persons can execute deceptions by violating any of Grice's 4 maxims. The quality maxim is most obvious, since it pertains to providing correct information. That, of course, presumes that the deceiver knows that his information is incorrect. The quantity maxim is relevant in that one readily can choose to provide too much or too little information in an attempt to misinform. The relation maxim also is easy to manipulate in ways similar to the quantity maxim in the sense that information is withheld that is at odds with the speaker's goals. And, finally, the manner maxim can be used to deceive when the speaker-preferred information is provided clearly and coherently, and any disclosure of speaker-non-preferred information is withheld, or provided in an unclear and/or incoherent way.

McCornack asserts that deceptions, in descending order of frequency, are those that violate quantity, quality, manner, and relation. That is, more people are inclined to omit all the speaker-non-preferred relevant information before they lie outright, to lie outright before they speak unclearly or incoherently, and to speak unclearly or incoherently before they interject information totally and obviously irrelevant to the subject at hand. That hierarchy of deceptive strategies seems obvious in parts, and counterintuitive in other parts. Accordingly, IMT2 takes pains to justify their system [lest they, themselves, be accused of violating the Grice maxims]. As I have done with other arcane topics earlier in this book, I merely will touch very briefly on the most essential features of the rationales for their hierarchy.

IMT2 emphasizes the roles of efficiency, memory, and means-ends, that I will call "the mechanisms of discourse production." Efficiency refers to our desire to expend as little energy as possible. Memory pertains to the ways in which we access and employ the information that we have retrieved. And means-ends is how we structure our conversations to achieve desired outcomes.

The McCornack group believes that truth tellers and deceivers use the same mechanisms of discourse production, but the latter do so exploitatively. One way deceivers exploit is by their corrupted "intentional states." That means that deceivers try to deliver misleading words and statements within their speech at times, and in ways that further their ends. For instance, if they feel compelled to admit some bit of information inimical to their intention, they could deliver it very early and briefly, followed by a lengthy, detailed ending that obfuscates and/or excuses the early inimical information. A second deceptive method of discourse production involves manipulating "cognitive load," the amount of working memory that one must devote to understanding. A burdensome cognitive load reduces the listener's ability to understand, and, therefore, to challenge the speaker. For instance, a deceiver might introduce a string of sketchily described technical information, such that you have trouble clearly remembering and/or understanding the earlier information that must be integrated to understand the later information. The third and final deceiver strategy is simply called "information manipulation." This refers to the deceiver's understanding the particular conditions that makes your specific manipulation more or less possible. The astute deceiver will have learned which deception is likely to work when. For example, he might realize that you are a person who can be duped only by being presented many compelling facts and figures that he currently lacks such data, and, therefore, plans the deception for a time when he has suitably deceptive data at hand.

In contrast to some theories, however, IMT2 posits that deceptions need not be planned in advance. Rather, they can evolve during conversation turn taking via a series of alternating truths and lies. That is, each element of deception very often is a spontaneous, real-time adjustment in the hope of reaching the deceiver's desired conclusion by communicating misinformation that is easiest to access and deliver. In the words of McCornack and Morrison (2012), "… people will commonly 'change it up' mid-utterance, from truth to deception (and back again), depending on dynamic changes in perceived discrepancies between initial states and desired end states."

Practical Implications of the Interpersonal Deception and Information Manipulation Theories

Let's consider how IDT and IMT2 might treat the same deceptive conversation. Imagine handsome, svelte Jack, a 36-year-old contractor, and Jill, a 43-year-old, average-looking single homeowner. The two are based in the same small town. From time to time they cross paths in a parking lot or local store, but the interactions have been limited to a quick "hello" and a warm smile. Having noticed the business sign on his truck, one day Jill asks Jack if he does stucco remediation. She explains that one of her windows has leaked slightly on a couple occasions after particularly heavy rainfalls. Jack offers a free stucco evaluation. The two of them exchange business-oriented information, and agree on a time for him to explain the service. One week later, Jack arrives at Jill's house where she greets him at the door after which Jack performs the inspection. Jack finds that Jill's problem could be solved by re-caulking, but he is struggling financially. He recommends extensive repairs because at the time he needs all the business he can get.

First, an analysis of their discussion via interpersonal deception theory is as follows:

They are meeting at Jill' house [a setting that should favor Jill]. Jack does 90 percent of the talking, sometimes even cutting-off Jill's questions [Jack is taking advantage of his expertise power position]. Jack claims that he is getting many service requests, and must choose quickly in order to "keep up" [The situation timeline is used to force Jill to make a quick, unreflective decision]. The two discussants have only a superficial, highly circumscribed history together [Jill must make a decision without adequate knowledge of the kind of person that Jack truly is]. Jack keeps the conversation as deliberately brief and vague as possible [This minimizes the chance of leakage regarding his manipulation. Moreover, those brief and vague conditions favor Jack who likely has well-developed deceptive behaviors that give him the upper hand]. To add to her vulnerability, Jill's personality is a liability [She entertains a high level of presumptive trust, and is relatively passive vis-à-vis her contractor-neighbor]. Radiant and fit, Jack also senses that he is very attractive to Jill [Jack distracts her with flirtatious antics]. Jill's infatuation also compromises her "theory of mind" (ToM) [She is disinclined to become suspicious due to her attraction to Jack]. Skilled in manipulation, Jack controls the conclusion of their discussion, and he ensures that he has little interaction with Jill from the time she signs the building contract to the time she signs his check. [That way she has little opportunity to recognize Jack's deceptive communications over time and topics].

They are meeting at Jill' house [a setting that favors Jill]. Jack does 90 percent of the talking, sometimes even cutting-off Jill's questions [Jack is taking advantage of his power position]. Jack claims that he is getting many service requests, and must choose quickly in order to "keep up" [The situation timeline is used to force Jill to make a quick, unreflective decision]. The two discussants have only a superficial, highly circumscribed history together [Jill must make a decision without adequate knowledge of the kind of person that Jack is]. Jack keeps the conversation as deliberately brief and vague as possible [This minimizes the chance of leakage regarding his manipulation. Moreover, those brief and vague conditions favor Jack who likely has well-developed deceptive behaviors that give him the upper hand]. To add to her vulnerability, Jill's personality is a liability [She entertains presumptive trust, and is relatively passive vis-à-vis her contractor-neighbor]. Radiant and fit, Jack also senses that he is very attractive to Jill [Jack, therefore, distracts her with flirtatious antics]. Jill's infatuation also compromises her "theory of mind" (ToM) [She is disinclined to become suspicious due to her attraction to Jack]. Skilled in manipulation, Jack controls the conclusion of their discussion, and he ensures that he has little interaction with Jill from the time she signs the building contract to the time she signs his check. [That way she has little opportunity to recognize Jack's deceptive communications over time and topics].

Next, consider the same basic Jack and Jill scenario with a few minimal changes to make it comparably analyzable via Information Manipulation Theory 2:

They are meeting at Jill' house [IMT2 does not emphasize the site of conversation, per se]. Jack does 90 percent of the talking, sometimes even cutting-off Jill's questions [The excessive wordiness contradicts the Maxim of quantity, and could operate against Jack]. Jack claims that he is getting many service requests, and must choose quickly in order to "keep up" [That communication is a lie, and, therefore, violates the Maxim of quality]. The two discussants have only a superficial, highly circumscribed history together [The manner maxim is used to deceive because Jill does not have enough history with Jack to have a chance to understand that he is being deliberately unclear and/or incoherent]. Jack keeps the conversation as deliberately brief and vague as possible. [Those brief and vague conditions favor Jack's well-developed deceptive behaviors that give him the upper hand]. To add to her vulnerability, Jill's personality is a liability [IMT2 does not explicitly address presumptive trust]. Radiant and fit, Jack also senses that he is very attractive to Jill [IMT2 does not explicitly address interpersonal attraction]. Jill's infatuation also compromises her "theory of mind" (ToM) [IMT2 does not mention theory of mind]as an independent variable]. Skilled in manipulation, Jack controls the conclusion of their discussion, and he ensures that he has little interaction with Jill from the time she signs the building contract to the time she signs his check. [This is one more instance of a quantity maxim violation by withholding information at odds with Jack's goals].

Although some features of the Jill-Jack scenario did not apply specifically to IMT2, others applied in ways different from the ways that they were explained by IDT. For example, the scenario did support that the idea that Jack's deceptions occurred as violations of quantity, quality, manner, and relation, in descending order of frequency. Similarly he had structured his comments and questions to use intentional states, cognitive load, and information manipulation —the mechanisms of discourse production—wittingly or unwittingly, and in ways that that manipulated the roles of efficiency, memory, and means-ends. Jill would have had to expend much energy, be able to access conversation relevant information, and assert herself sufficiently to structure her comments and questions in order to uncover Jack's deceptions.

The IDT and IMT2 analyses certify the common sense notion that some theories better explain some things, and some better explain other things. The scenarios were not presented to convince you which theory is correct, not which is correct when, and not even whether either is correct. However, by knowing fundamental theoretical notions of deception, you can select theoretical features that seem relevant and reasonable to you in order to better understand any given influence circumstance.

Restoring Trust after Deception and Manipulation

In the mid-1940s, Doris Fisher and Allan Roberts wrote the immensely popular song, "You Always Hurt the One You Love." They might have added to the lyrics, "You sometimes deceive and manipulate the one you love," as well. The latter would be the case for true-gooders who attempt to exert posfluence on you, and end-up delivering negfluence, instead. Although your trust has been violated, the true-good relationship is well worth redeeming. There are times, too, when you might be willing to restore your relationship with a garden-variety negfluence manipulator familiar to you who has done you wrong once, but only minimally. How can trust be restored in those kinds of relationships, since maintaining them makes it likely that the offender will be in a position to influence you again, for better or worse, in the future?

Books can be, and have been, written about establishing, maintaining, and restoring trust. Moreover, we all have our own theories and preferences about the best ways to do so. To simplify the issue in the context of influence, let's apply the common sense advice of Dr. Frances Frei (2018), professor of operations and management technology, at Harvard Business School. She simplifies the process of establishing, maintaining, and restoring trust to three parameters. Authenticity is one of the essential factors. To say so, is to state the obvious, since authenticity is virtually synonymous with trustfulness. However, would-be influencers often are so intent on taking control that they may forget the obvious. Of course, the more frequently you have interacted with the individual and the more varied the contexts, the more confident you can be in deciding that they are being inauthentic at any particular point in time. Frei's second factor is the rigor of the influencer's logic in delivering his message. When logic is shaky or absent, you might conclude that the influencer is deliberately or inadvertently misleading you. However, either their deliberate or inadvertently misapplication of logic can harm you. The last factor concerns empathy. Persons who lack empathy toward you cannot be trusted to care sufficiently about results of their influence upon you.

How do Dr. Frei's ideas translate to dealing with deception and manipulation of any type? When you are alert and clear-headed, you don't need me, or anyone, to tell you how to decide a potential influencer's authenticity, logic, or empathy. But it is precisely when you are least attentive and least clear-headed that you are vulnerable to influence. It is then that you call upon your ego strength—that you will remember is your understanding of your history, temperament, personality, and environments, and of how to make them work for you. Knowing your ego strength means knowing what you are susceptible to and knowing how to inure yourself against negfluence. Call upon ego strength insights to restore your attention and rationality. Thus restored, direct yourself toward assessing the influencer's authenticity, logic, and empathy. A true-gooder probably will receive passing marks on authenticity and empathy, but that does not mean that her logic is sound. A well-intentioned true-gooder who unwittingly dispenses faulty guidance due to ignorance still can cause you big problems. All other manipulators might fail on any or all of Frei's parameters, but especially authenticity and empathy. That is the case because, of the three parameters, you usually can more readily and reliably determine the logic of his suggestions. On the other hand, if you are dealing with an expert manipulator, only after extensive experience with him, or by exceptional intuition, will you be confident about his authenticity and empathy. That is especially true if, as most people, you operate according to Kramer's "presumptive trust" default assumption. After detecting negfluence, if you wish to give any influencer another chance, you must be able to ensure that person's manipulative tendencies are defused fully, both short- and long-term.

CHAPTER 10: "Good" & "Bad" Influencers

They Mean Well

Sometimes good people can lead you astray. The best of the good are our personal true-gooders who are authentic and empathic toward us. We know them, trust them, and often love them. All of those conditions make us open to their influence. In fact, those are the very conditions that can lead us enthusiastically to solicit their influence. When we request advice, we are less likely to critically evaluate that which is offered. First, we presumably asked because we assumed them to be knowledgeable about the issue in question. And second, we do not want to insult them by rejecting that which we solicited. But, as discussed in the previous section, although true-gooders are likely to relate to us with authenticity and empathy, they may not possess the requisite knowledge or deliver a logical explanation sufficient to make their advice helpful on any given topic. Even their authenticity and empathy occasionally can be suspect.

Regarding their authenticity, we all recognize that everyone at times, deliberately or inadvertently, misrepresents what they know and don't know. In the information age in which we live, our self-esteems are tightly connected to our being well informed. No one wants to look stupid, particularly in an area wherein they are presumed to be knowledgeable. The more eagerly and expectantly you have made your influence request, the more implicit pressure true-gooders might feel to produce an outcome. They might be reluctant to disappoint you, or to have your faith in them compromised. Either of those factors, or other ones, could cause the true-gooder unintentionally to influence you in a manner that later causes you harm. In that case, it would have been an isolated case of deliberate inauthenticity in their failure to admit their limitations, but not in their concern for your well-being. In other circumstances, the inauthenticity is inadvertent in the sense that the influencer has an inflated sense of his own capabilities. That is, he is inauthentic in his relationship to himself, and you are the unintended victim of his self-deception. Imagine, for instance, a well-meaning banker friend who fancies himself to be financially astute whom you ask about making a stock market purchase. The banker correctly believes that he knows bonds, but, despite never studying stocks, he blithely pronounces his faulty recommendation. He never intended to misguide you, but you suffered anyway due to his intra-personal inauthenticity rooted in his faulty self-awareness.

True-gooders also can cause you problems related to empathy. Empathy, of course, is not a constant. A trusted person can be empathic toward you in some sectors, and not in others. She might correctly understand and relate compassionately whenever you two discuss family issues. The trusted one knows you, knows your family, and has useful insight related to family problems that you express, and to their potential solutions. On the other hand, perhaps that same person has her own romance-related issues. She, for instance, might be conflicted or frustrated concerning such matters. She might even perceive you as more romantically successful than she, and be jealous of you only in that one narrow sphere. You are unaware of that jealousy. All you know is that her influence has been very helpful in family matters, and you incorrectly assume that she understands people, and will have something valuable to offer about your love life. Many, if not all, true-gooders likely have some life sector wherein they feel competitive with you. If you have a beloved sibling who is a true-gooder, for instance, odds are that she/he experiences some of the proverbial sibling rivalry toward you in some area. A case in point is the research of Annie McNerney and Joy Usner (2014), suggesting that 65 percent of their 20- to 25-year-old sample felt academically competitive with their sibling, but only about 30 percent felt that way about social relationships. Even with normally empathic relationships, the specifics of the relationship are critical.

If your friend presently is immersed in a loving relationship then, her suggestions related to intimacy might be just right for you; if she is alienated, they might be off base. But her influence is not limited to her verbal suggestion, her overt behavior counts mightily, as well. Psychologists refer to an interpersonal contagion effect. The contagion effect usually is insidious and, therefore, hard to recognize. When relationships are positive, we tend to think about and do things like those of our intimates. A close friend who develops a new interest in fishing will converse with you about it. During those discussions you naturally become more attuned to fish-oriented information and, perhaps, more willing to try fishing yourself. The same is true regarding more weighty issues. A friend who confides "exciting" details of her infidelity can pique your interest in its possibilities, making you more likely to be unfaithful yourself.

In "Breaking Up is Hard to Do, Unless Everyone Else is Doing it Too" McDermott and Fowler (2013) conclude that one is more likely to divorce if their friend divorces, even if a friend of a friend divorces. One could reasonably argue that when a friend's own relationships are negative, we should consider acting in our relationships in ways opposite to that which she recommends, but I am unaware of any empirical studies addressing that issue. There is research to suggest, however, that friends who gossip about the problems of third parties sometimes directly or implicitly warn each other not to fall victim themselves (Baumeister, Zhang, & Vohs, 2004). On the other hand, in risky situations, we should be especially cautious about the explicit advice that even our closest friend provides. Sarah Helfinstein and associates (2015) find that before one engages in risky behavior he typically is careful to consider all available information, but he is not nearly so careful before he recommends that same risky behavior to a friend. You always should consider influencer "skin in the game" (Taleb, 2017) when that person makes an important recommendation, especially when the recommendation involves obvious risk to you and to you alone.

All of this is not to say that you summarily should dismiss whatever your close acquaintances advise about you and your behavior. After reviewing seventy-five years of peer-rated personality traits, Joshua J. Jackson and colleagues (2015) concluded that peer ratings predicted the longevity of peer-rated persons better than their own self-ratings did. The review also suggested that men whom peers rate as conscientious and open to experience, and women peer-rated as emotionally stable and agreeable, lived longest.

If you accept Dr. Frances Frei's suggestion that the greatest risk with true-gooder advice occurs within areas wherein the advisor lacks the logical processing of whatever information they dispense, that notion needs no elaboration here. Presuming that the true-good influencer is being authentic and empathic at the time of influence delivery, you are left with the personal responsibility of assessing the factual accuracy and the rationality of that which is communicated to you. The question is: Are you willing to enact the due diligence?

The bottom line is that you need to be conscious that true-gooders can cause harm inadvertently. But they certainly pose the least threat, and, for that reason, I have chosen to spend the bulk of this chapter on those influencers who have no investment in your welfare. To reiterate the skin Taleb's skin-in-the-game advice, one simple, effective way to evaluate an influencer's advice—whether from a true-gooder, manipulator, or anyone in between—is to consider whether that which he recommends for you to do can either profit or harm him. If he only can profit from your decision or action, but can in no way be harmed by it, you had better be especially circumspect about applying his suggestions.

They Mean Ill

Let's now turn our attention to the polar opposite of a true-gooder. The worst of the worst manipulators evidence three aberrant personality traits—narcissism, Machiavellianism, and psychopathy—subsumed under the term "the dark-triad," a type of composite personality disorder rather than an emotional disorder per se. The hallmark of personality disorders, as opposed to purely emotional disorders, is that unlike neurotic people who are troubled by symptoms, such as by anxiety or depression, those with personality disorders are not troubled by their symptoms; their symptoms trouble others, as when dark-triad persons act out their grandiosity, emotional coldness, manipulation, and aggressiveness to the detriment of other people.

The three dark-triad traits have in common a gluttonous preoccupation with the self, and with everything self-associated. All three also are love-focused. The narcissist loves himself, and tolerates anyone who attends to and who dotes on him; the Machiavellian loves power and prestige; and the psychopath loves his emotionless unflappability that he wields as an ultimate weapon against others whom he regards as weak or vulnerable. As you no doubt have surmised, only highly permeable membranes separate the tripartite dark-triad personality. What distinguishes each triad leg is more quantitative than qualitative —all crave attention, love, power, and prestige, and all prey upon the weak and vulnerable.

Narcissism is the dark-triad's keystone, an inflated, self-absorbed preoccupation with feeding one's self-esteem and receiving acclaim. Machiavellianism describes a proclivity for manipulating and exploiting others, especially to attain fame and fortune. And psychopathy, a term somewhat eclipsed in the psychological literature by "antisocial personality," defines a personality trait in which one self-servingly acts out impulses in a virtually immediate and unrestrained manner without empathy, or regard to the consequences of the actions upon those around him.

Delroy L. Paulhus and Kevin Williams of the University of British Columbia (2001) have pioneered the dark-triad concept, and state that it entails "…a dark, socially destructive character with behavior tendencies such as grandiosity, emotional coldness, manipulation and aggressiveness." I want to underscore that despite the prerogative sound of the term, an individual with a dark-triad personality need not be insane or criminal, and he almost never evidences all the symptoms that define the condition. The dark-triad circumscribes an aberrant personality type that ranges from mild to severe; one person can be incapacitated by his dark-triad personality while another can manage it so skillfully that he becomes wealthy and/or, famous, and/or powerful. Each personality subtype of the dark-triad tends toward a particular influence style; although, here too, there is much overlap among them. The narcissist, the Machiavellian, and the psychopath all are prepared to deceive you in order to achieve their self-serving ends. But the three do not always use the same methods. To avoid being manipulated and exploited, be aware of their predilections. Know, for instance, that people are likely to initially perceive dark-triad individuals as physically and interpersonally attractive (Holtzman, 2012). The dark-triad ones know how to present themselves in ways to maximize the likelihood that you will give them a chance to implement their deceptions. Only over time will you realize how manipulative they are. And, by then, it might be too late. With that in mind, let's forearm you by briefly addressing each subtype of the composite dark-triad personality disorder.

Jones and Paulus (2017) produced empirical results that supported the well-established fact that the three dark-triad subtypes all engage in interpersonal exploitation. Although all tended to be dishonest, each subtype handled their deceit a little differently. The narcissist was the most inclined to engage in self-oriented deception, presumably to justify his nefarious behavior while maintaining some semblance of self-esteem. The Machiavellian and the psychopath, but not the narcissist, behaved deceitfully even when the deceit required them to lie intentionally and blatantly. When deceit exposed them to an obvious risk of punishment, however, the psychopath was not deterred, but the narcissist was. The Machiavellian, on the other hand, usually refrained from deceit when punishment was a definite risk, but not so when he was ego-depleted. For the Jones and Paultus study, ego depletion meant that subject had to focus his attention on ways to deceive while at the same time expending energy to block-out significant distractions from that deceptive effort.

For your mental health sake, you must be on-guard to resist dark-triad subtypes. The narcissist, Machiavellian, and the psychopath all are prepared to deceive you in order to achieve their self-serving ends. But the three do not always use the same methods. The fact that a dark-triad person possesses the characteristics of all three subtypes is one of their vulnerabilities. If you can recognize personality characteristics related to any of the three, you can be on the look-out for features of the other subtypes. Therefore, you can reduce your risk of being manipulated and exploited by being aware of the predilections of each subtype. Remember, too, that when you first meet a dark-triad person, you probably will be inclined to perceive him as physically and interpersonally attractive (Holtzman, 2012). He knows how to present himself in ways to maximize the likelihood that you will give him a chance to implement his deceptions.

So that you do not fall under their spells, let's learn just a little more about how influence is delivered by narcissists, Machiavellians, psychopaths, and dark-triad manipulators.

The Narcissist Influencer

The narcissist feels entitled to anything that he desires. He perceives whatever he does as grand, or, if not, he blames others for any semblance of personal failure or person limitation. Being so self-absorbed, he has limited space in his heart for empathy, since that would require him to prioritize someone else's needs and feelings above his own. Those character deficits make for an influencer unlikely to refrain from exploiting you. The one saving grace, if you want to call it that, is that a pure narcissist is a bit less inclined toward aggression than is a pure Machiavellian, or a pure psychopath (Vize, et al., 2016).

In an influence situation, you can imagine the narcissist being a charmer. Feeling superior, he exudes confidence. From his real or imagined power position, he presumes that he ultimately will be able to get you to accede to his wishes. Given that he feels so attractive, he can leverage his "beauty" into communicating the message that convinces you to play by his rules and, thus, benefit from your special connection with him. He expects that would be enticing, since everyone would know that you must be at least a little special to be on the inside with his majesty. Narcissist salespersons, for instance, might try to seal the deal by asserting that they, themselves, actually use the product or service they are peddling. Narcissist consultants might let you know that they have achieved fantastic successes by behaving in whatever way they are advising you. And narcissist politicians might attempt to convince you that they have special insight or privileged information that enables them to legislate whatever you need in order to make you healthy, wealthy, and wise.

The Machiavellian Influencer

Although a narcissist is likely to exhibit his narcissism in virtually all interpersonal venues, that personality consistency is not necessarily true regarding a Machiavellian. His aberrant behavior tends to be activated by situations that have a significant competitive or power component. And, when that is true, he can be extremely ruthless and deceptive. By definition, the Machiavellian behaves immorally or amorally when he pursues an important goal. His manipulations and cunning are legendary.

Given the Machiavellian personality, then, you must be careful when engaged in interactions with competition or power implications. Sounds simple, but it is not. That is because your perception of a competition or power situation might be quite different from that of the Machiavellian. He is inclined to imagine and to pursue opportunities in the least obvious places— a personality hallmark. Whereas you might volunteer for a community event because of due to your commitment to its cause, the Machiavellian would do so in the hope of making contact with and forming a partnership with the high profile person or organization that staged the event. You, therefore, might be targeted for Machiavellian influence intended either to exploit you directly, or to use you as a bridge to some other powerful person or institution to which you are connected. And, just as the narcissist tries to use his attractiveness to seduce you, the Machiavellian tries to use his power. That could be in the form of an outright bribe, or as a veiled threat in which he suggests that if you don't follow his advice, you will suffer harm of some sort. Although that harm could be physical, it more likely would be framed by him as your missed opportunity.

The Psychopath Influencer

From the start, I must acknowledge that the long-standing term "psychopath" has been a source of controversy over the last decade or so. If fact, it no longer appears as a stand-alone diagnosis in the Diagnostic and Statistical Manual of Mental Disorders Fifth Edition (DSM 5) which is the manual that mental health specialists use for insurance reimbursement and for research. Rather, psychopathy and sociopathy both are subsumed under the Antisocial Personality Disorder label. However, I will confine myself to psychopaths, since their primary characteristics overlap quite a bit with those of sociopaths.

As the notion of psychopathy has evolved over the years, the popular press has softened its negative connotations, applying the term to a wider variety of conditions. To my way of thinking, that dilution sometimes has been taken to an absurd level. One example is the Forbes.com article by Geoff Colvin entitled, *Why Great Presidents Are Often Psychopaths*. I do not dispute that presidents and other "great" and successful people can, and may be, psychopaths. In fact, in this book, I present evidence to that effect. But I do challenge the article for citing Kevin Dutton (2012) who concludes that America's three most successful presidents—Theodore Roosevelt, Franklin Roosevelt, and John F. Kennedy—were also the "most psychopathic." Since a detailed rebuttal about the selection of those three presidents would take us too far afield, I merely refer you to Hare (1996) who is widely regarded as the foremost world expert regarding psychopathy: "Psychopaths can be described as intra-species predators who use charm, manipulation, intimidation, and violence to control others and satisfy their own selfish needs." I trust that you will decide whether Theodore Roosevelt, Franklin Roosevelt, and John F. Kennedy fit that modal psychopathy profile. In any case, I believe you need to be alert to true psychopaths whom you are likely to encounter in your everyday life, rather than to alleged psychopaths diagnosed by journalists or historians. It would be easy to lower your guard when interacting with psychopaths, if you truly believe that they have much in common with three of our most popular presidents. That said, you definitely should be attentive to and concerned about politicians who are real psychopaths, and we will consider them in the following chapter.

However, you also need to be especially alert to psychopaths who are more likely to live in your neighborhood, and those, too, will be discussed. Dutton suggests that some common professions seem to attract persons inclined toward psychopathy, according to his lax criteria derived from the Self-Report Psychopathy Scale. Those are: chief executive officers, lawyers, persons in television and radio media, salespersons, surgeons, journalists, police officers, clergy, chefs, and civil servants. Notice that all of these professionals proffer some form of influence to others without necessarily having to follow that explicit or implied influence in their own lives. Although I do not agree to characterize them as psychopaths, not even as "psychopaths lite," you will notice that all, except chefs, are included on the Chapter 1 list wherein I enumerated professionals with the requisite training, opportunities, and resources to exert extraordinary influence.

Regardless of profession, an authentic psychopathic personality is similar to the narcissist personality in always being on-line. For that reason, if you observe influencers carefully you can determine who the psychopath is. When he talks about people, he eventually will betray his callous disregard for their well-being. The psychopath typically looks for the worst in others. Since he lacks empathy, he does not need to find reasons for his negative opinions and general cynicism, but he could present rationales for them, if he believes he needs those to convince you. The rationales also are likely to be presented when the psychopathic person knows that he has been observed committing an obviously insensitive act. On the other hand, if no one is in a position to detect his misdeed, he has no feelings of remorse or of behaving immorally.

Few psychopaths are easy to spot, since most of them are shrewd and cunning. As a group, they tend to be charming, sociable, and knowledgeable. They know how to present a façade of affability and congeniality. The successful psychopath, in fact, has been described as hiding behind a "mask of sanity" (Cleckley, 1982) that disguises his true personality and motivations. Behind the mask lies a person who lacks empathy. He has no trouble exploiting and manipulating others because he feels neither guilt nor remorse. He readily rationalizes away any personal responsibility for misdeeds. The psychopath operates according to the pleasure principle that permits him impulsively to pursue whatever he wants, including criminal activity when that serves his purposes. The future psychopath often exhibits problems early in life—in late childhood or early adolescence. There was a time when mental health specialists were taught that children who evidenced the triad of cruelty to animals, fire-setting, and extended periods of bedwetting were likely to become psychopaths. We now know that those behaviors are not limited exclusively to pre-psychopaths. However, they are the kinds of general behaviors that one would expect from them.

In influence situations, psychopaths represent the most danger to you. In addition to their callousness, amorality, and immorality, they frequently are impulsive. Therefore, there may be times when they take advantage of you on the spur of the moment for little tangible gain. Similarly, you might suffer from their characteristic irresponsibility. For instance, they make a promise, but either have no intention of keeping it, or later dismiss the commitment as being unimportant. You could imagine, for instance, a guarantee that hooks you into agreeing with the psychopath's request, and that later is found to be worthless. The lack of commitment to you is all the more likely, since psychopathic persons typically are here-and-now rather than future-oriented. Of all the misfortune that you might experience at the hands of a psychopath, however, you need to be most wary about your personal safety. You know, I'm sure, that extreme psychopaths can inflict injury—sometimes grave injury—on their victims. So, you never should allow yourself to be placed in an influence situation with them that compromises your safety. Those situations might range from your accepting an invitation to drive somewhere with them, to your inviting them briefly into your home.

The Dark-Triad Influencer

From a dark-triad person, you could expect influence tactics similar to those of a narcissist, a Machiavellian, a psychopath, or a combination of tactics derived from them. And the tactics could range from subtle to extreme. It is important to note, too, that narcissist, Machiavellian, psychopath, and dark-triad persons can be described along their own continuums, each condition being mild, moderate, or severe. Obviously, no dark-triad individual would be expected to possess an evenly distributed allotment of one-third narcissism, one-third Machiavellianism, and one-third psychopathy. Given what has been described so far, you almost certainly would be safest with a dark-triad person who possessed maximal narcissism and minimal psychopathy, but you never can be sure. When investigating dark-triad deception, Jonason, et. al. (2014) found that those highest in psychopathy and Machiavellianism tended to lie the most. The psychopath frequently lied for no apparent reason, and the Machiavellian's lies generally were less extreme than were the psychopath's. Not surprisingly, the narcissist's lies typically were deceptions to enhance his appearance, popularity, and dominance.

Of course, on a purely statistical basis, you are much more likely to encounter a narcissist, Machiavellian, or psychopath than a dark-triad person who embodies all three of the aforementioned dysfunctional personality subtypes. But because the dark-triad one is the most skillful of all negfluencers and the one with the most weaponry, you need to be especially well-informed about him. For the sake of that discussion, consider encountering a dark-triad influencer who poses as a financial advisor. Bernie Madoff probably was such a person, but let's take as our example someone that you personally have a greater chance of meeting. Financial advising has all the features that might attract a dark-triad individual. Narcissists would love to be on-stage in that exalted position. Machiavellians would relish the opportunity to compete, and to become a power broker in the financial arena.

And psychopaths would regard finance as a venue for crushing the opposition, and for playing excitedly and recklessly with another person's money.

Resplendently outfitted in a Tom Ford suit, Mr. Rich Beegspinder welcomes you into his cavernous center city office. At his invitation, you sink deeply into a plush, burgundy Boss Office Products Traditional Guest Chair. You scan walls replete with diplomas and oil paintings. Classical piano music echoes softly in the background. After an anemic, short-lived small talk interlude, Beegspinder reminds you of his supposed academic and business credentials, adding that he attended the same school as the current chairman of the Federal Reserve. He then requests all your financial statements whose presentation he had established as a prerequisite to agreeing to provide you this "free introductory session."

Rich Beegspinder studies the documents intently. He asks pointed questions about your other assets. He knows that you recently retired, and wants to understand your new short- and long-term financial objectives. So far, everything makes sense. Then his queries take an unsuspected turn. He quizzes you about your profession, and about those of your family and friends. He also wants to know what you would do in certain situations, such as how you would handle having bought a car from an acquaintance, and later discovering that he misled you about the extent of damage that it had incurred from a past accident. Beegspinder lavishes praise about each and every strategy that you describe to him, emphasizing your impeccable judgment. He manages to use your examples to show that they are fully consistent with the financial advice he is recommending. Through charts, diagrams, and written testimonials from satisfied clients, he explains at length how the program that he outlines will profit you and your loved ones. Without a careful reading, you sign a contract authorizing him to manage your money. One week later you receive a letter informing you that all future interactions between you and him will be limited to email. Over the next year, your assets slowly sink, but Rich's compensation remains constant. You consult an attorney who discovers that Beegspinder had been indicted in the past for fraudulent monetary transactions—mostly get-rich-quick schemes—but he was acquitted on a technicality. After looking over your contract, the attorney informs you that unfortunately Beegspinder apparently learned the hard way how to avoid being culpable for fraudulent monetary transactions; your contract teeters precariously on the borderline of exploitation, but you have no chance of winning a case against him.

What Just Happened?

The Rich Beegspinder, dark-triad financial advisor, saga can be dissected by applying the four primary influence vehicles. First, he used his person and alleged institutional connections as levers. Rich dressed and acted so as to project himself as eminently successful and connected. Diplomas were prominently displayed, and he name-dropped about sharing an alma mater with the Fed chairman. Second, Rich reinforced his influence by the objects and ideas he presented. The charts, diagrams, and accompanying client testimonials combined to provide what seemed to be a cogent argument for choosing the Beegspinder method. Third, the process flowed convincingly, as the financial advisor first described his qualifications, then inquired about your assets and goals, and, finally, gathered information from you that enabled him to relate his proposals precisely to your unique attributes and wants. Fourth and last, Rich Beegspinder skillfully crafted the situation as a whole. The combination of his person, institutional affiliations, charts, diagrams, explanations, and testimonials created an environment of competence and hope perfectly suited to you as a recent retiree.

Beegspinder's narcissism enabled him to present the facade of an extraordinarily successful, knowledgeable advisor. He exuded confidence. His Machiavellianism was incited by the sizable financial portfolio that you disclosed. He perceived you as being a reasonably powerful person who he needed to overpower. And Rich Beegspinder's psychopathy fortified him such that he did not hesitate to take advantage of you, despite previously having been indicted for similar tactics in the past.

Having discussed the best and worst influencers, we now turn our attention to the groups most likely to contain not only the best and worst posfluencers and negfluencers, but also the in-between influencers who either can be more or less helpful to us on an everyday basis. As mentioned previously, they are: politicians and other government officials, media controllers, celebrities, advertisers and salespersons, educators, and scientists. Every one of those powerful professionals has achieved social standing that they deliberately can leverage to enhance their abilities to influence everyday people. Their popularity and visibility also makes them attractive to those who crave parasocial relationships (PR)—one-sided faux relationships. Typically, within a PR, an ordinary individual devotes unreciprocated interest, attention, or other personal resources relative to the powerful one who often is totally aware of, and/or uninterested in the other's existence. Despite putting forth little or no effort to establish any single PR relationship, the more famous the influencer becomes, the more PRs he attracts. Fame begets fame and adoration. Most obvious are athletes and other celebrities who have publicists who make it their business to create early and strong PRs for them. When the publicists succeed, the athletes and other celebrities become central figures in the lives of the persons who have developed PRs with them. For instance, research suggests that athletes and actors sometimes contribute powerfully to adolescent identity formation. One relevant study (Gleason, et al., 2017) found that 61% of their adolescent sample regarded their favorite media person as a true relationship partner, and that boys usually established PRs with athletes, and girls, with actresses. Another (Hu, et al. 2018), claimed to show that persons who have strong

PRs with a media figure are quicker to accept a publicized apology from that figure when he has committed a transgression than from those with whom they do not have a PR.

CHAPTER 11: Politicians & Other Government Officials

Politicians and government officials should help our society run smoothly. They deliberately or inadvertently affect us all through their executive, legislative, or judicial duties. When doing so legitimately, they make decisions to allocate resources and facilitate actions that they sincerely believe will promote the common welfare. That is, ideally, they behave in a non-partisan manner, benefitting everyone regardless of their political affiliation. Whether the government is openly campaigning for an issue or surreptitiously nudging for it, they should not be promoting ultra-liberal or ultra-conservative values per se. Rather, their efforts should seek to advance policies that most people find desirable.

As a group, at their worst, these folks are all about exerting their power and control over us. They typically are from the most privileged of the privileged classes. Having been raised to believe that they are special and know everything about everything, they are intent on proving themselves to themselves. And the best way to do that is to get the masses to follow them to an assortment of promised lands. If thousands, even millions, of people vote for you and accept your rule, you've must be a titan. The more politicians and other government officials influence you, the more powerful and in control they feel.

Of all the intrusive influencers, then, politicians and government officials clearly wield the most power. They can alter your lifestyle radically, such as by demanding that you sell your home to allow the government's eminent domain use. They can punish you, even cause you to be incarcerated, if you fail to abide by the law they pass that you believe is unjust, such as one that you consider discriminatory. They can control your everyday behavior, such as requiring you to park your car on one side of the street and not on the other. They can reduce your wealth, such as by raising your taxes while at the same time reducing them for the wealthy or big business. Moreover, many negative government influences deleteriously can affect those whom you love, such their pain becomes your pain.

Think about the fact that government officials typically claim to have entered their professions to help citizens. They, for instance, speak of using their influence to "fight" for good schools, hospitals, health care, and infra-structure. Yet, many of these same civil servants also have campaigned to establish lotteries—44 states now are in the gambling business. Derek Thompson (2015) sounded the alarm in his The Atlantic article entitled "Lotteries: America's $70 Billion Shame" wherein he detailed their negative features. The article's subtitle is a shocker: "People spent more money playing the lottery last year than on books, video games, and tickets for movies and sporting events combined." Like others before him, Thompson explained that the poor are the biggest lottery losers, literally and figuratively. According to him, persons in the lower third of the income distribution purchase 50 percent of all tickets sold. Moreover, if they are lucky enough to win $600 or more, they must surrender 45 percent of those earnings back to the government. When all is said and done, lottery-supportive government officials have used their influence to legalize a system that offers mostly empty promises, and that preys primarily on persons of limited income. The lottery system, then, is a fairly transparent instance of what many people regard as government negfluence. There are many other government negfluences that are harder to define, and even harder to prove. It often "pays" to be wary of government officials professing to use their influence to help you.

Posfluence

A couple examples of primary motives especially germane to ethical politicians and government officials that they could use for posfluence would be:

Competency: to educate and direct us toward prosocial ends, such as community training activities.

Order: to promote efficient and effective outcomes, such as having clear guidelines for reaching community goals.

Stability: to help promote a more or less predictable environment, such as having a regular schedule to conduct community events.

Negfluence

As everyone knows, politicians and government officials do not consistently keep society moving smoothly. There is a fundamental, widely acknowledged, sometimes insuperable, flaw in the system: the great majority of those who control the executive, legislative, or judicial branches are elected to their positions. If they lose an election, those government-employed persons can lose their jobs. That stark, immutable reality often becomes the primary motivator of their decisions and actions.

Politicians and government officials, then, sometimes contribute to societal chaos and/or decay through their biased agendas. When doing so, they make decisions to allocate resources and facilitate actions that benefit them more than the common welfare. They might, for instance, coerce or nudge the populace toward self-serving ends.

Negfluences would be:

Power: when they pick and choose what to advocate and oppose according to their personal needs and preferences, rather than what is best for most of their constituents.

Money: when they primarily are motivated toward keeping their well-paying jobs that ensure them extraordinary health and retirement benefits.

Self-serving social connections: when they conspire with those who promote their own well-being rather than that of the citizens.

The Political Influencers

Joseph Goebbels

Most politicians are circumspect and circumscribed in their influence efforts. They usually prefer subtle nudging here and there that they can disavow later if the nudged position becomes unpopular. Not so with Joseph. From the start of his professional life, he presented his views directly, boldly, and pervasively. He knew what he wanted to promote, and how to sway popular opinion. Joe had an audience primed for his messages. They felt down trodden and humiliated. Their previously vibrant, relatively prosperous neighborhoods had become shabby and dilapidated. Food was scarce and of poor quality. At times, people literally had to fight to procure enough for them and their families to eat. The populace wanted someone to help restore their former lifestyle and bolster their spirits. They needed to believe that they were not responsible for their abysmal current condition.

The vicious Nazi, Joseph Goebbels, epitomized the worst of the worst politicians. His political career progressed from local party administrator, to district leader, to director of the National Ministry for Public Enlightenment and Propaganda. Goebbels, of course, considered himself more the enlightener than the propagandist, being convinced that he was engaged in a holy war for the German body and mind. A supreme irony was that Joseph and his crew did their best to exploit for propaganda the advertising tactics of Edward Bernays, the Jewish nephew of the Jewish psychoanalyst, Sigmund Freud.

Joseph Goebbels' employed all manner of propaganda delivery. In addition to controlling the press, books, and radio, he sculpted films, theater, art, and sports. Think about that for a minute. Here was a politician whose perhaps unprecedented influence permitted him to hammer forward Nazi-infused messages that assailed German citizens in every sensory modality and in every societal venue.

Fiery Nazi orators exploited mass assemblages, enunciating principles of proper living, and encouraging the populace to lionize Arians and to vilify Jews, Gypsies, and many other ethnics. The propagandists created an educational system and materials to ensure that German children would be thoroughly indoctrinated with the Nazi philosophy. And that child indoctrination was not limited to conventional schooling. So called "German Young People" and "Hitler Youth" programs for males began at ages 10 and 13 years, respectively. The former mostly emphasized physical fitness, while the latter, pre-military skills. Ten-year-old females entered the League of Young Girls that taught fitness, and at 14 they advanced to the League of German Girls where mothering skills training was added to the physical fitness regimen.

Goebbels and his assistants appealed to German pride and identity. Virtually all Germans were acutely aware of and smarting from the country's humiliating loss in World War I, and the harsh international retributions that followed. Many citizens were quick to accept Nazi misinformation that projected responsibility for all German suffering onto any and all available scapegoats.

What manner of man heartily would embrace a position that required outright deception and unspeakable cruelty? In Goebbels' case, it is reasonable to believe that his early history figured heavily. The facts that he had been born with a clubfoot and deemed unqualified for the armed forces certainly could not have bolstered Joseph's belief in his own personal Arian supremacy. And having been a University of Heidelberg history major likely stoked his allegiance to a long German militaristic tradition.

In Goebbels we have found a most extraordinary politician. As Minister for Public Enlightenment and Propaganda, he did not have to hide his influence efforts. The more partisan and manipulative he was, the better. He need not modify his extremist positions, either. Joseph Goebbels probably was animated largely by power and identity motivations. He needed to prove himself to himself and to the wider community. He craved the attention of der Führer whom he allegedly idolized. The minister, in fact, squandered his final days by living with Hitler in the Hitler bunker. After Adolf and Eva Braun committed suicide, Goebbels and his wife followed suit, but only after poisoning their six children.

Take Away

Presumably, you never will meet a Joseph Goebbels, but that does not mean you should ignore the implications of his manipulative methods. The German citizenry had authentic vulnerabilities, and so do you. You undoubtedly have suffered unfair treatment at some point or points in your life. Those mistreatments might have been related to your unique personal situation or to your group affiliations. Your family or other loved ones also might have suffered to the extent that you would want to avenge or protect them. Similarly, you possess features of your identity that are central to your self-esteem and well-being, and you strive to make the best of them. Powerful politicians can exploit your authentic vulnerabilities and desires. If you and your identity group want some special privilege, they can promise to secure it for you. On a mundane individual level, if you want a traffic ticket fixed, they can do that for you. More substantially, if you want a government job, they can intervene there as well.

Manipulative politicians rely on their staff and on computer data bases to determine what you and your group members want. Too often, this requires them to pick winners and losers. You could be on either side on any issue. If they refrain from influencing you, they risk losing your vote and support. That, you might say, is inherent in democracy. However, we are not talking now about promoting garden variety choices, but zero-sum-game choices that satisfy one person only at the expense of another. "Your" politician gives you what you want; their successor takes it away, transferring it to their own supporter. Politicians battle among themselves with you caught in the middle. The more you allow such government types to provide you special, extraordinary privileges, the more they expect from you. Your support is the weapon they employ in their war against each other. As their battles escalate, so does the likelihood that you eventually will become political collateral damage. What once you had perceived as posfluence becomes negfluence.

Eliot Spitzer

Our next politician is not notorious for brutality, but for hypocrisy. In 2006, Eliot Spitzer was a New York Democrat rising star, having just slaughtered his Republican opponent, John Faso, 69.0 percent to 29.2 percent in the gubernatorial campaign. That was merely the most recent in a string of impressive electoral victories. Before opposing Faso, Spitzer had crushed his 2006 Democrat primary rival, Thomas Suozzi, 80.74 to 19.26, and in 2002 he overwhelmed Republican, Dora Irizarry, 66.42 to 29.89 to become New York state attorney general. There were expectations that Spitzer eventually would run for president of the United States.

According to the Attorney General of New York website:

> As head of the Department of Law, the Attorney
> General is both the "People's Lawyer" and the

State's chief legal officer. As the "People's Lawyer," the Attorney General serves as the guardian of the legal rights of the citizens of New York, its organizations and its natural resources. In his role as the State's chief legal counsel, the Attorney General not only advises the Executive branch of State government, but also defends actions and proceedings on behalf of the State.

The Attorney General serves all New Yorkers in numerous matters affecting their daily lives. The Attorney General's Office is charged with the statutory and common law powers to protect consumers and investors, charitable donors, the public health and environment, civil rights, and the rights of wage-earners and businesses across the State.

The Attorney General's authority also includes the activities and investigations of the State Organized Crime Task Force and Medicaid Fraud Control Unit. While the Attorney General acts independently of the Governor, the Governor or a state agency may request the Attorney General to undertake specific criminal investigations and prosecutions.

The legal functions of the Department of Law are divided primarily into four major divisions: Appeals and Opinions, State Counsel, Criminal, and Public Advocacy.

Over 600 Assistant Attorneys General and over 2,000 employees, including forensic accountants, legal assistants, scientists, investigators and support staff serve in the Office of the Attorney

General in many locations across New York State.
(https://ag.ny.gov/legal-recruitment/overview-
functions-office-attorney-general)

Had you been a New York state resident under the reign of
Spitzer then, he would have been making decisions that affected
your daily life. Among other things, he could have had final say
on what you were or were not able to buy, where you invested
your money, the healthfulness of your environment in the
broadest sense, your basic human rights, features of your daily
employment, and job availability. He also could decide what,
when, and how to address potentially criminal activity impacting
you. In short, Eliot Spitzer had a profound influence on New
Yorkers' lifestyles, whether they realized it or not.

Such weighty responsibility certainly demanded someone with
the highest credentials and utmost integrity. Spitzer had the
former. He completed his undergraduate education at Princeton
and post-graduate training at Harvard Law School. After clerking
for a United States district judge, he joined three different law
firms before settling into the Manhattan District Attorney's office
where he remained for six years. According to the New York
Times, Eliot Spitzer became known as "Sheriff of Wall Street"
during eight years as attorney general. With a reputation for
personal probity and independence, he pledged to bring higher
ethical standards to the statehouse (Hakim & Rashbaum, 2008).
In the same Times article, Spitzer was characterized as having
spoken "with revulsion and anger" when explaining that in 2004
he had arrested sixteen persons responsible for a high-priced
prostitution business based on Staten Island.

After he ascended to governor in January 2007, Spitzer, the
politician, had everything going for him. In his head, he knew
just what to do. Unfortunately, his head did not inform his groin.
CBS claimed: "Investigators say Eliot Spitzer was clearly a
repeat customer who spent tens of thousands of dollars - perhaps

as much as \$80,000 - with the high-priced prostitution service over an extended period of time." Of course, Spitzer, the prosecutor, was never prosecuted. Instead, he resigned his governorship on March 12, 2008, after serving only about 14 months in office.

Did the former governor revise his influence ambitions? You know the answer to that: a resounding "no." After unsuccessfully trying out his residual influencer skills as a political commentator on CNN, first on October 4, 2010 when a co-commentator with the renowned political columnist Kathleen Parker, and then on his own, Spitzer signed off for the last time July 6, 2011. According to Wikipedia, the show "received consistently low ratings and there were reports of backstage fighting between Spitzer and Parker."

In 2013, Eliot Spitzer entered the New York City comptroller Democratic primary and suffered another defeat, although the contest was close: 52% for opponent Scott Stringer and 48% for the disgraced former governor. More recently the Spitzer saga took a most bizarre turn, described by Maria Perez in a January 9, 2018 Newsweek.com report entitled "Eliot Spitzer accused of threatening to stab man 'in the cock' at Manhattan restaurant." You can decide the veracity and relevance of that for yourself.

Take Away

When you choose to listen to a high profile influencer, think Eliot Spitzer. He had the schooling, the experience, and the social connections to be a posfluential politician. He repeatedly was lauded for multiple prosecutorial successes. If you paid any attention to New York elections, you almost surely would have been impressed by this campaigner who garnered 66, 69, and 80 percent of the popular vote. But you and those who voted for him did not know enough about Spitzer. Should you and they have trusted this hypocritical man who spoke with revulsion and anger about prostitution and then patronized prostitutes himself? Might Spitzer have been so wily as to use his intellect, knowledge, and connections to hide other non-prostitution nefarious activities? You never could be sure, could you? Perhaps you should heed the advice of Michael Kinsley (1988), a political journalist, who asserted that politicians commit a gaffe when they mistakenly admit to an obvious truth. Credentials and acclaim do not guarantee honesty and integrity. Many people are intimidated by influencers who proclaim themselves Princeton or Harvard graduates, concluding that graduates from those and other "good schools" must know what they are talking about. Ivy League types flock together, and can try to wow you with references to and/or appearances with their high profile compadres. Moreover, almost no one today gets elected to high office without having many millions of dollars and a battalion of staff behind them. Therefore, survival of the fittest suggests that it is a good bet that any politician who grabs your attention is one who is similarly endowed. You must be able to hold on to your self-esteem and self-confidence in order to resist being overwhelmed by the power radiating from and around all politicians.

To explain why we become gullible when dealing with politicians or with any high-profile influencer, let's apply the well-respected "personal construct theory" of George A. Kelly (1991). According to him, all people manufacture mental constructs to represent features of reality, whether of people, places, or things. Those constructs are joined together to produce systems of external reality and systems of internal personal reality. Most critical are the construct systems that yield our sense of identity and of our interpersonal relationships. The constructs that we create automatically reflect and automatically color our internal and external experiences. Returning to the Eliot Spitzer example, we might have developed constructs that apply to him, to us, and to him vis-à-vis us. Persons too enamored with the constructs that they have created relative to Spitzer, his education, profession, associates, or his acclaim, and too insecure about their own positive constructs might be loath to doubt him, and too eager to accept his influence. Moreover, there is compelling research (e.g., Smith, 2010) supporting the idea that the average citizen tends to believe elite counter-attackers enlisted to defend a politician who has received unfavorable media coverage. So, the politically powerful often make special effort to form strong bonds with media controllers.

Kelly's theory and the aforementioned Spitzer example also reasonably account for the extraordinary political career of Marion Barry of Washington, D.C. At minimum, Barry was the premier D.C. local politician from 1979 to 1999. From 1975 to 1979, he served on the district's governing council, and twice— 1979 to 1991 and 1995 to 1999—as district mayor. So what? The "what" is that Marion Barry was videotaped in a hotel room smoking crack in January,1990. In August of the same year, he was convicted of cocaine possession and later jailed. This man's criminal activities and indiscretions were far too numerous to enumerate here. Suffice it to say that, in the Washington Post, Bart Barnes (2014) described Barry's non-political history by commenting that "He was married four times, divorced three times and separated from his fourth wife. His extramarital liaisons and legal trouble over unpaid taxes made news." And when reviewing the former mayor's incarceration, Barnes wrote:

> "Late in December [1991], an inmate reported
> having seen a female visitor perform oral sex on
> the former mayor in the prison's family reception
> room. Mr. Barry denied it, but prison authorities
> ruled that he had engaged in sexual misconduct
> and moved him to a medium-security prison in
> Loretto, Pa. When he was released in April 1992,
> he returned to Washington like a hero, riding
> home in a limousine followed by six buses packed
> with praying, celebrating supporters."

Back home, Barry hit the ground running, seeking the Ward 8 council seat — in far Southeast Washington, the poorest, most isolated ward in the city and the only one he had carried in his failed 1990 bid for an at-large council seat. By a margin of 3 to 1, he crushed the incumbent, former political ally Wilhelmina Rolark, in the Democratic primary and then won handily in the November general election."

With all this so-called excess baggage, one might wonder how Marion Barry could have remained in politics. The answer, of course, is that constituents heartily, repeatedly voted for him after his convictions. Presumably, they had created constructs that exaggerated his positives and minimized his negatives. They considered his constructs to be aligned with theirs, ignoring all the negatives. The citizenry blinded itself to the incontrovertible realities of his offenses. Even after leaving office, Barry continued to exert strong influence over the people because they readily accepted it.

CHAPTER 12: Media Controllers

Let's travel back in time for a moment. It is 1915 and radio programs do not exist. Your receptivity to influence and capacity to influence are limited to directly-delivered spoken, written, or telegraphed messages. However, in five years, radio will offer some elite influencers the revolutionary opportunity specifically to access anyone having that machine.

According to the historyofinformation.com, the first known radio news program was broadcast on August 31, 1920 by a Detroit, Michigan station called 8MK that later evolved into WWJ. In 1922, regular wireless broadcasts for entertainment began in the United Kingdom from the Marconi Research Center 2MT in England (en.wikipedia.org). And United States television initiated the first prime time, seven day radio schedule in 1948 (http://www3.northern.edu).

Electronic media has progressed from influencing hundreds, to thousands, to millions, to hundreds of millions of people. Today, those who control radio and television possess influence power exponentially greater than any king or emperor ever dreamt possible. We all are painfully aware that contemporary media moguls relentlessly attempt to control our minds and wallets by using an assortment of electronic devices and the Internet whose combined power dwarfs that of all printed material. Let's think, for the moment, specifically about television as influencer.

Public service announcements (PSA) seem to be a great idea; after all, they have "public service" in their titles. I usually listen carefully to PSAs, hoping to learn something helpful to myself and to my loved ones. So, on April 28, 2018, I sat up a little straighter when Heather Marie Tom appeared on the screen and stated, "Do you know what to do when a child or an adult is choking? Make sure that you do. Go to redcross.org. You could save a love one's life…CBS cares." That was it: ten seconds, and nothing more.

I slumped and scratched my head. What thinking lay behind that PSA? If, as stated, CBS had ready access to life-saving information, and truly was interested in public service, couldn't they have stretched the 10 second PSA a bit, at least enough to provide the very basics of the most critical info?

Since CBS did "care" enough to have "redcross.org" subtitled on the screen, I went there. When I did not find anything on the homepage about choking, I used the search icon that produced the following: "Sorry, we are experiencing technical difficulties. We apologize but we are experiencing technical difficulties. If you wish to make a donation, register for a class or schedule a blood donation appointment, please call 1-800-RED CROSS. You can also text REDCROSS to 90999 to make a financial gift." [The Red Cross did manage to disseminate successfully the donations and financial gifts messages.] Undeterred, I went to the top of the page and clicked on the Training + Certification icon. The drop-down menu did not mention choking, either. But it did list CPR, so "click" again. One more "click" brought me to Child & Baby CPR. That information was fine, but, again, nothing specifically about choking.

I then proceeded to check out Heather Marie Tom on the Internet Movie Data Base website. There I learned that Ms. Tom is an extraordinarily talented soap opera actor who had won 5 Emmys, and who at the time was starring in the CBS show, *The Bold and the Beautiful*. Scratching my head once again, I wondered whether I earlier had watched a primary PSA with a secondary CBS commercial, or a primary CBS commercial with a secondary PSA. CBS Cares, but about what?

Posfluence

Media—electronic or print—obviously has the potential for tremendous good. In virtually every sector of human endeavor, media has something to offer. In a previous book entitled *Don't Rest in Peace*, I wrote about six essential sectors necessary for human physical and mental health, all of which can be promoted by media as in the following few examples:

Cognitive-Emotional – online lecture material and mental health resources.
Interpersonal Relationships – ability to communicate with people in real time, as with Skype.
Physical Conditioning – access to exercise-promoting information and videos.
Diet-Nutrition – information about the benefits and problems associated with particular foods.
Work – job search and in-service material.
Relaxation-Recreation – stress management guidance and vacation planning resources.

A couple examples of primary motives that could encourage media controllers toward posfluence in the six health-essential sectors would be:

Safety: when they can create and distribute stories and documentaries that highlight respect for the rights and well-being of others.

Autonomy: when they defy the money-making bias of their industry by producing material that is less lucrative, but more in accord with social welfare.

Transcendence: when they partner with creative persons having an avant-garde prosocial philosophy.

Negfluence

Media is only as good as its gatekeepers allow it to be. Media controllers sometimes specifically produce material whose central purpose is to sway the public toward their personal socio-cultural positions while denigrating or ignoring relevant, reasonable competing material. Michael Moore epitomizes that strategy, as is apparent in most of his works, such as the book *Stupid White Men* and the movie *Michael Moore in TrumpLand*. One can reasonably question whether any one person should be permitted to dispense to millions of citizens a totally one-sided political diatribe. Other media controllers manipulate us by furthering the careers only of television or movie stars who promote the media controllers' socio-cultural positions, either in their films or public appearances. Worse still are those elites whose celebrity coercion has included sexual exploitation, such as that attributed to the Hollywood producer, Harvey Weinstein.

A couple examples of primary motives especially germane to unethical media controllers that they could use to negatively influence us would be:

Money: when they produce lurid material that fills movie theaters and lines media moguls' pockets by appealing to the worst human instincts.

Power: when they use their high-profile positions to flood the airways with messages used to retaliate against persons whose views are discordant with theirs, effectively drowning out the opposition.

Sexual fulfillment: when they take unfair advantage of people, as has been alleged against Harvey Weinstein and many before him, and in so doing perpetuate the cultural expectation that one [overwhelmingly men] can use their power position to subvert law's meant to protect another [overwhelmingly women] from abuse and exploitation.

Media Controllers with a Transparent Agenda

Michael Moore

Michael Moore certainly is among the most transparent, outspoken agents using his media control to attempt to move citizens in his direction. Beginning in 1989 with the documentary *Roger & Me* in which he lambasted General Motors for closing factories in Michigan, he has produced a series of films designed to promote his agendas. Many of the films followed in the confrontational mode of the first documentary. That strategy has worked for him, so well at times that he has received critical acclaim, including winning the 2002 Academy Award with *Bowling for Columbine*, and the 2004 Cannes film festival Golden Palm with *Fahrenheit 9/11*. The former "attacked" gun control policies, and the latter, President George W. Bush's responses to the September 11, 2001 terrorism. One of his last completed films to date is *Michael Moore in Trumpland (*2016) that the Rotten Tomatoes audience gave only a 47% favorable rating, and the critics, 55%.

There are few media venues that Moore has not tried to exploit. In addition to producing movies, he has been a print journalist, magazine editor, television personality, one-man stage performer, and book writer. Many book titles offer ready insight into Moore's orientations. Among these are: *Stupid White Men and Other Sorry Excuses for the State of the Nati*on (a polemic mostly against George W. Bush and his kind), *Dude, Where's My Country?* (anti-George W. Bush, anti-2003 Iraq War, and anti-Enron), and *Downsize This! Random Threats from an Unarmed American!* (criticisms of American big businesses for caring only about their bottom line and ignoring the needs of their workers).

Although many agree with much of what Moore is selling, others question his personal integrity, and the accuracy and legitimacy of his messages. One measure of integrity of course is being able to take what you give and to justify your behavior. And those are the areas wherein Michael Wilson challenged the behemoth, Michael Moore.

In the early 2000s, the young independent film producer, Wilson, began following Moore, filming and attempting to interview him. That amounted to a "turnabout is fair play" maneuver, since much of Michael Moore's initial fame had resulted from similar tactics that Moore employed when in his Roger & Me, initial documentary, he had badgered General Motors chairman Roger Smith about the company's factory closings. Michael Wilson's pursuit did not please Mr. Moore who was neither cooperative nor pleasant with Wilson.

Michael Moore Hates America, the resulting Wilson documentary, indicted Moore for distorting facts within his films. Wilson alleged that Moore was primarily interested in influencing public opinion rather than in presenting unbiased information. Wilson suggested that Moore was distorting American society in order to make socialism look good. For instance, Michael Wilson claimed that the *Bowling for Columbine* film contained out of context sequences, spliced together to support Moore's biases.

What did others say about *Michael Moore Hates America*? Let's consider Variety magazine, a publication that Wikipedia claims endorsed Hillary Clinton for President, after never having promoted any candidate in its century-plus history. The article, written by Robert Koehler (2004), cites a number of criticisms of Moore. For instance, Koehler claims that a psychologist referred to Michael Moore as having a narcissistic personality disorder, and Penn Jillette, of the Penn and Teller magician duo, said that Moore employs deception and trickery in his film no less so than slight-of-hand artists do in their acts. However, the most damning remark is attributed to Albert Maysles, a nonfiction filmmaker guru, who is quoted as commenting that Moore is "tyrannized by his method, which is to simplify complex ideas."

Media Controllers with an Opaque Agenda

Harvey Weinstein

Whereas Michael Moore's influence attempts are obvious to any everyday citizen who views his productions or listens to him speak, such is not the case for the works and remarks of Harvey Weinstein. In fact, one might argue that more often than not, Weinstein's motion pictures reveal their biases subtlety, if at all. That is not to say that Harvey has no agendas, or that he does not promote them. Virtually every high profile person in Hollywood and Washington, D.C. knows Weinstein's social and political orientations, and their alleged importance to him. Allan Smith and Skye Gould (2017), for instance, wrote that "Hollywood producer Harvey Weinstein is one of the Democratic Party's most prolific donors," noting that from 2000 to 2017, he had given Democrats more than one million dollars. They even named names in their article, including support for Richard Blumenthal, Cory Booker, Hillary Clinton, Al Franken, Kristen Gillibrand, Kamala Harris, Martin Heinrich, Patrick Leahy, Barack Obama, Chuck Schumer, and Elizabeth Warren. So, one reasonably can assume that Weinstein could catch the ear of many of the nation's most powerful politicians in attempting to further his agendas.

At the height of his prominence, Harvey Weinstein's capacity for influence was not limited to Washington. He was able to extend his reach to every corner of the globe. Although many people ignore legislators, billions fall under the spell of actors. And Weinstein had scores of the most high-profile actors who wanted to and/or needed to curry his favor to further their careers. Amanda Luz Henning Santiago (2017) was among those who identified a few of the many actors who in the past had spoken positively and publically about Weinstein. They were: Ben Affleck, Penélope Cruz, Holly Hunter, Jennifer Lawrence, Gwyneth Paltrow, Meryl Streep, Billy Bob Thornton, Christopher Waltz, Dianne Wiest, Michelle Williams, Kate Winslet, and Renée Zellweger. Think about all the people who take notice when those superstars speak favorably of someone.

At the same time, some celebrity remarks about Harvey Weinstein, spoken in gest, provide insight into how he truly is perceived by those closest to him. For example, in her 2012 Golden Globes acceptance speech, Meryl Streep commented "I want to thank God: Harvey Weinstein. The punisher, Old Testament, I guess." And Jennifer Lawrence in the same venue the next year stated, "Harvey, thank you for killing whoever you had to kill to get me up here today." Jane Fonda also revealed the hidden side of Weinstein, although her statements were provided in all seriousness. For instance, after sexual allegations were made against him, Fonda said that Harvey was "not a nice man" and "didn't treat people well." As to her personal connection with his sexual indiscretions, she admitted in an interview with Christiane Amanpour (2017) that the actor, Rosanna Arquette, told her that Harvey Weinstein tried to induce Rosanna to touch his genitals. But Fonda did not reveal that abusive behavior to anyone. Jane excused herself by saying that she was not bold enough at the time to speak up, but now felt ashamed for not having done so. The remarks of Streep, Lawrence, and Fonda, then, strongly imply that Weinstein had a reputation as a powerful intimidator. Not surprising that, in the past, actors were quick to support and loath to oppose him, and his agendas.

But what about Weinstein films and the covert social and political influence contained within? Although most of his and other producers' and directors' movies convey a series of subtle messages that reflect the media mogul's biases, when aggregated, they provide a significant influence. For illustration, think about the Weinstein Brothers' film, *The Imitation Game*, released in 2014.

This film mostly presents a story about Alan Turing, and his role in World War II and its aftermath. Let's start with objective information, as abstracted from Wikipedia, for a point of reference. The relevant facts, as described there, begin with the central idea that Turing was a computer scientist and, more precisely, a cryptanalyst who specialized in discovering hidden codes within a computer system. It was Turing and his colleagues, working for the English government, who cracked the Nazi military codes, and in the process greatly accelerated the Allies' capacity to defeat the Germans. After the war, Turing continued and extended his groundbreaking work, such as by improving computing machines in general, program storage, and, even, mathematical biology.

Sadly, Alan Turing lived in an era during which homosexuality was a crime, and, caught in a homosexual relationship, he was prosecuted. Given the choice of incarceration or chemical castration in 1952, he chose the latter. Two year later, just sixteen days prior to reaching age 42, Turing was found dead of cyanide poisoning. Although at the time his demise was interpreted as a suicide, evidence later emerged to suggest that it could have been the result of an accident.

The Imitation Game accurately depicted much of the aforementioned objective information. However, it also presented story lines that likely were distorted to support Weinstein's social and political biases. Christian Caryl (2014) tried to set the record straight, as he saw it. According to him, the film depicted Turing as an oppressed, "tortured genius," instead of showing the full complexity of his character. To add pathos, Turing was rendered affectless and socially isolated. Surprisingly, despite his genius, Alan Turing was stereotyped in the film as a weakling who whined endlessly. Caryl took special umbrage at this characterization as the fatal flaw in the film. According to him: "This is indicative of the bad faith underlying the whole enterprise, which is desperate to put Turing in the role of a gay liberation totem but can't bring itself to show him kissing another man—something he did frequently, and with gusto. And it most definitely doesn't show him cruising New York's gay bars, or popping off on a saucy vacation to one of the less reputable of the Greek islands. The Imitation Game is a film that prefers its gay men decorously disembodied."

One might speculate about Christian Caryl's film critique in light of what we know now regarding Harvey Weinstein. There certainly is incontrovertible evidence that he embraces progressive political causes. And gay rights is a progressive cause par excellence. Any film producer or director who seeks to influence progressive politicians and progressive moviegoers must be an outspoken supporter of gay rights. One should wonder, however, how authentically Weinstein advocates for gays. Perhaps his gay rights support is as thin as his previous support for another progressive sine qua non: women's rights. Yes! Amazing as it seems, Weinstein was renowned as a campaigner for the women's movement. Thomas Frank (2017) reminded us that Harvey publically and regularly criticized sexism, prominently supported the group "Mothers Opposing Bush," and advocated for women-only scholarships. Whether it is his support for gays, women, or any other group, perhaps we should judge Harvey Weinstein based on what he does, not on what he says or portrays in his films. More important: perhaps we should resist his manipulative political and social influences altogether.

CHAPTER 13: Celebrities

Some celebrity influence of course is quite similar to that of their media bosses. Namely, celebrities literally have a stage from which to advocate. They cultivate personae that enable them to embody that which they want to communicate. However, unlike most of their bosses, celebrities are especially attractive and serve as role models. Whenever they want to influence us they can "book an appearance," either literally or figuratively, to garner publicity from which to dispense their opinions. Moreover, their agents frequently can get them "a gig" so that they can be paid for their influence efforts. And it would be unwise to underestimate celebrity influence power. In fact, research (Harvey, 2015) suggests that celebrities have more persuasive political power than actual politicians do. They are considered by the public to be more authentic in their advocacy, and their clout is further enhanced when they speak under the auspices of an established lobbying institution, such as the National Organization for Women or the National Rifle Association.

Posfluence

Social order: when celebrities commit to and advocate prosocial issues.

Tranquility: when they campaign for society enhancements, and they enjoy the contentment that comes with the proverbial "giving back."

Stability: when they advocate their prosocial positions over time and across circumstances.

Competency: when they devote their time, energy, and other resources to truly understand the particulars of what they endorse and how to endorse it.

Negfluence

Celebrities are taught to create social presence that further reinforces their fame and fortune, sometimes unscrupulously. Because they are so high profile, their negative influences can be particularly powerful, especially as it affects the young and impressionable. Virtually every celebrity has a publicist who directs them, no less so than a movie director does. The publicist proves her worth by sculpting the celebrity's persona so that it continually grows toward becoming as financially profitable as possible. You no doubt have heard the expression that there is no such thing as bad publicity. Sadly, sometimes the more outrageous the celebrity behavior, the more valuable it is to them. Our negfluence examples are:

Physical comfort: when the celebrity must have the biggest and the best of everything, and he manipulates the public to do so.

Power: when they lord over those who idolize them.

Safety: when they find solace by taking from others through creating zero sum games that benefit them only.

Competency: when they devalue competitors to enhance their own feelings of superiority.

Celebrity Influencers

A celebrity, by definition, is famous which leads naturally to the question: "Famous for what?' The answer could be virtually anything, but fame almost always is confined to some narrow sector of human experience. Often celebrity results from some extraordinary ability or even a single noteworthy activity. Rarely is someone celebrated due to their being superlative in multiple domains. In fact, many Americans reserve the word "celebrity" for actors who evidence superb acting ability. An actor is not celebrated for their pedagogical prowess.

Contemporary societies afford disproportionate opportunities for actors to exert influence. Media sometimes literally fight to obtain information about actors, and relentlessly promulgate that which they get. With all the media exposure, one can understand why actors— who make their living by looking their best and living big—set grooming and fashion trends. You may or may not like that fact, but there at least is a comprehensible rationale for it. Since grooming and fashion usually do not critically impact the quality of most citizens' lives, that extraordinary actor influence is tolerable.

Some actors, however, try to use their celebrity to exert influence in areas wherein they have no special expertise. They might do so because they want to elicit more publicity, because they sincerely believe in the position that they adopt, or because some other person, persons, or group seek to use the celebrity to achieve their own ends.

Aid and Comfort to the Enemy?

The helmeted soldier furiously cranked his antiaircraft gun into position, swinging and directing its barrel skyward. Grim-faced, he searched left and right for a target that never materialized. Then, erupting into a broad smile, he slid out of the operator's chair and leaped to the ground. Immediately thereafter, he was replaced by a slim, giddy young lady who smiled open-mouthed, clapped, and chortled like a child at the circus. A few minutes earlier, the woman had entered the area through a cordon of uniformed, armed soldiers who seemed genuinely pleased to be with her. Before mounting the antiaircraft seat, she had been videotaping the helmeted soldier as he performed his art for her. The woman also wore a helmet when she was videotaping, and she had draped around her neck a still camera and what appeared to be 2 telephoto lenses. The woman had the appearance of someone in the process of shooting a documentary, perhaps a complement to her hosts' documentary-like production of which she was the star. When exiting the video production site, the starlet turned to a group of grinning, clapping soldiers and made a final closed fist, extended-arm victory gesture.

Many persons reading this section correctly already have inferred that the woman star was Jane Fonda, the anti-aircraft installation was located in Viet Nam, and the soldiers were North Vietnamese. Fonda's visit occurred over a two week period in July, 1972 during which time she toured the country with her communist handlers and broadcasted anti-American radio programs for them. In the United States, the globally televised visit and radio broadcasts ignited a firestorm of outrage toward Fonda. Presuming a minimum of two loved ones mourning the loss of each serviceperson killed in Viet Nam, there were at least 116,440 reasons that the animus toward "Hanoi Jane" never abated.

The North Vietnamese reaped a spectacular propaganda coup from Jane Fonda's support. The propaganda included disseminating the fact that Fonda minimized the North's vicious torture of American POWs, and that she maligned some of the prisoners as "liars" and "hypocrites." By contrast, Jane pardoned the torturers whose torturing she labeled as "understandable" (New York Times Special, 1973). The POWs did not regard their torture similarly. For instance, Sam Johnson described his seven years imprisonment, including 42 months in solitary confinement, as follows:

> As a POW in the Hanoi Hilton, I could recall
> nothing from military survival training that
> explained the use of a meat hook suspended from
> the ceiling. It would hang above you in the torture
> room like a sadistic tease—you couldn't drag your

gaze from it. During a routine torture session with the hook, the Vietnamese tied a prisoner's hands and feet, then bound his hands to his ankles—sometimes behind the back, sometimes in front. The ropes were tightened to the point that you couldn't breathe. Then, bowed or bent in half, the prisoner was hoisted up onto the hook to hang by ropes. Guards would return at intervals to tighten them until all feeling was gone, and the prisoner's limbs turned purple and swelled to twice their normal size. This would go on for hours, sometimes even days on end. Aside from leg irons and leg stocks—both of which were used on me for months and years on end—the meat hook was a favorite instrument of torture at the Hanoi Hilton.

Later, Fonda also tried to reduce her own personal responsibility for the antiaircraft gun propaganda video, claiming that she did not realize that she was being manipulated until after the filming concluded. Two parenthetical facts also are worth noting: Jane Fonda blamed her father for her own 25 year old battle with bulimia (Abrahamson, 2016), and, as mentioned earlier, she reluctantly, belatedly admitted to Christiane Amanpour of CNN that she had known about Harvey Weinstein's sexual abuse of women and said nothing about it. (Luz Henning Santiago, 2017). In short, Jane Fonda, like most actors, should not be afforded extraordinary opportunities to communicate their personal moral, social, or political values denied to everyday citizens, especially when they attempt to rationalize away every criticism leveled at them,

The issue here is not whether Jane Fonda's views regarding the Viet Nam War were right or wrong. Everyone, including her, is entitled to their opinions. Rather, the issue is Fonda's disproportionate influence compared to yours. According to

Wikipedia, Jane was an "undistinguished student" who dropped out of college after her sophomore year, meaning that she had no real major course of studies. She was not educated about the conduct of politics, war, or the process of peacemaking. On the other hand, since childhood, Jane Fonda regularly had spent countless hours on film sets, either watching their productions or performing in them. Most listeners undoubtedly were unconvinced by her claims that she did not recognize immediately the propaganda significance of the North Vietnamese choreographed antiaircraft "movie setting" that she helped them stage, and that she, herself, was filming.

Dog Gone

Top athletes are celebrities in every sense of the word. Whether they like it, admit it, or not, they also are de facto role models to millions of youngsters across the world. Impressible minors scrutinize every action and attend to every word expressed by their sports' heroes. Many adults also pay close attention and often copy athletes. In football, quarterbacks are the undisputed kings, making the most money and commanding the most prestige and power. Michael Vick, an Atlanta Falcons signal-caller, satisfied all those criteria. In six years with the team, he earned a position in three Pro Bowls, and set a single-season record for most rushing yards by a quarterback.

As abstracted from Biography.com, Vick's personal history goes like this: Michael Vick developed into a first-rate football player during his two years at Virginia Tech. He, in fact, was so good that the Atlanta Falcons selected him as their first round choice in the 2001 National Football League draft, awarded a sixty-two million dollar, six year contract, and sweetened the pot with an additional fifteen million dollar bonus. Well on his way to becoming wildly famous and fabulously wealthy, Vick had been granted an opportunity of a lifetime. Would he rise to the occasion?

After mostly watching and waiting during his first year, Michael Vick played often and outstandingly well in seasons two and three. By season four, 2004, however, Vick's star already had begun to lose a little luster. Heretofore positive expectations faded, replaced by concerns that the quarterback was becoming increasingly arrogant, associating with undesirables, and making poor decisions. During the same year, police captured two men who were using Michael Vick's truck to run marijuana. Yet, the quarterback's financial future continued to streak upward and onward. Len Pasquarelli of ESPN.com wrote on Christmas 2004 that Michael Vick had just signed the biggest total pay package in pro football history to date, a contract extension that, if completed as intended, would have paid Vick approximately $120,000,000.

As his salary increased, so did Vick's crises. In 2005, he avoided a court date only by settling with a woman who claimed that he had infected her with a "sexual disease." In 2007, Michael Vick first denied then admitted to housing, funding, and running a dogfighting ring on his Smithville, Virginia property. By year's end, the former superstar received a sentence of twenty-three months in prison and restitution charges just short of one million dollars. As bad as it was, however, the situation got even worse. In two separate 2009 cases, the Royal Bank of Canada and Wachovia won a combined total of 3.6 million dollar judgments against Michael Vick for loan defaults, and the next year the United States Department of Labor claimed that he unlawfully had used over one million dollars from the pension plan of one of his businesses.

Of all of his troubles, the dogfighting conviction most threatened Michael Vick's short- and long-term future. As details of the abuse emerged, many Americans were incensed by the depth and breadth of its cruelty. An investigative report, published on August 28, 2008 by the United States Department of Agriculture,

Office of Inspector General, described the May 23 and June 5, 2007 testimony of "confidential witness, number one" who said that during public dog fights when interested persons paid admission to watch and/or wager, Vick stayed upstairs, fearing someone would recognize him. No wonder Vick was concerned, given the depravity of the enterprise that the witness detailed:

> Vick, Peace, and Phillips thought it was funny to watch the pit bull dogs belonging to Bad Newz Kennels injure or kill the other dogs… In mid-April of 2007, Vick, Peace, Phillips and Allen were rolling [testing fighting prowess] dogs at the property. Vick Peace and Phillips killed approximately seven dogs by hanging and drowning at this time. Allen did not take part in the killing of the dogs. Vick, Peace and Phillips hung approximately three dogs by placing a nylon cord over a 2X4 that was nailed to two trees next to the big shed. They also drowned approximately three dogs by putting the dogs' heads in a five gallon bucket of water. XX [name redacted on the transcript] also observed as Vick and Phillips killed a red pit bull dog, by slamming it to the ground several times before the dog died, breaking its neck or back.

In an August 14, 2007 interview, after he had pleaded guilty, Phillips spoke of having met Vick in 7th grade, becoming best friends, and playing middle- and high-school basketball and football together. He said that through an acquaintance named "Taylor," he and Vick became "involved" in dogfighting in 2001. On August 14 and October 9, 2007, Peace validated much of confidential witness number one's testimony, saying that

> In 2002, he, Vick, Phillips, and Taylor "rolled" (tested) dogs at XX [information redacted in the

transcript] to determine if they were good fighters. They would kill the poor fighters by shooting, electrocuting, or drowning them. Almost all the dogs they killed were buried on the XX [information redacted on the transcript] property. On occasion, he would want to give away a dog that would not fight. However, Vick stated "They got to go," meaning that they needed to be killed. Many times Vick, Phillips, and Taylor killed dogs when he was not present. Taylor would tell him about the dogs that did not test well, and would say "They didn't make it," meaning they were killed.

We see, then, that Michael Vick's dogfighting cruelty was a not a momentary, impulsive aberration; in fact, Vick treated animal torture so cavalierly that he produced shirts and head-bands bearing his Bad Newz Kennels logo to advertise his "business." As Vick emerged from prison on May 20, 2009, young men were watching, from sea to shining sea. Just as Pete Rose had disgraced baseball and was forever banned from his sport, Vick never would set foot on a gridiron again. Well, at least not for several weeks.

No. Michael Vick did not forfeit his "right" to play football—to hell with all that gibberish about the important of role models. Within three months after his feet hit the pavement outside Leavenworth Penitentiary, on August 13, 2009, Vick signed a two-year Philadelphia Eagles contract with a potential total payout of 9.8 million dollars.

Humane Society?

How did Michael Vick manage to finagle his way back into football? He did it through the most skillfully orchestrated and executed media and public relations scam. The stakes were high;

Vick's success would enable lots of "big" people—inside and outside sports—to augment their power positions, to make lots of big bucks, and to prove themselves eminently virtuous while doing so. You can be sure that every word by Vick and by every supporter was parsed, every sentence was rehearsed, and every action was pre-planned.

As is typical in conspiracies of virtually all types, we know little of the details of backroom deals brokered on behalf of Michael Vick. We do glean a hint of the intrigue, however, from the statements and writings of Wayne Pacelle, CEO of the Humane Society. On April 20, 2011, during a public radio feature regarding animal abuse, Marty Moss Coane spoke with Pacelle about the Vick case.

> Coane: …. the decision by the Humane Society to reach out to him [Vick]. Was that your idea?
>
> Pacelle: It was… actually he reached out to us, toward the end of his his ah prison term at Leavenworth Penitentiary. He, basically, through some of his intermediaries, asked me. My first response was absolutely not, no way, never. Ahm, I considered him radioactive. What he did was despicable …The second thing is, knowing as much as we do about dog fighting, we saw that the biggest growth area for dogfighting was in urban centers like Philadelphia, like Chicago, Los Angeles where young men and boys, often African American, not exclusively by any means, are getting pit bulls for the wrong reason and are squaring them up in fights - in abandoned building and back alleys, either on the street …

Coane: The reaction initially was that Michael Vick was using the Humane Society to try to get back into football.

Pacelle: There's no question that he needed to redeem himself. And, and we were a highly credible third party validator for him. But we were also looking to take advantage of his own story, his own experience, to try to leverage this case to do more good for animals …If Michael, you know, was playing me and working me, that's not going to embarrass me, that's going to embarrass him … I want to use creative strategies to attack the problem and I know we can't just do things the way we used to do them. We've got to reach out to this diverse community of people who are involved in so many forms and you know that this cause has been too Anglo. It hasn't had a conversation with

Coane: Too Anglo, meaning too white?

Pacelle: Too Caucasian, right. Too white. We need to have a conversation with these young kids who are not having a conversion about their responsibility to animals ….It's easy for this to get, you know, off-track which is what happened with Vick. He told me that he started dogfighting in Newport News when he was 7 or 8 years old. And all the kids were involved. They were chasing cats with pit bulls and killing cats; then they were fighting the dogs.

This interview begins with Coane naturally presuming that the Humane Society, in the form of their CEO, approached Michael Vick, but, of course, that supposition proved false. Rather, Vick's "intermediaries" did the approaching. This Vick-oriented "when you have a bunch of lemons make lemonade" strategy made perfect sense. There was no getting around Michael's record of cruelty, so let's just flip him from sinner to saint. After a minimum of seven years as a dog executioner, overnight he will become an evangelizing disciple of all that is animal humane and animal noble, an itinerant preacher, sauntering from one den of iniquity to another, preaching the gospel of St. Pacelle and saving wayward souls. Vick's motivation? Repentance, salvation? He entertained nary a thought of the fortune or fame that he could reap in the NFL. No way that he could have imagined making tens or hundreds of millions by playing a little more football.

In any case, the "everybody did it" claim is classic Michael Vick in that he implicitly projects blame for his personal criminality onto the neighborhood in order to get himself off the hook. The projection is fully consistent with material in *The Bond: Our Kinship with Animals, Our Call to Defend Them*, Wayne Pacelle's book, wherein he recounts Vick's initial reaction to being questioned about his animal abuse:

> Just two days after the raid, Vick denied any
> knowledge of dogfighting on the property,
> claiming that he rarely visited this home and that
> the people he allowed to stay there had taken
> advantage of his generosity. "It's unfortunate I
> have to take the heat," he told reporters in New
> York City on April 27 [2007], a day before the
> NFL draft. "Lesson learned for me." It would be
> several months before Vick would recant that lie
> and the many others he told following the raid.

Reinforcing Deviance and Forward Passing It

What of the Michael Vick's Humane Society collaboration? How did that go? Did it help?

By cooperating with Vick, The Humane Society had nothing to lose but their integrity, and everything to gain: animal rights publicity, entre into the African American community, sympathy, funding—even the marketing core of a book on human-animal bonding. Wayne Pacelle claimed that he and his Society decided to use Vick to do "good," and that is fine. But were there other ways to "use" him? For instance, couldn't the Society have capitalized on the Vick scandal by forming an African American, inner-city, permanent taskforce comprised of veterinarians or other animal-oriented resident persons living in the targeted communities? By doing so, the Humane Society would have put into place a self-perpetuating, self-reinforcing system that would endure over time and place. Moreover, it would have underscored the essential notion that everyday black citizens have the power to "rescue" their children and to take back their own neighborhoods. Instead, they got Vick whose sincerity Pacelle questioned in his book such as when the author noted that Michael justified his love of animals by saying, "I had pet birds. I love watching the Discovery Channel and nature shows."

Michael Vick's father, Michael Boddie, presented a portrait of young Michael's animal interests at odds with his son's pronouncements. USAToday.com on August 23, 2007 cited an Atlanta Journal-Constitution interview with Boddie in which he said that his son was dogfighting in the family's backyard, at least since 2001. Moreover, the father advised, "I wish people would stop sugarcoating it," that his son "likes" dogfighting, and has the finances to make it happen. In short, "This is Mike's thing. And he knows it."

If the Humane Society had a vested interest in cooperating with Michael Vick, it paled in comparison to the NFL's stake. The National Football League needed a good excuse to keep one of the most hyped, most highly paid, most coveted quarterback in history on the field, and to keep millions of football fans focused on his performance. The Vick handlers-inspired, Humane Society plan could not have been better, providing a perfect excuse to claim that Vick had been rehabilitated. Once the Eagles saw an opening, they jumped at the chance to grab Michael Vick and to dump their aging, first-string quarterback, Donovan McNabb.

Vick's Eagles, of course, are located in Philadelphia, a town with a large inner-city black population. MJD, a sports.yahoo.com author cited the Associated Press that reported how dogfighting surged after Vick came to town, rocketing from 245 cases in 2008 to 903 cases in 2009. Similarly, Vernon Clark, Peter Mucha, and Robert Moran of the Philadelphia Inquirer wrote on April 11, 2011 about the arrest of 17 people snagged in a police raid on a dog fighting ring. The article explained that police confiscated guns and large quantities of drugs, including heroin, cocaine, and marijuana. A preliminary investigation already had revealed that four suspects either had served time or were being indicted on drug cases and one had an earlier "cruelty to animals" conviction. Here, as often, we find a confluence of animal cruelty, gun violence, and drug abuse.

As if his negative modeling of animal abuse was not enough, Michael Vick even managed to communicate a crime does, in fact, pay message to young men within the City Brotherly Love. On December 23, 2009, the Philadelphia Eagles voted ex-con Vick the Ed Block Courage Award. No, Vick had not rushed into a burning building to rescue a trapped Rottweiler in respiratory distress. It was because.. ah… because. What was that courageous behavior? Well, what did Mikey Vick say was the reason? "I've overcome a lot, more than probably one single individual can handle or bear," said he. Oh yes, that's right! Another sterling, self-aggrandizing hero destined to inspire America's youth with his intrepid magnificence.

Almost exactly one year after Vick had won the Block award, President Obama also jumped on the I-love-Mike bandwagon, calling Philadelphia Eagles owner Jeffrey Lurie. Why? To say he appreciated that Laurie gave Vick "a second chance." So, soon after Vick comes out of jail, he manages a courage award from his team, a self-congratulatory soliloquy, and a presidential endorsement—a con job of the highest order.

Take Away

How many people had subscribed uncritically to Jane Fonda's or to Michael Vick's views simply due to their celebrity? Regardless of the correct demographic answer, the real question is, "Would you have?" That, of course, depends on a host of factors. First and foremost, you needed to have put forth the effort to understand the real issues. Second, you had to resist the social influence in whatever sphere to which you are most susceptible. That could be, for instance, Fonda's or Vick's celebrity per se, or implicit/explicit pressure from your family, friends, and acquaintances sympathetic to the celebrities' positions.

From my point of view, the celebrity issue assumes prominence because it too often causes people to short-circuit their own rational decision making. Many celebrities cultivate an aura of geniality, superiority and confidence that beguiles us to the point that we passively accept their influences. Celebrity actors are a particular concern. For instance, when Davison and Furnham (2018) compared everyday people with a sample of 214 professional actors, they discovered significantly higher rates of personality disorders in the latter group. Both the male and female actors evidenced higher rates of Antisocialism, Narcissism, Histrionics, and Borderline and Obsessive–Compulsive personalities. Moreover, male actors were found to be more inclined toward Schizotypal, Avoidant, and Dependent personalities than were non-actor males. One is left to wonder whether personality-disordered persons preferentially pursue professional acting careers.

CHAPTER 14: Salespersons & Advertisers

This is the group that we most associate with influence profiteering. Advertisers and salespersons make their livings by swaying our behavior, especially toward spending our hard-earned money. But money is for spending. As the stand-up comic George Carlin proclaimed, "We love our stuff." We want certain stuff and we need certain stuff; that's understood. Despite having done our own independent research before making a purchase, there usually is something to be gained by reviewing relevant advertisements and by talking with knowledgeable salespeople.

Advertisements and sales announcements are ubiquitous, and their influence attempts are not limited to selling stuff. They also try to sell ideas. As previously discussed, we continually are tracked whenever we use many smart devices, and our information is sold and traded to advertisers and sales people. Seth Godin (2003) links media controllers with advertisers, using the term, the "TV-industrial complex." He makes the point that, for decades, the advertising paradigm has been to flood the media-consuming population unceasingly with ads until they finally submit to the persuasion. However, Godin believes that the formula no longer works, since people do not attend to the same limited corpus of media anymore. He derides past flood-the-airways practices. Rather than trying to convert average people to your idea, he suggests marketing the message to those already interested in your general concept, and encouraging them to deliver it to other receptive persons. This of course is targeted marketing at its best. Harkening back to the value of celebrity, we realize that media stars are particularly well-suited for delivering targeted messages to their targeted audiences. Young males are more likely to be attracted to macho-oriented ads and salespeople who are promoted by muscle-bound twenty- or third-something actors that appear in action films. And women are more inclined to follow those endorsed by "drop dead gorgeous," supposedly sophisticated, young actresses.

Posfluence

On the plus side, advertisements and salespeople can promote our well-being. Anything that popularizes values and activities leading to physical and mental health, for instance, would be a posfluence. In the former category are campaigns that highlight physical fitness activities. The advertisements could be ones that raise our consciousness about fitness in settings where youngsters congregate, such as displaying posters in a local mall. The placement of advertisements is critical, since they are maximally effective when located in a space where they are most likely to cue behavior at a time during which it can be enacted. The "salespersons" could be any attractive, fit people who have access to boys and girls, and who can provide concrete examples of how to be more fitness-conscious, as well as how to follow through on actions consistent with the fitness philosophy. Of course, the more the salesperson is seen as approachable, successful, and similar to the target, the more powerful their influence. Some potential posfluences are:

Safety: when they promote products that reduce dangers.

Autonomy: when they sell an item that contributes to the buyer's self-sufficiency.

Excitement: when they facilitate healthfully stimulating experiences.

Meaning: when they contribute to another's understanding in important lifestyle sectors..

Negfluence

Continuing with the youngster-oriented theme, the examples of negfluencial advertisements and salespersons are so numerous as to be overwhelming. Let's take one: music. Any adult who has had the misfortune of being subjected to most rap knows exactly where I am going with this. The ads are songs replete with racist, misogynistic, and misanthropic overt and covert messages. The salespersons are young male "singers" who conform to a hyper-masculine stereotype. They frequently embody "dark-triad" personality characteristics, already defined as meaning that they tend toward extreme narcissism, Machiavellianism, and psychopathy (Paulhus & Williams, 2001). Their negfluence is: bask in my beauty, power, and prestige, and model yourself on my asocial, antisocial persona.

Some other potential negfluences are:

Safety: when they advertise items with unintended negative consequences.

Money: when they sell products that are significantly overpriced.

Meaning: when they hype something to the point that it creates unrealistic expectations.

Social connections: when they exploit group members to market inappropriately among themselves.

Salesperson and Advertiser Influencers

No one can fault salespersons and advertisers for trying to influence us, since influence is their stock in trade. They are in business to sway us to their benefit, not to promote our wellbeing. The most effective salespersons and advertisers are ones who employ judo-like maneuvers, leveraging you against yourself. They achieve their ends by telling you what you want to hear and showing you what you want to see. In the words of Nobel Prize winning economist Richard Thaler (2015A), "It's easier to make money by catering to consumers' biases than trying to correct them." As always, the issue is the particular ways that they try to cater to our biases and otherwise exert their influence, especially how legally and ethically they do so. Thaler (2015B) expresses concern. After first saying he believes that the countries with which he has worked most closely—the United States and Britain—ethically have used the nudge swaying technique that he has advocated, he adds, "But the private sector is another matter. In this domain, I see much more troubling behavior."

Salespersons

If you believe the Guinness Book of World Records, Joseph Samuel Gerard is one of the greatest salespersons of all time. His story epitomizes how, through shear grit, a garden variety salesman evolves into a great one. Joe Girard.com provides the autobiographical details. According to it, Joe's Sicilian-born father immigrated to America for a better life. He reportedly was an overly stressed man who could be emotionally and even physically abusive to Joe. The emotional abuse included predictions that Joseph would never succeed in life. Fortunately, Joe's mother provided such unconditional love that it compensated him for his father's behavior.

Irrespective of the source of his motivation, Joe developed a superior work ethic. At age 9, he began shining shoes. At 11, he added a news carrier job to his routine. Within a year, he competed in and won a new reader solicitation contest which rewarded him with his first bicycle. Unfortunately, by the time he reached 14, his abusive father regularly ejected Joe from the home, causing him to sleep in railroad boxcars or in flop houses. At about age 16, the high school principal slandered Joe about being Sicilian, an argument ensued, and Joseph was expelled. Now free to work full-time, he secured a brief job as a six-day-per-week, 12 hour-per-day stove assembler. Next, Joe joined a vegetables and fruit vender, but soon tired of that.

By 18, Joseph Girard had had enough of conventional work. Instead, he joined the United States Army. Once again, the plan proved unfruitful, as a result of Joe's falling from a military truck and quickly being Honorably Discharged. But, the next two years of civilian life was no better, at least employment-wise. Then Joe got a break, snagging a job with a benevolent, aged building contractor. Their relationship grew so close that when the contractor eventually retired, he passed the business along to Joseph. Could it be that Joe finally turned the corner? Not even close. In fact, things got even worse. After taking control, Joseph failed in his attempt turn a profit on several homes that he built. Instead, he lost $60,000.

During the next year, Joe Girard and his family teetered on the brink of total poverty. Desperate for work, he literally begged for a salesman job at a local Chevrolet franchise, and his plea was heard. By the end of the next month, he had managed to sell 19 cars. Incredibly, however, the owner of the franchise fired him, because other salesmen alleged that Joe's style was too aggressive. But Girard had found his calling and there was no stopping him now. He quickly secured a job at another Chevrolet dealership and began his meteoric rise to car salesmanship fame.

Guinnessworldrecords.com describes Joseph Samuel Gerard as follows: "The all-time record for automobile salesmanship in units sold individually is 1,425 in 1973 by Joe Girard of Detroit, USA, winner of the No. 1 Car Salesman title each year since 1966. His commissions in 1973 totaled $189,000 (then £78,750). His 1974 total was 1,376." He allegedly remained number 1 from 1963 to 1978—a record of consecutive auto sales that stands to this day.

Joe Girard helps us to better understand the mind of a master influencer. You will notice that he possessed an intuitive sense of the principles of persuasion long before they were researched and popularized by psychologist gurus, such as Robert Cialdini. Girard writes extensively about rules for sales success. He and Robert L. Shook (1989) published *How to Close Every Sale*, and it has been a compass for many would-be sales experts. What follows is my edited version of thirteen seminal principles contained in that book.

Principle One: Understand Sales Resistance

Society often portrays salespeople negatively.
The sales process often is regarded as adversarial.
To their detriment, salespeople often ignore their client's schedules.
Clients often recall unsatisfying sales experiences.
Salespeople often develop negative attitudes.
A common negative salesperson attitude is the conviction that a client does not really want what they are selling.
Many clients are so averse to saying "no" that they avoid sales situations at all costs.

Principle Two: Sell Yourself First

When it comes to making a sale, the salesperson is their most important product.
Impress the client with your company's reputation and your trustworthiness.
Fully believe in your product.
Be positive but realistic about making a sale.
Specifically tell the client that you use the product that you are selling.
Visualize yourself clinching the sale.
Cultivate a positive self-image that includes but is not limited to looking like a professional.
Thoroughly know your product and its competitors.
Clearly communicate that you value the client.

Bring the client into your space and structure that space to impress.
When appropriate, disarm the client with humor.
Bestow inexpensive gifts.
Make sure that the client leaves the transaction feeling good.

Principle Three: Assume That the Sale Will Be Consummated

Specifically but subtly imply to the client that the sale is a foregone conclusion.
Deal quickly with any objections.
Make statements or ask questions that reinforce the implication that the sale is about to be concluded.
Give the client a chance to try out the item or service.
When referring to the prospect of the sale, say "when," not "if."
Whenever possible, say "we" and "us," not "me" and "you."
Promise outstanding service during and after the sale.

Principle Four: Learn the Client's Buy Signals

Carefully scrutinize client externals, such as clothing and jewelry, to have a sense of their budget.
Use the externals only as a rough guide, don't stereotype based on them.
While giving the client a chance to handle a product, look for signs of approval and disapproval.
Listen carefully.
Notice how the client behaves in social situations.
Determine whether the client is risk seeking or risk averse.
Get a sense of the size and qualities of the client's ego.

Principle Five: Know How to Deal with Objections

Use objections as a chance to make your counterpoints.
Differentiate flimsy from more solid discontents.
Don't abet client defensiveness by mishandling them.

Know how to rebut "I can't afford" what you are promoting.
If a decision requires agreement by partners, ensure that both are present so you can address their issues, too.
When a client states, "I have a friend who can satisfy my needs," have a reasonable reply handy.
If a client wants to shop around, be able to introject information that undercuts the competition.
If a client want you to leave information so that he can contact you, instead elaborate the positives that you already presented.
For clients with a great number of reservations, choose the strongest one and overcome it soundly.
After addressing objections, be silent and let the client process your information.

Principle Six: Cope With Client Procrastination

Facilitate decision making.
Increase client confidence, even if you need to convince a trusted client confidant of the wisdom of your advice.
Emphasize as early as possible in the negotiation that time is of the essence.
Appeal to his self-concept as a responsible adult who is capable of making correct choices.
Introduce some well-established, compelling adage about expedient action, such as "strike while the iron is hot."

Principle Seven: Take Charge

Be sure to sell with animation.
Eliminate all distractions.
Never answer your phone.
Communicate via dialogue, not monologue.
Demonstrate superior knowledge of all relevant information.
Always thoroughly explain value before quoting any price.

Principle Eight: Be Able to Execute a Variety of Closing Strategies

Combine assumptive and closing comments, such as "This car is so fuel efficient that next week you will be driving for pennies on the dollar."
Lead the client through a few small decisions that result in a final big decision. For instance, ask how he plans to pay, the time for delivery, and whether he wants paper or internet documentation of the sale.
Explain in detail how failing to take your simple advice now will cause him great harm eventually.
Provide no more than three choices in order to avoid information overload.
Rather than being rejected, reduce your request, as when you suggest a more economical item over the one you had promoted earlier.
Explicitly admit that you very much want the client's business.
If all else fails, help the client write a pros and cons list that over-weights the former.
Underscore that what you are trying to sell is very special and limited to a select few.
Use emotional appeal, as when you suggest that your advice would be best for his loved ones.
Refer to some high prestige person who does exactly what you want him to do.

Principle Nine: Introject Time Pressure

Claim that your offer is time-limited.
Suggest that the price soon will rise.
Make the client feel that his particular demographics make a quick purchase necessary.
If your product is unique, drive that point home
Try to get potential buyers into a bidding war.

Principle Ten: Don't Oversell

Don't be paralyzed by fear of getting a "no" from the client.
Limit your pitch information necessary for the client to make his decision.
Provide time for the client to consider what he has been told.
Ask the client whether he wants more information.

Principle Eleven: Go All Or Nothing

Make your strongest pitch right from the start. The more time that elapses, the less likely your influence.
Explicitly explain that you cannot be available to the client beyond the near term.
Strive to make the biggest sale that you can. Do not try to be incremental.
Remind yourself that failing to make a single sale does not sully your career.
High-pressure strategies sometimes can work on some select clients.

Principle Twelve: Take Steps to Eliminate Risks of Buyer's Remorse

Close the sale with sincere appreciation.
Compliment the client on making what you know is the best decision.
Linger with the client after the sale. Subtly remind him of why he chose as he did.
Immediately after the close, prompt the client to directly interact with the product or ideas.
Follow up soon after the close.
Ask why the client accepted your specific presentation.

Principle Thirteen: Make the Client Your Advocate

Provide continuing superior service.
Choose to work only for a customer-focused company.
Maintain an enduring relationship with your clients.

Takeaways from the 13 Principles

Summarized below are the principles and some of their implications for you as the target of influence:

Principle One: Understand Sales Resistance means: The salesperson will be ready to overcome quickly most objections that you offer.

Principle Two: Sell Yourself First means: From the outset, she/he will pack on the charm.

Principle Three: Assume That the Sale Will Be Consummated means: She/he will be prompting you—subtly or otherwise—to develop a completed sale or completed idea frame of mind.

Principle Four: Learn the Client's Buy Signals means: She/he will pay close attention to whatever you like about what they are offering.

Principle Five: Know How to Deal with Objections means: She/he will quickly respond to whatever you label negatively.

Principle Six: Cope With Client Procrastination means: She/he will try to speed you along.

Principle Seven: Take Charge means: She/he will attempt to lead or channel you toward their ends.

Principle Eight: Be Able to Execute a Variety of Closing Strategies means: She/he will tailor their close to your demeanor and inclinations.

Principle Nine: Introject Time Pressure means: She/he will strive to get you to sign on the dotted line, even before you are ready.

Principle Ten: Don't Oversell means: To the extent that they can, she/he will pace their presentation so not to be off putting.

Principle Eleven: Go All Or Nothing means: If you seem to tolerate an intense salesperson she/he might adopt that stance at the start. If you don't, they might adopt that stance as a last resort.

Principle Twelve: Take Steps to Eliminate Risks of Buyer's Remorse means: She/he will not stop selling so long as you are present.

Principle Thirteen: Make the Client Your Advocate means: She/he will do whatever they can to encourage you to sell for them, such as prompting you to talk to your friends and neighbors about her/him and their ideas/objects.

Advertisers

When it comes to advertisements, nothing on earth receives the hype and attention that Super Bowl commercials do. So, rather than focus on a single advertiser, let's look at what Alex Fitzpatrick and his colleagues (2017) at Time magazine called, "The 25 Most Influential Super Bowl Ads of All Time." Doing so should allow us to peek into the minds of some of America's most high profile advertisement creators to determine how they seek to influence us. In the interest of brevity, only 12 of the ads are considered, but they will be carefully evaluated via the four primary influence vehicles. You will not be surprised to see that several commercials exploit the extant American preoccupations of their day. Some are heavily sexualized, some heavily racialized. Only a couple ads emphasize the product per se—the majority exploits primal instincts and social identities. Obviously, the following commercials are just ones chosen by the Time authors who, of course, have their own agendas, biases and preferences.

Good Old Fashioned Sex

1973
Person(s)/Institution: Joe Namath (NFL quarterback with a playboy reputation) and Farrah Fawcett (blonde superstar actress); Noxema. Procter & Gamble
Object/Idea: Noxema shaving cream makes you sexually attractive.
Situation: Gorgeous woman rubs man's face, snuggles, and sings to him in a sultry manner.
Process: Man opens the scene by jubilantly exclaiming, "I'm so excited; I'm gonna get creamed" after which the woman rubs his face and sings. At the end, while the woman is holding him close and again rubbing his face, the man smiles broadly and says, "You've got a great pair of hands."

1992
Person(s)/Institution: Cindy Crawford, 2 young boys; Pepsi
Object/Idea: Pepsi's new cans are beautiful and the drink is as good as ever.
Situation: Two young boys are standing behind a fence, out of sight. A gorgeous, sexy woman drives up in a fast car, stops abruptly, exits the car, and purchases a Pepsi from a vending machine in front of a gas station. Song "Just One Look" plays.
Process: The boys watch her long drinks. The first boy asks, "Is that a great new Pepsi can or what?" The second replies, "It's beautiful." Neither mentions the woman whom they had been watching. The scene ends with a voice over: "same great taste, a new way to look at Pepsi and Diet Pepsi."

2001

Person(s)/Institution: Britney Spears, dancers; Pepsi
Object/Idea: Pepsi incites exuberant joy.
Situation: Workers transform into hedonists immersed in revelry
Process: Pepsi logo fades out. Woman within a garage wearing work clothing, strips them off to reveal a skimpy Pepsi logo outfit. On each side of her are Pepsi trucks. Raucous music explodes. Men leap out of the trucks. She flings open the garage doors. All begin dancing wildly. From time to time images of Pepsi flash by. Woman drinks a Pepsi. More dancing. The woman is shown on top of and beside a Pepsi logo. Scene ends with the printed statement "Joy of Pepsi."

Women's Liberation

1984
Person(s)/Institution: Unknown athletic female, automaton-like people; Apple
Object/Idea: Overcome the tendency to mindlessly accept the status quo, break barriers, and achieve liberation.
Situation: A procession of men and women in prison-like garb mechanically march into an assembly hall accompanied by guards while a Big Brother instructs them all via a huge video screen.
Process: Athletically dressed woman runs into the hall, spins, and hurls a sledge hammer at the screen. The screen explodes and a printed and spoken message begins, "On January 24th, Apple Computer will introduce MacIntosh. And you'll see why 1984 won't be like '1984.'"

2002
Person(s)/Institution: Elton John and Melanie Amaro; Pepsi
Object/Idea: Replace an imperious male status symbol
Situation: A royally crowned and gowned white male king and a Hispanic female singer battle for dominance.
Process: The king summarily dismisses a tone deaf singing male entertainer by ejecting him through a trap door and into a

dungeon. A Hispanic female singer assumes the entertainer's position. While singing "Respect," she overwhelms the king with her vocal power. She then declines his offer of a Pepsi, dispatches him into the dungeon, and proclaims, "It is Pepsi for all!" A message appears,
"Where there's Pepsi, there's music." In the dungeon, a black male, dressed like a Viking, mockingly shouts "Get up boy!" at the white king who is lying on the floor.

Silly Boys

1993
Person(s)/Institution: Michael Jordan and Larry Bird basketball superstars and on-court rivals; McDonald's
Object/Idea: sandwich/exceed everyone's wildest beliefs of perfection
Situation: Two basketball players compete to determine who can make the most amazing set shot.
Process: On a basketball court with only the two men present, Bird sees Jordan sitting down to eat and asks, "What's in the bag?" Jordan: "Lunch. Big Mac, fries." Bird: "Play you for it." Jordan: "You and me for my Big Mac?" Bird: "First one to miss watches the winner eat."

As music plays, the two alternate back and forth, each shooting their shot that must be matched by the other player. After a few shots accompanied by players' comments, it is a standoff. Jordan interjects, "I think we'll be here a while. I suggest you get a Big Mac." The contest continues uninterrupted. Shots become exceedingly difficult, progressively reaching a farcical level. For instance, in the last scene, while the two stand outside on the roof of a building, Jordan points down to the street and challenges Bird to make the following shot: "Off the expressway, over the river, off the billboard, through the window, off the wall, nothing but net." The commercial ends: "Swish."

1999
Person(s)/Institution: Everyday young African American men;
Budweiser
Object/Idea: Lighten up, have fun, drink beer; Budweiser
Situation: The males are having uproarious fun phone-calling or
otherwise calling out to other present males, shouting,
"whassup."
Process: The first man calls another, asking "what's up" to which
the second replies, "Watching the game, having a Bud." The
second asks the same question of the first, and receives the same
answer. A third man enters the room where the second is on the
phone and screams, "Wassup?" while raising his hands high over
his head. The second then screams "Wassup?" into the phone.
Scenes are consecutively shown in which other American males
call and yell "whassup" into the phone and loll out their tongues
while doing so. In the final scene, the original first and second
men, still talking on the phone, calmly ask each other again what
they are doing, and they calmly repeat that they are "Watching
the game, having a Bud." The commercial ends with the
Budweiser logo, and the spoken and the written word, "True."

Race Exploitation

1980
Person(s)/Institution: Charles Edward Greene (AKA: Joe
Greene), National Football League defensive tackle and a small
boy; Coke
Object/Idea: Intimidating, distant figures really can be tender and
nurturing.
Situation: Soda brings people together.
Process: Ad begins with a black male, renowned for his
nickname "Mean Joe Greene," and for his formidable size, speed,
and aggressiveness. In full NFL playing garb, holding on to a
railing, he painfully and stiffly is walking off the field and into
the football stadium tunnel after a game. A small white boy
behind him asks, "Mr. Greene, do you need any help?" The boy

continues, "I just want you to know that I think you're the best ever." Joe stops and turns to the boy: "Yeah, sure." Boy raises his soda: "Want my Coke? … It's okay. You can have it." Joe: "No, no." Boy: "Really, you can have it." Joe: "Okay" and takes the Coke. Joe, with a huge smile to the boy, drains the soda, straight down. Boy watches the Coke despairingly, shrugs his shoulders in disappointment, and turns to walk out of the tunnel, toward the field. Giving a backward, anemic wave, he murmurs, "See you around." Joe, again smiling, calls to him: "Hey, kid" while throwing the boy his game jersey. Boy, with an equally big smile, catches it: "Wow!, thanks!" Commercial ends with background singing ("…I like to see the whole world smiling with me…") and with the printed statements, "Have a Coke and a smile" and "Coke adds life." The commercial, then, suggests that Coke can bridge gaps that exist between the most widely diverse people.

2010
Person(s)/Institution: Unknown black male; Old Spice
Object/Idea: Become an ideal sexual and life partner object.
Situation: Look good and all good things will follow.
Process: Slim black male with washboard abs appears in front of a shower, wearing only a towel that is slung down to a level just above his pubic hair. There's a can of Old Spice shaving cream in his hand. Staring straight into the camera, he confidently and seductively instructs, "Look at your man, then back to me, then back to your man, then back to me." He continues, "Sadly he isn't me, but if he stopped using lady scented body wash and switched to Old Spice, he could smell like me." Scene changes; the man, now wearing only tight white pants, appears on the deck of a yacht. He commands, "Look down, look up, look down, look up. Where are you? You are on a boat." A towel drops from the sky and surrounds his neck, like a scarf. The man puts down the Old Spice and picks up an open oyster, and states, "It's an oyster with two tickets for that thing you love." The tickets fall from the oyster and are replaced by small flowing shiny stones: "Now it's diamonds. Anything is possible when your man smells like Old

Spice, like me." The scene changes to him on a large white horse on a beach with the ocean behind. As the commercial ends, he stares provocatively into the camera and observes, "I'm on a horse." Simultaneously, the printed message appears, "Smell like a man, man." And the words "Old Spice" are presented to the right of the man.

Even the Unaware Instinctively Understand Our Message

1984
Person(s)/Institution: 3 unknown elderly white females/Wendy's
Object/Idea: sandwich/product value. Don't allow yourself to be duped by deceptive product presentation.
Situation: The grey-haired ladies are standing at a fast food ordering counter, scrutinizing a sandwich on a plate. Behind them is a maze-like construction and on the wall, a sign: HOME OF THE BIG BUN.
Process: Woman 1: "It certainly is a big bun." Woman 2, looking over 1's shoulder, "It's a very big bun." Woman 2: "A big fluffy bun." Woman 1: "It's a very big, fluffy bun." She opens the bun, revealing a tiny hamburger topped with cheese and a pickle. Woman 3 loudly: "Where's the beef?" Voiceover: "Some hamburger places give you a lot less beef on a lot of bun." Woman 3 loudly: "Where's the beef?" Voiceover: At Wendy's, we serve a hamburger that we modestly call a single. And Wendy's single has more beef than the Whopper or Big Mac. At Wendy's you get more beef and less bun. Woman 3 loudly: "Hey, where's the beef?" Commenting on the absence of a server, 3 adds, "I don't think there's anybody back there!" Voiceover: "You want something better. You're Wendy's kind of people."

1995
Person(s)/Institution: 3 frogs in a pond on lily pads/Budweiser
Object/Idea: Beer. Think Budweiser beer

Situation: Nighttime scene during which each frog sequentially repeats a call that together sounds like, "Budweiser."
Process: Frog 1 croaks, "Bud". Frog 2 croaks, "weis." And Frog 3 croaks, "er." They "sing" that song, over and over. The camera then fades back to include a cabin-like bar next to the pond with a sign flashing the word "Budweiser" and its logo.

Take Away

The commercials described above cost billions to produce and distribute. They were created by people whose job is to know how to seize your attention and how to manipulate your thoughts, feelings, and actions toward the goals of the commercials' funders. More than anything else, the commercials reveal what the creators and funders believe about you and your vulnerabilities. They prey on your identity, biases, longings and so forth. And recall that they do not care whether you are conscious of their ads after they play, only that they influence you in the desired direction. The latter is what gets them more business and makes them more money. That is all that counts for them.

The commercials that they develop are focused myopically on moving you in ways that satisfy the funders. And that myopia can have unfortunate consequences. Consider the two commercials that I classified as racial exploitation. Those who created and funded the commercials would never accept their being classified as "exploitation." If anything, they might insist that the ads, in fact, fight against racial bias. But one thing is undeniably true: the commercials reveal their beliefs about the collective human psyche. In the case in question, that means they believe you will be hooked by a racialized commercial, whether that commercial works to the benefit or detriment of society.

CHAPTER 15: Educators

Here we consider all persons who present themselves as educators of any kind. They speak from the alleged authority of their credentials and knowledge, believing they have wisdom to impart to you. The educators range from certified, traditional professionals to fringe, iconoclastic anarchists. In all cases, their impact depends on the extent to which you buy into their messages. Research (e.g., Pulford, et. al, 2018) suggests that people who possess knowledge that they believe is correct are most confident in themselves and most persuasive to others. Therefore, since professional educators, by definition, should have mastered their subject, they (and scientists whom we will discuss in the next chapter) usually possess extraordinary influence power over us.

Human beings have dominated the biosphere due to their ability to learn. From our first to last breath, everyone needs to be educated in one way or another. In the earliest days of life, our parents are our educators. They almost always know the basics of what we need, and they almost always have a stake in selflessly teaching us. Parents, then, should be, and usually are, what I previously have termed "true-gooders." Having been introduced by them to the importance of education literally from the cradle, we naturally gravitate toward those who we believe have something valuable to teach us. Therefore, we are extraordinarily vulnerable to influence from authentic or bogus educators, and to the posfluences and negfluences that follow from what they espouse.

Posfluence

A properly designed and implemented formal educational system enables us first to learn the basics and then to progress toward advanced skills. That also is true for a well-crafted informal educational system, such as a physical fitness program at the local gym. Those who formally or informally seek to educate wish to have us as long-term "students." Moreover, once we come on-board with the system, we are likely to want to grow within it. So, educators typically are not only imparting skills, they are promoting a kind of philosophy. With the right educator, you can learn to be healthier in body, mind, or spirit, and fashion a more successful, satisfying lifestyle.

Competency: when they teach valuable ideas and skills.

Meaning: when they help impart understanding of universal truths.

Order: when they structure teaching environments that make learning easier.

Transcendence: when they facilitate a student's ability to exceed her/his modal levels of functioning.

Negfluence

Since the posfluences of education are so obvious, there is no need to dwell on them. That is not the case concerning negfluences. In the past it was almost a contradiction in terms to say that you were educated in a manner that undermined your body, mind, or spirit. However, in the 21st century world of misinformation and rampant manipulation, education and negfluence are common bedfellows. We will consider several examples of negfluential bed-sharing in formal education institutions.

America presently suffers from the negfluence because some educational institutions and educators believe that it is their jobs not only to tell us what to think, but also to restrict our access to views contrary to theirs. Later, we thoroughly will consider the University of California, Berkley, the school that prided itself on having been incubator to the free speech movement (FSM) that began during September of 1964. Although the movement started with the Berkley student body and the university initially resisted it, by January, 1965 the educators relented and institutionalized the program by designating their Sproul Plaza as an area that allowed open discussion of all types, most notably political discussion. That free speech policy quickly spread throughout the nation's institutions of higher learning, especially the elite ones.

Unfortunately, over the decades, university faculties increasingly have become dominated by liberal professors for whom education includes indoctrination into liberal ideals and opposition to alternative views. In some universities, free speech now is selective free speech, being exclusively determined and adjudicated by the university and their staff. For instance, Condoleezza Rice—a female African American, former Secretary of State, former Stanford University professor, and near concert-level classical pianist—had to withdraw from giving the 2014 Rutgers University commencement address because of protests from professors and students regarding her political positions. That outrage is just the tip of the silence-the-opposition iceberg, however. The university "unfree speech movement" has become so extreme that even Nicholas Kristof, an avowed liberal, in a New York Times OP-ED entitled, "A Confession of Liberal Intolerance' (2016) grudgingly admitted:

> WE progressives believe in diversity, and we want
> women, blacks, Latinos, gays and Muslims at the
> table — there, so long as they aren't
> conservatives.

> Universities are the bedrock of progressive values,
> but the one kind of diversity that universities
> disregard is ideological and religious. We're fine
> with people who don't look like us, as long as they
> think like us.

Notice the identity politics tone of Kristof's admission. Although he made no reference to the despicable treatment that Condoleezza Rice received in 2014, his criticism would be an indictment of any racist orientation to free speech. However, it would not acknowledge that a white, male conservative also deserves to be able to speak his mind—even at an Ivy League commencement.

For us, this issue is all about the forces of influence. Universities not only educate us and our children, they also educate the nation's leaders. The more elite the university, the more leaders they teach. Most Americans presume that education is all about promulgating objective facts that everyone can apply in accordance with their own ideals and needs. However, today nothing could be further from the truth. To an unprecedented level, every fact that virtually every contemporary educator utters is filtered through her/his ideological/political belief system. Too many educators believe that they must toe the party line in order to keep their jobs and "be on the right side of history"—a history defined exclusively within their formal and informal university "history' departments. And the overt pressure for them to conform to that party line can be completely overwhelming.

Whenever an educator presents their ideas, be alert to their spoken and unspoken, emotion-laden and objective, overt and covert messages. Pay attention to how they are trying to influence you. After carefully evaluating their evidence, make your own decisions based on your own standards.

Some additional negfluences are:

Comfort: making some students feel that their moral beliefs are inferior.

Power: summarily dismissing a student's opinion when it contradicts that of the teacher.

Stability: changing established requirements post hoc to punish unpopular ideas and/or unpopular students.

Competency: denigrating a student's skill or beliefs because those skills or beliefs are not valued by the teacher.

Educator Influencers

Teachers are second only to parents in their power to influence us during our most formative stages. That fact is obvious, of course, during our minority, especially when we are young children. But young adults and fully mature adults also place themselves in dependent positions vis-a-vis teachers to earn a degree, continuing education credits, or virtually any unmastered skill. Given their socially conferred power, most of us want to trust teachers. Most important, we desperately want to trust them with our own children. We need to believe we are doing the best for our progeny when we send them off to school. In light of the vulnerability of children and our responsibility to them, let us first focus our discussion of educator influence primarily by considering public school teachers.

If we accepted George Bernard Shaw's line from the play Man and Superman that "He who can, does. He who cannot, teaches," we never would allow our children to set foot in their local elementary schools. In fact, for 2016-2017, about 1,598,905 school-aged children, three percent of that entire population, were home-schooled. The reasons for doing so are as varied as the parents who chose that route (A-to-Z of Homeschooling.com., 2017). However, researching several surveys and anecdotal evidence, Calvert Education claims to have found that the five major reasons for homeschooling are: Make A Change From A Negative School Environment, Get A Higher Quality Education, Improve Social Interactions, Support A Learning Disabled Child, Educate Children During A Family Relocation To Another State

Or Country, And Other Reasons
(http://www.calverteducation.com).

Since about 97 percent of our children are schooled outside the home, most teachers presumably are doing at least an adequate job. If we can identify and understand when that posfluential teacher effect fails and take steps to correct those problems, however, America's young people will be all the better for it.

Let's Raise Those Test Scores

Feedback is absolutely essential for learning and teaching. Both learners and teachers need to be evaluated and adjusted regularly. Accordingly, schools conduct building-wide standardized testing, using it to decide student progress and teacher effectiveness across the district, state, and nation. As you probably know or surmise, such testing is a very big deal. Aside from "proving" the district's educational value, results of tests often are used to decide student placement in classes for remedial or advanced instruction, and for deciding teachers' and administrators' compensations. Teachers and administrators do their utmost to influence the opinions and conclusions of parents and school boards when it comes to test results. Testing time is pressure cooker time.

Selected as Atlanta School superintendent in 1999, Beverly L. Hall needed to prove that she could reverse the district's abysmal academic record. And did she! The children's test scores rocketed upward. The meteoric rise received nationwide publicity which culminated in her being awarded National Superintendent of the Year from the American Association of School Administrators on February 20, 2009.

The applause for Beverly Hall barely had faded when The Atlanta Journal-Constitution published several 2009 articles questioning the district's too-good-to-be true test results. Thus began an initial informal scrutiny of the system that raised issues so serious that Governor Sonny Perdue in 2010 appointed special prosecutors to investigate the burgeoning scandal. By the next year, the inquiry had issued a report disclosing that no less than 44 of Atlanta schools engaged in systemic deception. Thirty-eight of the principals and approximately 180 employees had colluded to fudge student test scores and achievements in general. In the words of The Atlanta Journal-Constitution:

> Hall inculcated an atmosphere that encouraged using any means necessary to achieve test-score targets, the indictment said, and then "publicly misrepresented the academic performance of schools throughout APS." Pressuring subordinates to produce targeted scores, the indictment said, "created an environment where achieving the desired end result was more important than the students' education." (Judd & Cook, 2013).

The Atlanta School District cheating operations were uncommonly sophisticated and "professional." For instance, the New York Times reported that one principal wore gloves when she changed children's test sheet answers, and that the superintendent and her assistants had "created a culture of fear, intimidation and retaliation" that had permitted "cheating — at all levels — to go unchecked for years" (Blinder, 2015). Other sources suggested more specifically that the duration was from about 2005 to 2010. Judd and Cook claimed that from the time of her arrival in Atlanta, Beverly Hall intimidated her teachers, even threatening their job security. She used carrots as well as sticks, however, offering monetary rewards for elevated student test scores. The superintendent also wanted her own carrots, since her bonuses were partly test score dependent. And she ultimately received enough bonus carrots to satisfy Bugs Bunny—$580,000 during her 10 year tenure.

Atlanta parents had entrusted their children to a high profile, apparent superstar superintendent and her big city staff, expecting their children to reap the benefits. The educators had all the influence weapons that they needed. They controlled 100 percent of the data that could be used to decide student progress. They controlled the narrative by which the data would be disseminated. And they controlled when, where, and how the district parents could access any relevant information. Students and parents had virtually no chance to resist the educators' influences.

Just Get the Students to Come to School

Lest you think that Atlanta School District fiasco was an isolated event, briefly consider Community School (CS) of Ann Arbor, Michigan as described by the Brafmans (2014). CS was another sad story of chronic pupil underachievement. However, its problems included abysmally poor student attendance, as well. One would have expected better, since the school had been created specifically to be extraordinarily welcoming and pupil-focused. Rules were few and often lax, purportedly to enable students to flower with minimal extraneous interference. In fact, at first CS proved to be a sensation. During registration, prospective students literally lined the block; so many applied that the district created a waiting list for future admissions.

Unfortunately, the CS experiment soon foundered. The lax rules inspired lax attendance. What to do? Maybe throw some money at the problem. And that is precisely what CS did. Teachers were offered a bonus equivalent to 12% of their salaries for improved student attendance. To earn that increase, they had to have at least 80% attendance when, during the last week of each semester, their attendance rolls were checked. The program worked fabulously. Within a few years, attendance had climbed from 51% to 72%. How did that happen?

The improvement came after teachers had increased markedly the number of in-class parties and field trips. Those "goodies" primarily were delivered to the students during the last week of each semester when attendance was measured. The teachers then got their own goodies on paydays. Unfortunately, students' achievements declined severely. So, once again, the educators had asserted their influence to personal advantage. Teachers used their power positions to structure the school environment and to manipulate the students in ways to ensure that their own goals took precedence over those of the pupils.

The most outrageous teacher influence attempts, however, sometimes bear no relationship whatsoever to the school district curriculum. For instance, a California history teacher decided to inflict his biases on a high school captive audience. Gregory Salcido—El Rancho teacher, Pico Rivera city councilman, and former mayor—tried to persuade his students that military personnel are degenerates. For instance, referring to those who fight for our country in foreign countries, he said, "Think about the people you know who are over there. Your freakin' stupid Uncle Louie or whatever. They're dumb s - - - s. They're not high-level bankers. They're not academic people. They're not intellectual people…They're the freakin' lowest of our low" (Hunt, 2018). When you send your children to school, do you expect their teachers to try to sway them toward the teachers' personal views of patriotism and/or morality?

Finally, one especially sad commentary on childhood educator influence. Most everyone reading this book will recall the horrendous slaughter in which 17 people, 15 of whom were children, were shot to death by a 19-year-old former pupil at Marjory Stoneman Douglas School in Parkland, Florida on February 14, 2018. Less than one week after that carnage, well-positioned educators—from Atlanta, Georgia (Parker, 2018), Roxbury, Massachusetts (Dougherty, 2018) and more (Gibbs, 2018)—exuberantly announced that they would fund student trips to view the just-released Black Panther movie. It was not quite the 2017 *Rooted in Peace* film that featured such luminaries as the Nobel Peace Laureates Mairead Maguire and Archbishop Desmond Tutu. No. Instead, according to the IMBd parent's guide, Black Panther exposed the children to a violence-saturated Hollywood blockbuster described as follows:

> There are battles with swords, spears, guns and fantastical weapons. Violence includes slashes, stabs and hand-to-hand combat. A character breaks another's arm, and a person's throat is cut, but without strong detail.
> Violence in Black Panther is more intense and realistic than other Marvel films, with blood regularly visible during combat. Characters are impaled and slashed with spears and swords, the blood and wounds not always focused on by the camera.
> There are tons of violent scenes. How about 12+
> A man is stabbed in the chest, another the same, another stabbed in the abdomen.
> A man is cut numerous times during a fight
> A large battle/ civil war takes place with friends fighting each other. Not clear if anyone actually dies, though bodies are thrown, trampled, stabbed, etc.
> Security guards are shot, some at point blank range, another shot in the back unexpectedly (and gratuitously)
> 2 main characters are shot, one at point blank range (off screen). Bullet wounds are shown (though not much blood)
> A man is beheaded - though it is actually hard to see and not apparent at first (if at all).
> (http://www.imdb.com/title/tt1825683/parentalgui de).

Opening Students' Minds to a Liberal Education

Having concentrated mostly on school-age children so far, it is fitting to spend a little more time addressing teacher influence on mature, post-high schoolers. To do so, let us return once more to the University of California, Berkeley (UCB) as a seat of premier educator influence on young adults. After the university institutionalized the FSM, free speech became a defining feature of its academic and campus life. Virtually any radical message, short of genocide, received thoughtful consideration. Since at least 1965 then, UCB educators have had extraordinary power to sculpt and sway the evolving socially-relevant thoughts and moralities of their students, and they have exercised it with gusto.

Fast-forward from the 20th to the 21st century. At UCB, speech no longer is free; it is expensive and miserly controlled. Only politically correct speech is tolerated. Those who do not conform to sanctioned political correctness usually are not invited. Censorship ideally is implemented a priori to avoid exposing the campus-located thought police to unflattering public exposure and potential criticism. If a politically incorrect speaker does inadvertently, miraculously slip through the "Big Brother is watching" cordon, she/he is shouted down, maligned, or threatened. UCB and similar universities don't want outsiders to defile the campus with their blasphemous messages.

Abby Jackson (2016) wrote about dis-invitations by a variety of elite universities during the 2015-2016 academic year. Those dis-invited included distinguished women and men, some of whom were minorities. The prestigious, dis-inviting schools mentioned were: Brown, California State University at Los Angeles, University of California at Berkeley, University of Chicago, George Washington University, Trinity College, Hampshire College, University of Pennsylvania, San Francisco State University, Virginia Tech, and Williams College. Jackson noted that even such die-hard liberals as Barack Obama and Michael

Bloomberg "warned about political correctness gone awry" at elite liberally-oriented universities.

Take Away

Obviously, people seek educators who they believe fully are capable of providing the instruction sought. Typically, teachers have some form of credential that some form of government institution had issued to them. And most educators have manuals and curricula designed to govern their teaching. Those credentialing and manuals can lull us into a false sense of security. We let our guards down, believing that the most important vetting has been completed for us.

As implied earlier, teachers have considerable control over objective measures of their effectiveness. They know the evaluative tests that will be given and the content of those tests. They know that they will be judged according to their pupils' test scores. Educators can teach excessively to the test, or worse, they can change answers on scoring sheets.

For high school and post-high school students, teachers have incredible opportunities to influence their charges in ways pivotal for character development. Most vulnerable are the "good" students who want "good" grades. They are likely to have the greatest need for teacher acceptance, and, therefore, are inclined to uncritically embrace what they are told. Since accepting students often gather together, they inadvertently reinforce teachers' messages. Thereafter, teachers' messages become peer messages, making them all the more resistant to challenge. These so-called good students from good schools become captains of industry and education. What began as teacher influence in a circumscribed sphere can explode exponentially, such that persons from elite institutions become conduits who pass-on the biases inculcated into them by their teachers. When those women and men become post-graduate students, teachers, and administrators at top-tier universities like Berkeley, they sincerely believe that they know what is best for everyone, and have no tolerance for any opinions but their own. You must be particularly cautious, then, whenever you or your loved ones are in the presence of all education influencers, but especially those from elite institutions. Do your best to uncover their biases and intolerances before you accede to the guidance that they offer.

CHAPTER 16: Scientists

There is one class of influencers defined by their objectivity: scientists. They are expected to observe, question, hypothesize, experiment, confirm or disconfirm, and then to report valid, reliable findings with no bias or preconceived agenda. Of course, since scientists are human beings, we do tolerate minor deviations from the standard, but only the most minor ones. We feel betrayed when we discover that scientific results have been fabricated in order to profit the scientist in some way.

We often consider scientists to be educators in a general sense, but they need not necessarily be. Some provide information or other products that have resulted from their work, but not with the specificity that would enable anyone to reproduce the work. In fact, some scientific information or other products are purely proprietary: the scientist keeps some or all features of their discovery secret, perhaps to make money from it. Since scientists typically know what we do not know, we are at their mercy. They can tell us things that are perfectly correct or totally wrong, and we have little chance of knowing how accurate or inaccurate they are. Their influence can be unassailable and powerful. Because the general public often is in awe of science, scientists and scientific data often are used to convince us of the value of a product or an idea, even when the science bears no authentic relationship to what is being advocated. That exploitation is particularly common regarding neuroscientists and neuroscientific findings—so common that the practice has its own acronym: SANE, standing for "the seductive allure of neuroscience." For instance, an advertisement for a new metal bracelet, alleged to reduce pain, might include a diagram illustrating connections from the wearer's bracelet-encircled wrist, through his peripheral nervous system, spinal cord, and into the brain's pain center.

Posfluence

The foundational sciences, such as mathematics and physics, provide granular processes that enable many less precise fields of study. Chemistry and biology reveal practical insights into ways in which the inanimate and animate worlds impact our environments and bodies. And so-called "soft" sciences, including psychology and sociology, while lacking the mathematical rigor of the aforementioned "harder" ones, compensate by giving concrete, practical advice that we readily can apply in our daily lives.

Human scientific advances are the lifeblood of modern civilization. No one need defend their value. As with formal educators, scientists exert positive influences over virtually every aspect of our lives. Their machines keep us warm in winter and cool in summer. Their medicines literally can mean the difference between our living and dying. Some specific benefits that scientists make possible for us are:

Physical comfort: when they create labor saving devices that we use to prepare and cook raw food.

Excitement: when they make vehicles, such as reliable, safe fast cars and realistic, engrossing video games.

Order: when they produce advances in information processing so that we can keep better track of our important data.

Safety: when they introduce new detection devices that monitor the safety of our homes.

Negfluence

The more dependent we are on scientists, however, the more vulnerable we are to science misuse. Over the past few decades, a new word increasingly has appeared in the English language: monetize. The term became especially popular when dotcom companies were popping up like dandelions. These, usually high tech, businesses had something innovative and flashy to distribute to the public. For instance in the middle to late 1990s particularly, a host of new web businesses appeared on the scene that had attractive ideas, but no revenue. They needed to figure out how to monetize their business in order to survive. As everybody knows, Facebook learned how to do so spectacularly well. Most, however, failed miserably. Drkoop.com, a pioneering health information website, was one of the surprising failures. Debuting in June, 1999, the site initially was ranked as the number 1 of its kind. But in 2000, Drkoop.com began losing tens of millions dollars every quarter, and by 2002, it was gone. The so-called burst dotcom bubble taught the technologically sophisticated—and all attentive scientists—that they need to be as adept at making money as they are at creating innovations. Although the financial incentive may not be an all-consuming need for many scientists, most, like all human beings, do want to be compensated and recognized for their breakthroughs.

The financial imperative and the narcissistic needs of some scientists can lead them astray. As a result, they might create and/or promote bogus ideas or products that impede rather than empower society. That means that you and I can be harmed by bad science, whether the creator inadvertently or deliberately caused the problem. Potential problems are:

Social connections: when they create Apps that they allege will keep us in touch with our friends, but that are designed to simultaneously exploit our relationships to reap financial gain.

Autonomy: when they provide just enough information to incite a need in us, but make it increasingly complex and critical over time, such that we must pay them for frequent updates.

Tranquility: when they disrupt our peace of mind by suggesting dire consequences if we do not follow their suggestions or buy their products.

Competency: when they create a purportedly user-friendly product with vast potential utility that no one except a highly trained expert ever can get to operate consistently and correctly.

The Piltdown Man

Charles Darwin's groundbreaking theory of evolution in the mid-1800s made him a superstar, surely feeding his ego. And the book, *Origin of the Species*, that broadcasted his ideas across the world, amounted to a clarion call for all interested scientists. Any naturalist professional, or their sponsoring country, could achieve fame by uncovering a missing link that bridged apes and people. Two countries were especially keen on solving the riddle: England and Germany. The battle was on.

Germany struck first. In 1907, in the town of Mauer, a quarry worker found a jawbone buried in the sand. Having earlier been told to be on the lookout for such fossils, the worker promptly delivered his specimen to Otto Schoetensack, an anthropology professor at nearby Heidelberg University. The next year, Doctor Schoetensack published his findings, claiming that the jaw belonged to a new species intermediate between Neanderthal man and Homo sapiens.

In 1912, the English countered with their own missing link candidate. Near Piltdown village in Sussex, England, Charles Dawson, a fossil-hunting amateur, claimed to have found a few teeth, an ape-like jaw bone and a human-like skull, among other things. The esteemed paleontologist, Sir Arthur Smith Woodward, joined with Dawson to investigate further. After two additional years of digging and studying, Woodward and Dawson concluded that their finding revealed an approximately one-half million year old creature, midway between ape and man. The English anthropological society could not have been happier, since the bones—teeth and jaw like an ape and brain-vault like a man—were precisely the characteristics that they had expected from the prototypic creature.

For 40 or so years, the bones of Piltdown Man were displayed, and his story was taught in school. In the interim, fossil dating technology progressed. New fluorine testing, conducted by geologist Dr. Kenneth Oakley in 1949, suggested that the Piltdown bones actually were only one-tenth the age—50,000 years old—than initially had been believed. The disclosure opened floodgates of skepticism that prompted Oakley to join forces with Drs. Joseph Weiner, a biological anthropologist, and Wilfrid Le Gros Clark, a human anatomist. The three ultimately found that Dawson's specimens did not come from one missing link creature but from two conventional ones: a human being and an ape. More damning was that the bones deliberately had been stained to appear old, and the ape teeth had been filed to simulate those of a human. In short, the Piltdown Man was an elaborate scientific scam, presumably designed and skillfully executed by Charles Dawson.

The Taung Child

At the end of the first quarter of the 20th century, the United Kingdom had a second chance to rock the world of evolution science, but this time an Australian was the prime mover. After completing a biology post graduate program at the University of London, Raymond Arthur Dart accepted a Professor of Anatomy position at The University of the Witwatersrand, Johannesburg, South Africa. There he conducted field and laboratory work in both paleontology and anthropology, encouraged by knowing that Charles Darwin believed that Africa might be the location wherein humanity first evolved. Dart was especially interested to learn that workers in nearby limestone quarries were regularly discovering primate fossils. And Dart let it be known that he would welcome being shown any promising specimens.

The wish was granted spectacularly. When at the home of a friend whose father managed a quarry, one of Dart's former students, Josephine Salmons, inquired about a primate skull that lay on the mantel. After she showed Raymond Dart the skull, he excitedly declared that it was one of ancient origin, and once again asked that any similar bones be sent to him. Not long afterwards, Robert Young, a visiting geologist, asked the quarry manager about available specimens. The manager eventually presented a large number of fossilized skulls to Young who promptly mailed them to Dart. Among the crated bones was a juvenile primate skull, including teeth, and an endocast of the creature's brain. Raymond Dart strongly suspected that he had specimens of major significance.

The more he scraped and cleaned debris from the bones, the more convinced Dart was that he was about to make a historic paleoanthropological contribution. The editor of the prestigious journal *Nature* agreed, publishing the journal article "Australopithecus africanus: The Man-Ape of South Africa in which Raymond Dart described his findings. Having been uncovered in the village of Taung, Dart's Australopithecus africanus soon became known as the Taung Child.

Ordinarily, having a paper appear in Nature virtually guarantees that the author will be embraced by the scientific community. Not so for Dart, however. High status anthropologists resisted accepting Africa as the cradle of human evolution. Some suggested that the Taung Child was really nothing more than a prehistoric ape. The Piltdown Man better satisfied their popular notions about European origins. In fact, three of Raymond Dart's most outspoken critics had an obvious conflict of interest in that they had been strong, early supporters of Piltdown.

It was not until about 1947 that the tide turned decisively in Dart's favor. Le Gros Clark, a renowned English anthropologist, argued that the Taung Child definitely was a humanoid, not merely an ape. The defense was so convincing that one of the former most outspoken critics of Raymond Dart's specimen, wrote a *Nature* published paper in which he admitted that he had been wrong. Thus, the ascension of Dart's Taung Child as a legitimate, early humanoid that predated the decline of Dawson's Piltdown Man as counterfeit by about two years.

Almost Free Energy

The invention of the transistor was undoubtedly one of the most important developments of the 20th century. Formerly, radios, television, clocks, and almost all electrical devices, depended on bulky, inefficient, short-lived vacuum tubes to amplify their electronic signals. Scientists across the globe knew that there had to be a better way, and set out to find a vacuum tube alternative. Fortunately for America, in 1947, Bell Laboratory got there first, due to the work of the lab's phenomenal physicists William Shockley, John Bardeen, and Walter Brattain who created the first transistor. Over the next seventy-plus years, the transistor evolved in ways that no device ever had before, becoming exponentially smaller and more efficient. Pivotal was the pioneering work of Jack S. Kilby who in 1958, while at Texas Instruments, managed to aggregate transistors into integrated circuits. Three years later, Kilby, along with Robert Noyce, introduced the silicon microchip that to this day continues to be the platform of choice for integrated circuits. The latter physicist combined forces with Gordon E. Moore in 1968 to found Intel Corporation, the planet's first microchip creating powerhouse. It was Moore who almost correctly predicted that science would progress such that the number of transistors per square inch of microchip would double each successive year. "Almost" because 21st century chip makers eventually realized that miniaturization was slowing, and in time would cease to grow entirely.

Accordingly, physicists commenced a frantic but futile search for a silicon chip alternative.

Enter Jan Hendrik Schön, a 1997 Ph.D. from the University of Konstanz in Baden-Württemberg, Germany. Schön stunned the world of physics with his meteoric rise to prominence. Peers marveled at the rapidity and quality of his research and publications. He was setting standards to an extent not seen since Albert Einstein. Among his many accomplishments, Jan Hendrik demonstrated that the conventional transistor might be replaced by organic dye molecules, thus overcoming the aforementioned miniaturization limitations of silicon chips. The high tech world seemed on the brink of the most massive improvement since the creation of the transistor, itself. Awards and commendations pursued Schön like hounds after a rabbit. Among those were the Outstanding Young Investigator Award of the Materials Research Society, the Otto-Klung-Weberbank Prize for Physics, and the Braunschweig Prize. One example of Jan Hendrik Schön's prowess is that he had eight papers accepted by the journals *Science* and *Nature* in the year 2000, a stunning, unprecedented accomplishment for even the most seasoned researcher.

It was a *Nature* paper that eventually led to Schön's professional demise. The journal editors contacted him after being alerted that he had reported some of the exact same data for two different studies. But Schön easily sidestepped that challenge, claiming that it had been an error due to insufficient attention. Nature accepted that explanation, but more complaints soon followed. Before long it was apparent that Jan Hendrik repeatedly had been creating false data to support his research hypotheses. The silicon chip retained its preeminence. But Schön lost the job that he had been holding at Bell Labs, his journal articles were deleted, and the University of Konstanz revoked his Ph.D., an extraordinary disciplinary action for any institution of higher learning.

Take Away

Together, the Piltdown vs. Taung and the Schön stories drive home that science is not immune to bias. Piltdown demonstrates that when the scientific establishment broadcasts its expectations, enterprising tricksters can exploit them. Taung is the mirror opposite. Those who buck prevailing scientific orthodoxy sometimes must be prepared to fight tooth and nail for their ideas, and strive to elicit support from open-minded colleagues. And Schön reveals that when science is desperate for a solution, the hierarchy may be overly eager to embrace enticing but bogus ones.

You might not care too much about Piltdown, Taung, or Schön per se. However, the three stories should make you nervous about the effectiveness of institutional checks and balances. You probably will concede that when the most prestigious scientific organizations and publishers are so thoroughly duped, less savvy purveyors of information are infinitely more vulnerable.

To the extent possible, we, on the receiving end of science, must be proactive in differentiating the good from the bad, the useful from the superfluous. Most people reading this book probably would be more cautious and discriminating about new, radical innovations, and reasonably so. However, old, established ideas are not necessarily correct, either. Just as the Piltdown Man endured over decades as a scientific fact for British anthropologists and citizens, bogus ideas have been accepted by American science professionals and everyday people. For many years, we erroneously were taught, for instance, that all fats caused health problems, and that all carbohydrates were health enhancing. The science community's opinion about coffee and your heart has alternated from its being helpful to harmful and back again. And in March, 2018, California Superior Court Judge Elihu Berle ruled that coffee sellers in the state with ten or more employees must label their coffee as containing the carcinogen acrylamide (Rosenberg, 2018). Does that mean that citizens who buy their coffee at an establishment with less than ten employees deserve protection any less?

It is even more concerning that your physician regularly has been lobbied and rewarded by pharmaceutical representatives who wish to sway her to their products, including widely prescribed medications. In December, 2018, the New York Times published an eye-opening article, penned by Charles Ornstein and Katie Thomas entitled, "What These Medical Journals Don't Reveal: Top Doctors' Ties to Industry." They detailed two major issues. The first was that many of the nation's most influential, most powerful doctors who have received millions of dollars in payment from drug companies either failed to disclose or inadequately disclosed the payments, a violation of The Physician Payments Sunshine Act (PPSA). The second, and related issue, concerned the conduct of and dissemination of drug-relevant research. In some cases, the doctors did not acknowledge their drug company affiliations, and in others, their research was not adequately vetted by the prestigious journals that reported their results to the world-wide medical community. As a result, your physician and mine might have been misinformed about the value and/or applicability of information contained in the medical literature that guides their practice. In short, you and your local physician can be deleteriously influenced, either deliberately or mistakenly, by the nation's "top docs" and the nation's top journals.

How about a concrete example of potential physician-drug company exaggerated oversell? You undoubtedly know many people who take statins, and you may be among the over 20 percent of Americans aged 40 to 75 who do so to prevent a first heart attack or stroke, meaning for "primary prevention." Your doctors might have advised you to take the medication, or you might have petitioned them for it. In the first case, the physician presumably did so based on available research and in the second, you might have succumbed to advertisements or other publically available information extolling the virtues of statins. Perhaps the statins were perfect for you, or perhaps not. Not all medical professionals believe that statins are the wonder drugs that virtually everyone should take. Michael Nedelman, (2018) cites one particularly outspoken critic, Dr. Rita Redberg, the editor-in-chief of the *Internal Medicine* magazine of the *Journal of the American Medication Association*, who suggests that most people have unrealistically high expectations of the drugs. According to her, for every 100 patients who take primary preventive statins only one, or perhaps two, avoids a heart attack, and no one will live longer because of the medication. Moreover, many statin users will suffer cognitive deficits, diabetes, fatigue, and muscle pain as side effects. Since much of the research supporting the use of statins is funded by the pharmaceutical companies who sell them, you would do well to think twice about jumping on the statin bandwagon. Look to a responsible, ethical physician who can help you decide whether statins are right for you and for your unique health needs.

One final thought about the science, scientific medicine and their influences. We occasionally hear doctors complain that our system is oriented toward curing people after they are ill, and woefully inattentive to preventing illness onset. The argument usually continues that many of the most debilitating diseases—such as diabetes, hypertension, and obesity—could be short-circuited or ameliorated by better educating our citizens about their lifestyles. In the latter case, the Harvard Medical establishment would be a powerful resource. And, not surprisingly, the Harvard Health Publishing division advertises that **Harvard Medical School offers special reports on over 60 health topics. Visit our website at** http://www.health.harvard.edu **to find reports of interest to you and your family.** [To check it out for yourself, you can go to Harvard Medical School (healthbeat@mail.health.harvard.edu)]

The Harvard information comes in both email and hard copy formats. As an example, the publishing division sent me the following email: ***Don't let depression rob you of life's joys. Discover 12 strategies to break the chains of depression, and free yourself to live every day to the fullest!*** Its 3 bold-printed headlines were that ***Depression is treatable — and beatable! You'll meet the strategies that can change your way of thinking!*** and ***A dozen strategies with one goal.*** Also, on the page was a text box explaining ***"Inside Understanding Depression, you'll discover: What is depression? Causes of depression, Diagnosing depression, Seeking treatment, Finding the right medication, Psychotherapy, Brain and nerve stimulation therapies."*** The information influenced me sufficiently that I decided to "Click Here to Learn More." At that point, I was forwarded to a page that advised me to send $20 for the print book, $18 for the ebook, or $29 for the print and ebook downloads. On another occasion, Harvard Medical sent me an email correspondence entitled, ***7 reasons why you may need a medication check-up: New medications and side effects warrant an evaluation.*** That got my attention sufficiently for me to click again. After a one paragraph teaser introduction, I was informed, ***To continue reading this article, you must login.*** The next click disclosed ***Online Account Activation.—Don't have a username and password? Activate your account and gain access to your subscriptions and purchased electronic special health reports.*** The solicitation that was most offensive to me, however, was ***Discover the Best Ways to Heal Your Heart and Mind After Losing a Loved One*** that offered no immediate guidance, but did advise the reader to ***Click here to order your copy of Grief and Loss. We're pleased to offer you 30% savings off the regular $29 cover price to help you at this difficult time.*** That solicitation struck me as exploiting grieving people at the time that they are most vulnerable.

According to a Congressional Report, Harvard was worth $37.6 billion in 2015. Given that the institution and most of its research is funded by the monies that you and I pay in taxes and other fees, shouldn't Harvard Medical offer us the preventative information as a token of their gratitude, and as a concrete example of their alleged commitment to public health? Or, could it be that Harvard is more interested in receiving income than in promoting wellness?

CHAPTER 17: Control & Choices

Control

Influence amounts to a bid for control. The influencer seeks to steer you toward their end as surely as you steer your car toward a parking space. Psychologists have shown that our well-being usually is enhanced by an internal locus of control (ILOC) which basically means that the individual looks within herself to evaluate circumstances, and to decide what is right and wrong for her. Conversely, well-being usually is diminished by an external locus of control (ELOC) that directs one's attention to what other people believe is proper.

Sometimes locus of control (LOC) is global (GLOC), influencing large swaths of thought and behavior, and sometimes it is specific (SLOC), limited to a given situation. For instance, a person with a predominantly ILOC who usually looks within himself in making decisions might be insecure about his retirement, and cede full responsibility to his financial advisor for that financial decision only—an instance of a specific external locus of control (SELOC). Another person permits his financial advisor to decide all monetary issues—a global external locus of control where money is concerned (GELOC). The final LOC dimension is temporary-permanent. To continue the financial decision example, a person who always had made his own financial decisions might experience a devastating stock loss that prompts him to grant time-limited full financial responsibility to his advisor—an instance of temporary, specific, external locus of control (TSELOC), or the experience might have been so traumatic that he, thereafter, cedes full enduring responsibility for his advisor to make all of his financial decisions,—a permanent, specific, external locus of control (PSELOC). In short, there are three interrelated dimensions relevant here: internal-external, global-specific, and temporary-permanent, and all three affect a person's independence and self-esteem.

Obviously, LOC is a relative thing. Some issues are more easily addressed via an ILOC, such as choosing a car, and some are more suitable for an ELOC, such as being advised about choosing the best medical procedure for life-sustaining surgery.

Whether one is more inclined toward an ILOC or ELOC is believed to be rooted in core self-evaluations, meaning that self-appraisals predispose how we perceive our experiences and our environments. The concept is important because core self-evaluation correlates positively not only with tendencies toward ILOC, but also with feelings of esteem and capability, and general emotional stability. Psychologists have been uncertain about the particulars of the core self-evaluation and ILOC relationship. For instance, is ILOC separable from core self-evaluation, and, if so, what are the implications for how one determines environmental influences?

Russell E. Johnson and his colleagues (2015) considered all the above issues in four experimental samples. They teased apart when ILOC was most salient for our well-being, when ELOC was most salient, and when neither was significant. Results indicated several noteworthy conclusions: LOC, in general, correlated with job satisfaction, supervisor ratings given to workers, and life satisfaction. However, all such positive correlations were stronger for predominantly ILOC than for predominantly ELOC persons. That is, an individual who believed that she controls her own fate was more likely to do well in all three areas than were those who looked toward external control.

The lesson is clear: know when to look more internally and when to look more externally to make decisions. The two foci need not necessarily conflict. Although an ILOC is a good default, there are times when any reasonable person would look outside herself. That said, ELOC guidance first must always be filtered through an ILOC. For instance, if you need guidance to decide about a medical procedure, you should not passively receive that guidance. You must embrace the guidance proactively. Take what you have been taught externally and work it through internally in your own unique manner. That ILOC approach to ELOC guidance is effective whether you are endeavoring to learn chemistry, to stop smoking, or to develop a more consistent exercise habit.

Choices

Whether adopting an ILOC, ELOC, or a hybrid approach, you ultimately must choose how to behave. Even when they cannot exert their external control, influencers desire to bias your independent choices to suit their purposes. They can do so by structuring and/or limiting your options. One way is to provide false dichotomous choices as when they suggest that "You can have this one or that one" as though no other possibilities exist. They also might use other choices parameters that research has shown to be effective. For instance, presented with two coats for sale, one costing $200 and one costing $50, an individual likely would choose one or the other based on that individual's unique standards regarding coat purchase without necessarily relying heavily on price. However, if a third coat priced $100 is placed alongside the others, that same person quite often will select the $100 one, inferring that it is neither too expensive nor too cheap—a common human tendency to gravitate toward the "magnetic middle" (Goldstein, Martin, & Cialdini, 2009).

The LOC issue underscores that influencers need not be "the bad guys and gals." Rather, **you** must be the responsible one who mindfully attends to influencers, evaluates their utility, and uses them in the manner most constructively suitable for you. Although one almost never should adopt a permanent, global, external locus of control, some variant of external locus of control occasionally is worth considering.

Choice Architecture

Within your home or workplace, your behavior is guided by the space architecture. If you have two bedrooms but six children, they must share their nighttime accommodations. If your car has five seat belts, you make a big mistake if you choose to transport more than four passengers. Such architectural choices obviously should, and usually do, limit the houses and cars that we decide to purchase. However, when influencers talk about choice architecture, they have a more inclusive definition in mind. To them, choice architecture is **any** feature of the physical, socio-cultural, or administrative environment that can affect the choices you make. Recall that I have used the term "situation" to include environment as environment pertains to the influence scenarios, so I sometimes will use "situation" and "environment" interchangeably.

Once choice architecture is explained, most people readily recognize that it well accounts for many common situations (such as how meeting a professional in their office adds to their power position). So, for purposes of our current discussion, I will narrow our focus to a most germane, non-obvious, very important issue investigated by Hannah Perfecto and her associates (2017). Although Perfecto specifically emphasizes that understanding choice architecture is invaluable to politicians and marketers, any would-be influencer could use choice architecture to their great advantage.

Before beginning, I must warn that even though I am diluting the material, the reading might require you to concentrate and process a little more deeply than usual. However, that reading effort is mere rehearsal for the more important real-world effort you need to maintain vis-a-vis determined influencers. I do promise that by this discussion's end, you will better comprehend how minutely influencers calculate and execute the twists and turns of their interactions with you: their "target."

The Perfecto group concentrated on "how choice options are arrayed and described." More specifically, they scrutinized subjects' choices in terms of their decision confidence and consensus estimates, the latter meaning whether they did or did not believe their choices to be relatively common or relatively unusual. Five related choice studies were created with two decision *frames* being manipulated—"choose" or "reject"—and two *response options*— "positive" or "negative." The researchers used the phrase "attribute matching" to designate the relationship between the frame and response. Regarding the frame, the "choose" attribute was deemed consistent with the "positive" attribute and, regarding the response, the "reject" attribute was deemed consistent with the "negative," and both cases being considered attribute matching. Given the complexity of the studies and the fact that each one complemented the others, I briefly will describe only the particulars of Study 1, and then explain general conclusions derived from the entire group of studies.

In Study 1, middle-aged men and women were told to select female models for an advertising campaign based on head-shot photographs. Sixteen pairs of photos were presented—eight pairs that previously had been rated by a separate group as attractive and eight pairs, as unattractive. Half of the subjects were asked: "Which woman would you choose?" and the rest, "Which woman would you reject?" In other words, all decisions were framed in terms of beauty (attractive/unattractive) while those within the former half were framed with a positive valance option (choose) and the latter half, with a negative valance option (reject). After answering the valance questions, the subjects indicated their confidence in the photo evaluations that they had submitted (consensus estimate).

As anticipated and predicted, when presented two attractive models, subjects instructed via the positive valance option (asked to *choose the better* model candidate) expressed greater consensus confidence in their decisions than did those instructed via the negative valance option (asked to *reject the worse* model candidate). On the other hand, when two unattractive model candidates were presented, the opposite effects resulted. Namely, subjects instructed via the negative valance option (asked to *reject the worse* model candidate) expressed greater consensus confidence in their decisions than did those instructed via the positive valance option (asked to *choose the better* model candidate).

The four other Perfecto group studies altered the Study 1 conditions to achieve a more fine-grained understanding of the ways that choice options are arrayed and described. Their hypotheses and conclusions were:

Study 2 altered the Study1 by expanding the valence options from merely two levels (positive and negative) to four (extremely positive, slightly positive, slightly negative, and extremely negative). The reason was to determine if slight emotion was sufficient to elicit Study 1's effect. The hypothesis was supported, since the choices labeled "slight" yielded the expected attribute matching outcome.

In Study 3, the conditions of 2 mostly were retained, except for two differences. First, the researchers limited subject responses to the "extremely" options. And second, the researchers looked at the subjects' ease of response, time to respond, confidence, and consensus beliefs. It was anticipated that in attribute matching conditions, decisions would feel to be easier and be completed faster. And again, the study's hypotheses were confirmed.

Study 4 wanted to determine whether the Study 3 results were attributable to subjects' own decision confidence rather than to the researchers' having changed the study conditions. The Perfecto group expected that subjects would believe the former. To differentiate the two possible explanations, after the subjects made their choices but before they made their subjective ratings, half the group was told that it was the researchers having changed the study conditions that influenced the subjects' ease of response, time to respond, confidence, and consensus beliefs. Once again, as expected, that half did not show the enhanced confidence and consensus estimates that the other half did. The researchers, therefore, concluded that self-attributed ease of decision making was critical for subjects' experiencing enhanced confidence and consensus estimates.

The final study—Study 5—included a major shift. Rather than showing the subjects stimuli of positive or negative *subjective* valence, they were presented a series of food pairs—one *objectively* high in calories and the other *objectively* low in calories—and asked to say which of the two had either more or fewer calories. This was an important condition, since the decision was no mere opinion, but a scientifically-certified *objective* reality. The researchers' hypotheses were correct once more. The subjects' confidence and consensus beliefs were stronger when frames and response options matched. In fact, even their *subjective* opinions about response ease were higher when attribute matching occurred.

Let's take this study's results from the laboratory to your neighborhood. Perfecto-savvy influencers know much about choice architecture. They want to know how to present and describe your choices in a manner that impels you to accept their politics and products (and anything else they are peddling). If they get it right, you not only will respond "correctly," but also be more receptive to their future entreaties. They desire to know your particular style of framing and optioning. Do you tend to frame things in terms of attractive-unattractive, economical-expensive, popular-unconventional, or else wise? Would choices arrayed as "Vote for me" versus "Don't vote for her," or "Pay in full now to avoid interest fees" versus "You can get this today and comfortably pay over the next three years" be more enticing? In short, the influencer always will attempt to control the choice architecture and to communicate in ways consistent with your framing style, and with your attribute matching proclivities.

Putting It All Together

Where are you? Here. What time is it? Now.

Those two questions and answers pretty much describe the "veridical" —true— reality of our lives. You are influenced by agents in the here and now, and you resist that influence in the here and now. In the final analysis, nothing else matters. Therefore, the more you are grounded in the veridical reality of here and now, the more autonomous you can be. This advice is akin to the now familiar notion that we fare best when we are mindfully "in the moment." In influence situations, consider the here and now in terms of our previously discussed four primary influence vehicles which, once again, are:

The person/institution ("human" influencer)
The object/idea (concrete item or abstraction that is being promoted)
The situation (the environment where the influence is provided)
The process (how the object or idea is packaged and presented)

Although no one can or should be on guard at every moment (that would be counter to mindfulness), when you do become aware of a potentially significant influencer, be especially attentive to the here and now of the present person/institution, object/idea, situation, and process.

You can control the four primary influence vehicles only if you fully embrace the opportunity. Since control means accepting personal responsibility, sometimes it is far easier, but, also, far riskier, to adopt a bad faith attitude that overtly or covertly consigns outcomes to fate, or purely to external influences. Whether you like it or not, you always have some measure of choice. Usually that means that a default internal locus of control (ILOC) is your ideal starting point. As long as you accept that you always can assert control, after careful introspection, you can delegate the breadth, depth, and duration of control that is best for you in any given situation. But you must never forget about that situation to the extent that your self-control muscle atrophies, monitoring must be ongoing. Sometimes just knowing and embracing that stance is enough to enable you to live your life adaptively.

Regarding choices, never accept false dichotomies. Do not allow yourself to be drawn mindlessly to the magnetic middle. Just because one member of choice array seems moderate, does not mean that it is desirable. You make the independent calculation first, and then gather additional data to evaluate your initial independent conclusion.

Be your own choice architect so as to structure your decisions in all spheres, not just the physical, socio-cultural, or administrative environments. Consider all of the primary influence vehicles: person/institution (human influencer), object/idea (concrete item or abstraction that is being promoted), situation (the environment where the influence is provided), and process (how the item or idea is packaged and presented. Know your vulnerabilities, preferred frames, and optioning inclinations.

Finally, don't lose sight of the fact that influence does not just come from without. You are your own most powerful influencer. You deliberately or unwittingly can do to yourself virtually anything that someone else can do to you. In fact, you might be your own worst influencer, especially when you are driven by, unconscious, automatic self-defeating personal habits. Whenever you detect someone manipulating you, evaluate whether you do a variant of that same thing to yourself. Introspection is your friend: embrace it.

CHAPTER 18: More Than Mere Talk

To be influenced is to totally change, or at least to modify, your pre-existing position. As emphasized here repeatedly, succumbing to an influence—anything from making a new purchase to accepting a new idea—can be positive or negative. However, most people tend to resist major change. Their default is the status quo, since it usually requires less effort to continue to feel, behave, and think the same way that they always have.

In the realm of thought, resistance to influence, called "belief perseverance" occurs when a person refrains from rejecting a personally held status quo belief even when he becomes aware of evidence inconsistent with that belief.

Alex Filipowicz, Derick Valadao, Anderson Britt, and James Danckert (2016) wanted to understand whether surprising new information was more or less likely to cause individuals to "update" status quo beliefs. Their research participants included non-surprise controls and experimental subjects who were induced into one of three levels of surprise intensity—low surprise, medium surprise, and high surprise. Overall, surprised persons updated faster than did non-surprised controls. And in general, the more surprising the information, the quicker the updating tended to be. However, some in the high surprise condition updated more poorly than others did. The investigators suggested that for some unknown reason, those poorly-updating high surprise subjects placed more faith in information with a longer track record as opposed to newly acquired information. One might infer that the confidence of those subjects was so very threatened by the highly surprising information that they had to dismiss it summarily in order to maintain their self-esteem.

What else could determine whether or not one uses available information that contradicts his personal status quo ideas? We can find some clarification by applying a few communication principles mentioned earlier when we discussed Information Manipulation Theory 2. You will recall Herbert Paul Grice's four conversation guidelines:

Maxim of quality - We seek correct information.
Maxim of quantity - We seek just enough information, no more and no less.
Maxim of relation - We seek the most relevant information.
Maxim of manner - We seek information that is expressed as clearly and coherently as possible.

To concretize this application of belief perseverance in a posfluential way, imagine that you always have thought that the benefits of exercise are being over-hyped. You feel so because you never exercised, and you consider yourself to be quite healthy. Your blood pressures always have been solidly normal. And your blood sugars have been virtually ideal. Your skepticism has been fueled by contradictory information about exercise and health promulgated in the popular press. So, you always ignore factoids that advocate exercise as a biological cure-all.

You subsequently talk to your doctor who tells you about a new, comprehensive, state of the art National Institute of Health research project. The study specifically was designed to determine the health areas that exercise does and does not help. Your doctor addresses every one of your health-relevant study questions, presenting all this in a concise and crystal-clear manner. Now, it is up to you to process the doctor conversation through the Grice maxims, and decide whether to change your status-quo belief, or to continue with your belief perseverance.

Moved by Conversation

Like all animals, we are sensing and acting machines intent on surviving and thriving by literally or figuratively moving toward the good and away from the bad. The sensations that we experience and the actions that we take reciprocally affect each other, and determine our decisions. However, unlike all other animals, we have language. Sensing, acting, and language are tightly related. Therefore, influencers regularly use conversation to induce us to sense what they are promoting and to prompt us to act upon it. What others say to us and what we say to ourselves skew us toward some decisions and away from others. For instance, often when people are in intimidating social situations, they reduce both their overt physical movement and their conversation, a phenomenon called the "elevator effect" (DeWaal, et al., 2000).

Through conversation we verbally can move toward or away from our conversational partner—an affiliation-disaffiliation dimension. To move toward is to decrease our isolation and/or to increase our interdependence. And to move away is to increase our isolation and/or independence. Those two diametrically opposite movements render us, respectively, more and less susceptible to the influence of a conversational partner—whether the conversation is casual, with a friend, or formal, or with someone unfamiliar to us.

Conversation discloses both parties' optimism-pessimism, analogous to their tendency to apprehend the world as good/pleasant/positive as opposed to bad/unpleasant/negative. Conversational material permits us to make such intra-psychic inferences as to whether each speaker is relatively fulfilled or frustrated emotionally and socially; we also can consider whether the speaker's conversational style is likely to endear or alienate him from his speaking partner. This does not depend merely on the words that conversation partners use, and it is not merely a sterile, academic endeavor. When we scrutinize spontaneous conversations, we hear not just the words, but also a speaker's prosody, the "music" of discourse, including the inflection and rhythm of verbal communication. Juslin and Laukka (2001) emphasize the importance of such elements, stating that voice cues in general and loudness or talking speed in particular (Planalp, 1998) are among the most central conversational features by which people "…judge the emotional states of others in everyday life." Robert Krauss and his colleagues (2002) show that merely by listening to the voices of speakers without ever seeing them, naïve subjects can estimate the age and height of such speakers almost as well as can naïve observers who see photographs of the same speakers.

In addition to dispensing such emotional resources as succor and affiliation, the people who attempt to influence us themselves comprise a major component of our emotional environment. Such people influence our emotional environment because we are impacted affectively by their personal traits, moods, and emotions. As used here, "traits" refers to their enduring personality-based emotional response predispositions, "moods" to their background emotional tone that persists from hours to days, weeks, or months, and "emotions" to their brief, intense episodes of feeling that are accompanied by emotion-specific physical changes, such as the flush of embarrassment or the pallor of fear (Buck, 1999).

Because conversation moves us, you should always be attentive to how it is influencing you. Be aware of the simple fact that being in conversation is affecting you positively or negatively, irrespective of the content. Conversing as an activity is making you and/or your relationships better or worse. You also will feel better or worse about yourself and about the influencer. And, of course, the intensity of the better or worse feeling usually is related to the content being discussed. Both relationship and message always impact you to some extent, and they always impact each other. A very endearing influencer can convey destructive information to you, and a very obnoxious influencer can convey constructive information to you. By taking the time and putting forth the effort to understand the motivation behind a conversation, you will be able to benefit from that which is helpful in it, and ignore the rest.

Since I advocate default skepticism, I advise that you to beware of the legendary "smooth talker" who either tries to overpower you verbally, or to lull you into uncritical, passive complacency. Sometimes the trick for you and your susceptibility to influence is your ability to disentangle relationship and message to make the best autonomous decision. You must become a "smooth listener" who knows what to listen for and how to handle both the conversation relationship, and the conversation message being delivered.

You can better deal with conversation relationships, and conversation messages by being cognizant of the fact that you always are listening consciously with your two physical ears and unconsciously with your third, mental, ear, the one that Theodore Reik (1948) believed hears the hidden meanings of what we say and do not say when conversing. These three ears, attuned to the self and others, account for a wide variety of well-recognized conversational facts. Two examples illustrate my point: The cocktail party phenomenon (Moray, 1959) designates the fact that often we can hear someone whisper our name over the clamor of a noisy party when other words spoken more loudly are missed. It is as though we have a personal, automatic radar continually scanning the conversational environment in its own relentless search for spoken self-references. "Coensthetic reception" (Spitz & Cobliner, 1965) describes a personal, automatic self-referential process. In this case, we exhibit an extra-sensory-like awareness of the self-other relationship aspect of conversation. Coensthetic reception is the ability to know intuitively, for instance, that a conversant partner took offense to something that you said, despite the fact that other observing persons present at the time detect no signs of upset from the person that you correctly "feel" was aggrieved. The speaker's listening to herself is analogous to her looking in the mirror, gazing at oneself in a mirror reveals the physical self while listening to oneself in conversation reveals the social-emotional self.

You need to apply the third ear insights whenever aware of being in an influence situation. Think third ear about yourself and third ear about the influencer. Take concrete steps to test out your third ear intuitions, and use them to minimize unwanted influences.

Handling the Influence Conversation to Your Advantage

What to Expect

Professional advisors teach professional influencers ways to control the conversation. Jeff Haden, for instance, recommends that his clients implement "Nine Secrets of Incredibly Persuasive People" themuse.com). He wants the influencers to appeal to emotion by making "bold" statements rather than equivocating. The emotion appeal, he believes, can include a couple curse words to create a sense of urgency about whatever he is promoting.

Haden also wants his acolytes to appeal to the intellect. He subscribes to Grice by directing influencers to be clear and concise. The emphasis must be on positives associated with the promoted position, but he concedes that there is a definite advantage to raising and resolving potential negatives. Haden wisely teaches that the influencer must know her audience, and adjust accordingly. Begin the "pitch," he suggests, with statements with which the listeners almost certainly will agree, and then slowly and carefully move toward less acceptable information. Do not pressure the reluctant; give them time to reflect.

The Haden method raises gender as a possible influence issue. In his words,

> As a general rule, men tend to feel competitive in person and turn what should be a conversation into a contest we think we need to win. (Be honest; you know you do it sometimes.) The opposite is true if you're a woman hoping to persuade other women. According to the researchers, women are "more focused on relationships," so in-person communication tends to be more effective. But if you're a guy trying to convince another guy you know well, definitely communicate in person. The closer your relationship, the more effective face-to-face communication tends to be.

Finally, Jeff Haden voices support to fast talking as a conversation influence factor. He recommends fast talk when the listener disagrees so there is less time to formulate a rebuttal. And he regards slow talk as better when the listener agrees, the rationale being that the agreeing person has more time to process and incorporate their own substantiating ideas into the equation.

I do not present Haden's advice as gospel, but merely as a sample of what some would-be influencers are being taught. Morgan (2013) is another "expert" who provides advice, albeit obvious advice, for conversation dominance. Simply stated, he offers four suggestions to prospective conversation influencers. First, take advantage of your position—talk mostly with persons of lower status. Second, speak passionately. Third, speak about subjects about which you have special expertise. And, finally, use non-verbals, such as body language, to control the conversation.

Understanding the Dynamics of Conversation

Now that we have a sense of how influencers seek to dominate conversation, let's learn some of the most essential aspects of casual conversation that we can turn to our influence-resisting advantage.

The Self and the Other

When two people converse, each is at least dimly aware of his self-presentation, and of the other person's self-presentation. Accordingly, anything that affects one's sense of himself, or his understanding of the other's sense of himself, will affect conversation.

Humans are highly self-conscious creatures. A sense of self is demonstrably present at least as early as two years of age (Harley & Reese, 1999). We constantly think about the impression that we make on others—how we are "coming across" and what people think of us (Goffman, 1967)—and there is reason to believe that this process operates unconsciously (Koole, et al., 2001). Many psychologists contend that adolescents consider themselves to be scrutinized by an omni-present "imaginary audience," and that that belief causes them to be extremely self-conscious about visible aspect of their being, from the way they talk, to the way they walk. Frankenberger (2000), however, presents research suggesting that many adults, at least as old as thirty years, are no less self-conscious than adolescents are.

Conversation, itself, promotes a particularly unique and automatic self-consciousness in everyone. That is true for at least four reasons: conversation is self-presentation par excellence, it is public, it is subject to explicit or implicit criticism, and it always communicates both message and relationship information. We converse for the same reason that we usually do anything else—to cause ourselves to feel good, better, or, at least, homeostatic (GBH). For our purposes, "good" means a pleasant/comfortable physical and/or mental state. "Better" means an improvement in pleasantness, regardless of the level of pleasantness of the preceding state. And "homeostatic" means a state of usual internal balance and/or relatively familiar level of tension. Regarding homeostasis, it is possible, for instance, for us to seek a physical or mental state that is not good, not better than the current state, but is at least familiar enough that we derive some comfort, however perverse, from it. An extreme example of homeostasis desire would be a masochist who intentionally seeks out physical or emotional pain. Such a person might readily engage with a manipulator whose conversations and influences cause them obvious harm. Those with manipulative or masochistic tendencies have an affinity for each other.

So, we relentlessly pursue message and/or relationship to make our physical-mental "self" feel GBH. Moreover, the self always is involved in conversation because we always are trying to "save face" when conversing (Goffman, 1967). Even when I ask the most straightforward, objective, message-oriented question, it is obvious to myself and to all listeners that I am responsible for asking it. Was it a dumb or a smart question? Was it relevant to the topic? Should I have known the answer? Relationship-oriented remarks clearly involve the self in a way that invites evaluation of the speaker. If I say or imply that I like or dislike something or someone, I betray my preferences, and my preferences represent much of what constitutes my personality. Thus, during conversation, we not only are trying to communicate objective ideas, but also to position ourselves (Drew et al 1999) favorably in order to get GBH—message or relationship. We are trying to make the presentation of ourselves such that it enhances our GBH efforts.

Because conversation is vastly more self-conscious than is self-thought, conversation sometimes makes us especially sensitive to the words that we use when expressing ourselves. Word sensitivity could be word sensitivity concerning the objective meaning of words, as when we feel that we have not expressed ourselves clearly enough. But, more often, it is word sensitivity in the sense of the social-positioning implications of our word choices—concern about how we as a "self" are "coming across" to our conversational partner. If I say that I am a "cosmologist" or "cosmetologist," the message conveys the same essential objective fact about me, my job title. However, the effect on the listener, the social positioning or social fact, is vastly different for me to call myself a cosmologist than it is for me to call myself a cosmetologist, since my conversational partner will make very different assumptions about me as a person based purely upon the two job titles.

The converse of self-awareness is other-awareness. For conversation, an especially important aspect of the latter involves what we already have discussed as "theory of mind" (ToM)—the human ability to think about the thought of others.

Conversing partners need a sufficiently clear ToM of their counterpart as a prerequisite for developing the "empathic accuracy" (Icker, 1993) necessary to read correctly the thoughts and feelings of the partner. Those who lack adequate empathic accuracy are prone to giving either too little or too much detail to their counterpart when conversing. Although all conversational partners are vulnerable to empathic inaccuracy, those having more intimate and more long-term relationships are less so.

ToM makes conversation both possible and complicated. Since conversation is a non-obligatory behavior initiated for GBH purposes, an individual starts to chat in the expectation of satisfaction. He does so because, through use of his ToM faculties, he believes that he knows how his conversation partner generally will react to his overture. At minimum, he expectantly hopes that by conversing on his chosen topic in a particular way, he has a fighting chance to attain GBH—message or relationship. The complication that arises is that ToM capabilities permit some individuals sometimes to perceive conversation as a zero sum game, meaning that he imagines that his GBH gain can only occur as a result of a loss on the part of his conversation partner. Such a mindset promotes destructive, duplicitous conversational games in which each person is intent not only on satisfying his own needs but on undermining the needs of the other. The Transactional Analyst Eric Berne (1968) wrote about these games, such as the "Now I've Got You, You Son of a Bitch" game in which the purpose of conversation is to expose the other's lie or foible. The GBH for the "snagger" perhaps is the satisfaction coincident with being one-up on the person with whom he is speaking.

To summarize, the self-conscious tendency is a direct consequence of the valuing process by which we automatically tag thoughts, stimuli, experiences, and the self as good-bad. We have at least an unconscious awareness of our own evaluating proclivity and of a similar proclivity by others. The self-conscious self is at the center of conversation. The speaker is conversing in an expectant, self-centered search for GBH, "arguing" for his position and "arguing" for his self-conscious self in order to obtain GBH. The speaker's desires and preconceptions determine what he will say. As he speaks, he, at least unconsciously, wonders what his partner's response will be. His anticipation of the partner's understanding and response to it is biased toward what the speaker believes and against whatever ideas that he does not share with the partner. The listener, usually unconsciously, wonders, "Why is he saying that now?" The listener eventually becomes the speaker who operates according to the very same dynamics that the previous speaker had operated by. It sounds tedious and complicated, but it usually works effortlessly and effectively, simply because it is so automatically and unconsciously orchestrated.

You Think You're Conversing, But You're Being Mined

Grice's maxims and everyday experience suggest that everyday people usually try their best to converse honestly. That is, they speak and listen in order to deliver and receive accurate messages, and to create and sustain positive relationships. However, professional influencers frequently have an alternative intention; they listen for anything in your conversation that they can use to sway you toward their ends. That speech mining has become a very popular, highly refined science and practice called "speech analytics." The speech analyst scrutinizes every feature of your spoken language, from your inflection, to your hesitancies, to your word choices and avoidances. Their preferred mining method is to record your verbal communication so that they can analyze it minutely via sophisticated, specialized speech analytics software. Telephone transactions are particularly ripe for recording and analysis. The telephone is ideal because there is evidence to suggest that over 90 % of businesses and over 50 % of consumers prefer using the telephone to conduct business (Bailey & Staples, 2014). Therefore, whenever you use the telephone and hear a statement such as, "Calls may be recorded for training and quality purposes," beware.

Although we have just focused on telephone conversations, influencers mine every communication that they can. On December 18, 2018, for instance, PRNewswire wrote that "Fleishman Hillard today released 'Tech Trends 2019: The Fads. The Fears. The Future,' a new report offering insights and predictions for the technology industry. The report features an analysis of 1 billion tech-focused consumer conversations on Twitter between 2017 and 2018, along with insights from more than 25 technology thought leaders from around the world." Yes, you read that correctly: 1 billion tech-focused consumer Twitter conversations. Perhaps yours were among them. The PRNewswire release said that Fleishman Hillard's global managing director, Sophie Scott, claimed that her company's analysis of those communications would enable companies to better understand consumer expectations and plan their brands accordingly.

CXO Today (2018) suggest that almost nothing in the consumer contact market is growing as quickly as is the use of speech analytics, rising from 49 percent use in 2016 to 90 percent in

2017. The article argued that the speech analyses enabled businesses to understand the negative and positive features of conversations between customers and company representatives, as well as ways to improve revenue. Forty percent and twenty-six percent of speech analytics' business benefits were reported to have accrued in customer experience and in cost savings, respectively. CXO Today claimed that a 2017 intercontinental survey disclosed: over half of the companies performed the analytics to determine specifics of their customers' frustrations and to determine how to optimize their workforces while slightly less than half of the companies sought to identify customer intentions or to resolve existing issues. The site described a Garner Inc. report (Davies, 2014) explaining how speech analytics can reveal speech emotions of both staff and customers engaged in business oriented telephone conversations. The start-up, Chorus, (https://www.chorus.ai/solution/) is one of many companies attempting to capitalize on the speech analytics revolution. Chorus promises to "Turn your conversations into revenue" by using artificial intelligence to "…capture, summarize and enter call notes into your CRM [Customer Relationship Management], enabling humans to do what they do best - build relationships."

Influencers, then, regard conversation as a means to control you. No matter what you think is occurring, when you talk with potential influencers there is nothing casual about casual conversation; never assume for one minute that it is. Your chit-chat is not her/his chit-chat. Particularly when you are on a telephone with a business, government, or other power agency, there is a good chance that your every word and every emotional inflection is being captured, analyzed, and distributed.

Thus far, we primarily have explored conversation in terms of an individual speaker, but, of course, conversation involves at least one speaker and one listener. So let us now dig down a little deeper to understand, and underscore dyadic and contextual features of verbal discourse.

CHAPTER 19: Conversation Under the Influence

In addition to being self-conscious, conversations are dyad-dependent and context-dependent. Just as three converging lines define every triangle, every discussion is defined by three main vectors, one representing each speaker and one representing a topic. You must understand the dynamics of conversation, if you are to resist verbally delivered unwanted influence. The speaker, the conversational partner, and the topic are all affected by each person's beliefs about what the other knows. Your personality, your influencer's personality, and the context determine what is said, what is heard, and the actions, if any, that result. You are about to learn about the conversational triangle, the conversational meadow, and conversational synchronicity, all of which are important in every conversation, but are especially salient whenever you relate to an influencer. Be acutely aware that anyone can attempt to sway you by embedding her/his influence within casual chit-chat, or by using casual chit-chat to soften you up for a subsequent influence.

The speaker, his conversational partner, and the topic are most affected by the knowledge that each person ascribes to his counterpart regarding the topic being discussed. Nickerson (1999, 1998) suggests that people often erroneously presume that their conversational partner knows more of what the speaker knows than is true, and that this is at the heart of many communication problems. Citing the work of Nickerson et al. (1987), Rainer Bromme, Riklef Rambow, and Matthias Nückles (2001) describe his three central hypotheses:

> The correspondence hypothesis. It states that one
> is more likely to impute a bit of knowledge to
> others if oneself has it than if oneself does not
> have it. We call this the correspondence
> hypothesis because it says that the estimations will

show some sort of correspondence with the estimator's own knowledge.

The overestimation hypothesis. This one says that persons tend to overestimate the commonality of their own knowledge.

The expertise hypothesis. The third hypothesis indicates that persons who possess an extraordinarily high level of knowledge in a certain domain will tend to overestimate what other persons know about this domain.

Fortunately, the correspondence, overestimation, and expertise effects usually are reduced among frequently conversing partners. On the other hand, although the entire universe of ideas connected to a topic is open to them, their conversation largely is governed by their relationship history together. Conversational partners with a long history are unconsciously biased toward some topics and some topic details, and away from others. Imagine, for instance, that I ask my next-door neighbor, "Eugene, How's your brother, Keith?" Given his extensive past and present history with his brother to whom he is emotionally very close, Eugene can respond in any one of a million ways to my interrogative. However, he instantly replies, "Great, his practice is going well." I did not specifically ask about his brother's professional/financial life, but that is the response I received because in the past, Eugene and I have mostly spoken about his brother in his professional capacity. Our conversational history together and the fact that I am a psychologist primed Eugene's thought process, so that he assumed that I am asking about his brother as it relates to his being a psychologist. Had I been his brother's fishing buddy, Eugene probably would have had an entirely different set of associations triggered. It would be surprising if Eugene responded to the fishing partner with the very same answer that he had given to me. Had he done so, the response would have indicated that when his brother is the topic of conversation, Eugene's own internal psychodynamics dominate his brother-oriented conversations rather than does the extant conversational relationship, and the topic history that he has with the conversational partner present.

The Conversational Meadow

When you think about it, the fact that people tend to have conversations about the same things—conversational template-like—with the same people is rather astounding. You and your partner literally could talk about anything from the most remote past to the most remote future. You even could discuss fantastic ideas that defy classification. That you tend to be repetitive is more evidence in favor of the view that you and your partner are not just conversing to converse, but are looking for GBH in the places where you expect you will find it together. You could go anywhere, but instead you hang around the same conversational territory.

The conversational terrain is like a huge, unobstructed, fully-accessible meadow that can be entered from any direction and traversed in any way. When addressed or when addressing, each conversational partner can wander anywhere conversationally, so long as she can make some reasonably relevant connection among the ideas presented. Yet, as discussed above, conversations between frequent speaking partners typically follow familiar, historically salient routes. Just as Eugene always responds to my question about his brother by focusing on the bother's professional/financial life, most people have prototypical topics and topic development specific to their conversational partner. Why is this? It is because, in addition to having our GBH needs, we have expectations about where, and to what extent, our current conversational partner can satisfy them, and he has similar expectations about us. He and we take the path of least resistance that offers the greatest promise of GBH with the least expenditure of effort. This is due, in large measure, to our conversation history with this person, and to the rewards that we have enjoyed in the past. To take another conversation entry point or to traverse a new route is to place ourselves at risk, to jeopardize the GBH satisfactions that have kept us conversationally connected to this speaking partner in the past. When we do take the risk, we open ourselves and our partners to new influences that we hope will lead to new GBH satisfactions. We will have much more to say about conversational direction and conversational consistency later.

Conversational Synchronicity

We need to stroll the meadow in time with our partner. In conversation, as in all of life, timing, or synchronicity, is critical. For conversation to be sustained beyond the briefest comments, there must be a synchronicity of conversational partners in process and content. Conversation process synchronicity refers to conversational partners volitionally engaging in discourse at the same moment. They need to be sufficiently committed to talk then and there, rather than to any other "action" or topic that competes for their mental energies. Conversation content synchronicity refers to conversational partners discussing similar subject matter then and there, rather than to any other subject matter. To be in synchrony, conversational partners need to be mentally attuned to, or at least receptive to, one or more certain mutually shared body, environment, thought. or feeling (BETF) experiences. [BETF will be explained in full later, since the four comprise critical sources of tension and satisfaction that conjointly determine our physical and mental well-being.] Persons excessively focused on overt, physical action, rather than on verbalization, and on narrow, esoteric topics, rather than on wide, broadly held ones have a reduced probability of achieving the process synchronicity and/or content synchronicity that helps conversation unfold readily and smoothly.

Conversation content synchronicity often takes the form of our mirroring the talk of others by using their very words or metaphors. Two especially relevant and common types of mirroring are lexical choice and conceptual pacts. In lexical choice mirroring, conversational partners use identical or tightly related terms to refer to the same concept, as when I say that I feel that I am a "ship at sea," and you advise me to seek a "safe harbor." Brennan and Clark (1996) demonstrate that in conceptual pact mirroring, conversational partners use their shared lexical choice conceptualization repeatedly in the current or subsequent conversations, even when other word choices would be more linguistically economical. Speaking specifically of dyads, Niederhoffer and Pennebaker (2002) suggest, "If one person uses a high number of positive or negative words, words that signal concrete thinking (e.g., articles) or sentence complexity (e.g., prepositions), the other does too." Over time, conversational partners often conjointly modify or abandon their conceptual pacts—another example of the ubiquitously co-constructive nature of conversation. Davis and Rusbult (2001) show that close conversational partners tend toward "attitude alignment," changing their individual opinion about a given subject when the issue is salient and central to the partners' self-concepts.

When discussed this way, the necessity for conversational synchronicity seems obvious and trite. Yet failure of synchronicity is a major impediment to effective, satisfying conversation. How often have you begun talking with someone only to lose interest because your partner was not "there" with you? She may have been doing something else, such as glancing down at her cell phone, and obviously not paying attention to your interaction (process), or her irrelevant or tangential comments may have signaled that her current issues were discontinuous with your own (content), such as when you speak about your job, and she replies about her parents' new car.

In addition to process and content synchronicity—the conversation essentials—there is also the non-essential, but highly desirable, affective synchronicity. Whether our relentless, expectant search is for message or relationship GBH, we desire to speak with someone who is "in time" with us emotionally. If we are solemn, we usually want a serious partner. If we are effusive, we usually want an emotionally reactive one. It's a matter of "misery loves company" or "laugh and the world laughs with you." This does not mean, however, that we always want our conversational partner to mirror the exact same feeling that we do. Conceivably, there are occasions when we search for someone who evidences emotion at variance with ours in order to snap us out of our current mood. The synchronicity in this case is that we want our partner to do the "snapping" then and there, at the very moment that we need it.

Is it All in Your Head?

Since conversation begins in an individual mind, intra-personal mental factors profoundly influence what will be said. But conversation of course is not just intra-personally determined. The inter-personal environment, too, determines conversation, because conversation always is co-constructed collaboratively, on-line, and relative to the person with whom we speak. Usually the intra-personal and inter-personal factors combine seamlessly and automatically, constraining some conversations and enhancing others.

Lewis Carroll's oft-quoted "Words mean just what I want them to mean, nothing more and nothing less" has much merit. Words do mean only what people use them to mean, and words in conversation mean only what both conversing persons understand them to mean. Willard V. Quine (1977), a preeminent language philosopher, seems extreme in claiming that there is no intrinsic meaning behind words. But he does underscore the indisputable fact that dictionaries are insufficient to capture the meanings of words in conversation. When I use a word while conversing, if I am using a conventional dictionary definition at all, I am focusing only on one small part of it at that moment as I strive to communicate my thought. This is especially true because the word I choose always will be an insufficient expression of my total thought gestalt. To converse adequately with me, you need to ignore all the other meanings listed in the dictionary or in your head, if you are to react appropriately to mine. And the only way our meanings will match is if we share enough mental content, baseline consciousness, and speaking standards that permit us to communicate the all-important nuanced meanings of what we want to say. If we are of the same mind linguistically, we are said to be entrained.

When relating to an influencer, the inter-personal environment activates the social self—the feature of personality acutely aware of and sensitive to the current social relationship. And, of all that defines the social self, nothing is more important than social comparison of the self with other people. Stapel and Tesser (2001) suggest that the mere activation of a personal sense of oneself promotes his/her social comparison, and a search for what makes him/her both separate from and similar to the person with whom they are relating. In their words,

> often people's goal is 'being the same and different at the same time.' That is, people derive their sense of self or identity from a fundamental tension between their need for validation and similarity to others (being the same) and a countervailing need for differentiation and individuation (being different). Individuals are concerned with obtaining a certain level of being the same and being different, called optimal distinctiveness (Brewer, 1991). From the present perspective, self-activation is thus likely to activate optimal distinctiveness concerns. Such concerns can only

be addressed by reference to other people, that is,
by social comparison.

Social comparison is endemic in social relationships (Kelly, 1955). We automatically compare and contrast ourselves with significant others as well as with strangers, and we react affectively based on our conclusions, especially in terms of the extent of self-relevance of that which has being evaluated. Beach and colleagues (1998) found that when a married person compares himself or herself with their partner, they are less likely to be bitter about the partner's superiority, or less likely to gloat over their own superiority than they would in comparisons with strangers. For dating couples, by contrast, pleasure in the partner's superiority, if present at all, is most likely to be restricted to comparisons of low self-relevance. An intense attachment seems necessary, if we are to be "charitable" in our self-other comparisons. Moreover, when social comparisons involve decisions, we incline toward a "person sensitivity bias" by which we ascribe too much credit to others when things are going well, and too much blame to them when things are going poorly (Moon and Conlon, 2002).

Whether another person influences us or not, then, is significantly affected by how we handle both the intra-personal and inter-personal experience. Although both dimensions are impacting us, one is prepotent at any time in a given conversation. And the balance often depends on our desire to maintain our self-esteem. According to Rusbult et al. (2000) people maintain a positive sense of self in part by selective attention, encoding, and retrieval of self-reinforcing information, by interacting with others who support one's positive beliefs, and by having a broadly-based corpus of readily retrievable positive self-facts. Similar processes are employed in the attempt to maintain a positive sense of one's inter-personal relationships. Concerning the latter, Rusbult and his colleagues emphasize several social comparison strategies including: Downward comparison by which one views her relationships in contrast to others deemed less positive; dimensional comparison by which one focuses on particular aspects of her relationships that are especially salutary; manipulation of surrounding dimension which finds reasons to discredit the attractive features of others' relationships; and avoidance of comparison which blinds her to anything that depicts her relationships as inferior to those of someone else. However, as Stapel and Tesser (2001) note, we are two selves—a personal self, with a tendency to look within for self-centered, often secret, GBH goals and desires, and a social self, with more broadly shared, outwardly-directed goals and desires.

The dual character of personal self-definition and of social self-definition in relationships is critical in conversation wherein the individual both contributes thoughts and feelings and reacts to the thoughts and feelings of her immediate social environment, that is, of her conversational partner. The dual character also is apparent in the subpart of the self that we specifically call "self-esteem"—a subpart that remains prominent in all conversations. Heine and his colleagues (1999) assert that, in Western culture, "People have a need to view themselves positively. This is easily the most common and consensually endorsed assumption in research on the self (e.g., Allport, 1955 ; Epstein, 1973 ; James, 1890 ; Maslow, 1943 ; Rogers, 1951 ; Steele, 1988 ; Tesser, 1988). In fact, positive self-regard is thought by many to be essential for achieving mental health (e.g., Baumeister, 1993; Leary, Tambor, Terdal, & Downs, 1995; Taylor & Brown, 1988)." Tafarade (1998) states that self-esteem is comprised of the individual's feelings of self-competence, and his standing in the wider society, the last of which he calls "self-liking." Tafarade regards self-competence as an individual's assessment of his ability to "impose his will on the environment," meaning the veridical and presumed environment, and, as such, it is an autonomous, personal evaluation. By contrast, self-liking is seen as "one's worth as a social entity with reference to internalized standards of good and bad" that derive not so much from the individual's autonomous values, but from values embraced by people in his reference group. In conversation, then, an individual's self-esteem derives from the extent to which he can talk himself into getting whatever GBH that he wants (self-competence) while abiding by the social mores of proper conversational behavior so that he can mentally represent himself as being inter-personally appropriate (self-liking).

Take Away

In all cases, but especially when exposed to influence from persons with whom you have a significant history, you should strive to be conscious of how your personality, their personality, and the context come together. Your conjoint history is likely to be very powerful in determining what is said, what is heard, and the subsequent actions. You and the partner most often will be looking for GBH in places that have been fruitful in the past. All else being equal then, you are likely to avoid novel issues, unless one or both of you is seeking some new satisfaction. A new uncharted topic certainly might be of benefit to you both. However, be open to the possibility that, wittingly or unwittingly, your familiar partner could be seeking a previously unsought unilateral benefit that might lead you into an area of negfluence. And, of course, when you converse with an unfamiliar person, their negfluences on you can come from virtually anywhere.

CHAPTER 20: You as Resistance Warrior

Your internal self-oriented conversation—what you tell yourself about yourself— is especially crucial for all of your decisions. When being pressured by a persuader and/or by a choice, you need to engage in what psychologists call positive self-affirmations (Epton et al., 2015), meaning self-statements that provide encouragement consistent with a more-or-less accurate reality orientation. There even is evidence that a person in a trying situation can benefit from bringing to mind accurate self-affirmations regarding *unrelated* self-affirming situations (Kang et al., 2015). The rationale is that the positive focus increases one's sense of competence and ability to endure.

Ideal self-affirmations are ones that are reasonable, concrete, and behaviorally specific. It is not enough to say, "I will do better in resisting peer pressure." You must tell yourself, in concrete detail, your personal qualities that make resistance and success possible, and how you behaviorally will exploit those qualities when you need them.

Positive self-talk is one aspect of general emotion regulation. We all need to learn to manage our emotions better when making decisions and when resisting unwanted influence. Management ideally includes preventing and minimizing negative decisions, and promoting and maximizing positive ones. Folk wisdom offers some advice for short-term emotional coping such as reducing anger by counting to ten, and coping with sexual tension by taking a cold shower. Other useful ideas are exercising to reduce anxiety, or listening to soothing music to induce a feeling of comfort. In the long-term though, self-conversation is a very effective emotion regulation strategy, and its power extends far beyond positive self-affirmations to include all emotion-relevant, supportive self-talk.

One somewhat gimmicky aspect of self-talk deserves mention, since there is a reasonable amount of psychological research to support its judicious use: Introspective talk during which one refers to him- or herself by name or with a non-first person pronoun (e.g., he or she) can improve anxiety regulation and, even, performance, especially performance in social influence interactions (Kross, et al., 2014). Implementing this strategy tends to promote a more objective view of highly personal situations. However, "self-distancing" is insufficient. You need to have an full armamentarium of strategies to successfully resist unwanted external influences.

Recognize the Emotion Present Within Your Talk

To be empowered to regulate your emotions through self-talk, you must understand that emotion suffuses the very fabric of language. The evaluative, or connotative, dimension of words contrasts with the denotative dimension. The latter has the dictionary as its principal accuracy arbiter. A Merriam-Webster readily can provide the denotative definition of "mother." To communicate with any degree of reliability, we tacitly must accept some basic denotative features of "mother." But this word, and the overwhelming majority of words, has innumerable connotations as well. For some persons, "mother" is a virtual god; for others, she's the devil.

Consider for a moment the multifaceted, fluid relationship that governs the denotative and connotative features of words in our mental lexicon. As a constant in mental life, emotion is a powerful element in words. Some words clearly are emotion-words, words that describe feelings. These can be found in a standard thesaurus, and include terms like angry, hate, gloom, love, compassion, and hope among many others. Psychologists have used emotion-words to explore the nature of emotions and personality, pointing out that emotion-words and words to describe personality often are identical (Plutchik, 1997), as when we use the word "anxious" to describe a type of emotion or a type of person.

Extensive intra-cultural and cross-cultural research has affirmed that the good-bad continuum of connotative meaning is the single most powerful non-denotative dimension for explaining the significance of words, accounting for two-thirds of the expressive language similarities between people (Osgood, 1957). That is, we automatically perceive most words as connoting something good or bad—even apparently non-emotional words such as "aardvark"— and there is substantial, although certainly not perfect, agreement about the affective valance of a given word across people and cultures. For example, using a 9 point scale, with 9 being most positive and 1 being most negative, subjects in a study conducted by Warriner, Kuperman, and Brysbaert (2013) produced the following affective word rating averages: aardvark (6.29), aggravate (2.55), ballerina (6.79), barren (3.8), purpose (6.70), pushy (3.10), salesman (4.10), and science (6.32).

In influence-relevant contexts, listen carefully to the connotative aspect of your self-talk, of how you talk with others, and of how they talk to you. If you do, you often will be able to improve your emotion regulation, and, therefore, your decision making and how you handle external influences. Attend to the frequency with which you and influencers use positive and negative words, and to the strength of the positivism or negativism. Positive words will raise other positive associations in your own mind and in the minds of those with whom you converse. Research (Gottman, 1993) suggests, for instance, that marriages are in danger when the ratio of positive to negative communications is less than 5 to 1. That, of course, implies that any influencer who manages to communicate an absolute minimum of six congenial interactions for every tense one is more likely to win you over.

Maintain an Internal Locus of Control

Since LOC mostly consists of the previously discussed three interrelated dimensions of internal-external, global-specific, and temporary-permanent, understand where you tend fall on the three continua. Although you probably do not show the same dimensional profile all the time or in all situations, everyone has their characteristic LOC tendencies. What are the areas in which you are most externally inclined? Why? What, if anything, can you do with that self-awareness to minimize your susceptibility to deleterious influences?

Look to your past to find circumstances during which you did and did not manage to maintain control in the face of overt or covert manipulation. What affected you then, and what was it about those circumstances that caused you to succeed or fail? Have the courage to face all future manipulation, not necessarily in an aggressive way, but with enough vigor to counter the manipulator.

Focus on Your Competencies

Your core self-evaluations also warrant close attention. According to Judge et al. (1997), LOC is, in fact, one component of core self-evaluation. The other components include self-esteem, generalized self-efficacy, and emotional stability as essential components. So, these four are the personal components worth considering.

Self-esteem can be a slippery concept. However, most psychologists would agree that several characteristics usually differentiate high from low self-esteem persons. The former exhibit a greater readiness to: confront challenges, accept deserved praise, maintain a measure of optimism during failures, and gravitate toward situations that support their extant self-concepts.

Generalized self-efficacy is consistent with high self-esteem. Persons high in generalized self-efficacy have an indomitable "can do" perspective and possess good faith as opposed to bad faith. They believe that they can achieve virtually anything to which they put their minds. Most often these persons embrace an internal, specific, and temporary LOC orientation. They are unlikely to seek external excuses. They trust that personal effort produces beneficial results, that the benefits are specific to given challenges, and that they will last only as long as they sustain their efforts.

The consistency of one's LOC depends of course on the consistency of their mental stability. Behavioral science research supports the notion that everyone's personality can be described by her/his position on a neuroticism-stability continuum. Herein, "neuroticism" is defined as predominantly moody, negative emotions whereas "stability" refers to predominantly positive emotions. The neurotic person is easily rattled and insecure, especially during times of uncertainty, whereas the stable one is better able to maintain their composure whether things go right or wrong.

To maintain control and to forearm yourself against unwanted influence, keep a close watch on your core self-evaluations. Influencers make it their business to "read" you. They want to know how externally or internally oriented you are. They want to know the areas wherein you are high and low in self-esteem and in self-perceived effectiveness. And they want to know how emotionally stable you are. With that knowledge, manipulators customize their approach to get you to think, feel, and behave in ways consistent with their motives. Even when the specifics of your personal self-evaluations are inaccessible to them, the influencers try to control you via your reference groups. Presuming that you share key self-evaluation and other personality features with your affiliation groups, they attempt to treat you as they would treat anyone with those affiliations, hoping that your desire for social acceptance (Cialdini's social consensus) will sway you to their positions.

To ensure your autonomy and well-being then, maintain a justifiably paranoid frame of mind and attend to your core self-evaluations. Understand and counter habits of thought, emotion, and behavior that render you vulnerable to unwanted influences. Resist your natural human proclivity to mindlessly and automatically respond to external influences by becoming mindful and deliberate relative to them.

One potential complication is that your core self-evaluations include your personal sense of group membership. The highly refined human self-concept requires a conception of others as well. The meaning of self always occurs in an interpersonal context, even if the context merely exists in our minds, as when we incorrectly believe that people regard us in a particular way when they do not. The self is evaluated and perceived in terms of the behavior of other persons and vice versa (Sullivan, 1953). We consider ourselves to be good by contrasting what we regard as our virtuous behavior with what we see as the dastardly behavior of someone else (Kelly, 1955). That is, your core self-evaluations often are "contaminated" by your group identities. Life is a continual struggle between behaving in a fully autonomous manner, and behaving as a group member. Adopting either extreme tendency literally can be deadly. Just be aware that you must determine when and to what extent you do better in adapting a more autonomous-oriented versus a more affiliation-oriented stance.

Time Perspective

How we self-talk to frame situations time-wise also exerts an especially powerful effect on our decisions. Some people are strongly biased toward immediate gratification—the pleasure principle—while others more readily sacrifice now to reap higher returns later—the reality principle. Since rational decisions tend to favor those with a long-term, reality principle horizon, impatient people usually choose poorly. Research (e.g., Kooij, D., et al., 2018) suggests that persons with a long-term orientation usually make wiser choices regarding health behavior, risk behavior, well-being, achievement, and retirement planning. Conversely, wise results rarely accrue to slaves of the pleasure principle—to those impatient for a quick fix. Incremental, continuous, reality-based effort is most likely to facilitate overall achievement and happiness.

The particulars of one's time orientation definitely contribute to emotional tone and can be the difference between seeing decision delay and decision effort as an intolerable, acute burden or a worthwhile, long-term process. And there is another personality-relevant aspect of time orientation that must be considered: the paradox of time perspective, a concept pioneered by psychologist, Philip Zimbardo.

Zimbardo (2009) takes the three basic time orientations with which we are familiar—present, past, and future—and subdivides them regarding their personality implications. His scheme suggests six perspectives: present-hedonistic, present-fatalistic, past-positive, past-negative, future-oriented, and transcendental-future. The terms are largely self-explanatory except for transcendental-future by which he means an approach that considers life mostly to be preparation for an after-life. Importantly, Philip Zimbardo does not regard time-perspectives as immutable. Quite the contrary, he proposes that people must learn to match the correct time perspective to each given situation. In his words,

> So, very quickly, what is the optimal time profile?
> High on past-positive. Moderately high on future.
> And moderate on present-hedonism. And always

low on past-negative and present-fatalism. So the
optimal temporal mix is what you get from the
past -- past-positive gives you roots. You connect
your family, identity and yourself. What you get
from the future is wings to soar to new
destinations, new challenges. What you get from
the present hedonism is the energy, the energy to
explore yourself, places, people, sensuality.

Applied to the decision process, the Zimbardo scheme advises
you to draw on the best of your past learning and long-term
support systems, reach deep down within yourself for your
current personal resources and skills, and establish a fierce
commitment to do all necessary to make the right choice rather
than the automatic, expedient one.

Time orientation is especially important for decisions enacted
under stress. Research in the 1940s confirmed the commonsense
notion that the intensity of your apprehension for a negative
situation increases as you approach that negative situation, and
the intensity of your eagerness for a positive situation increases
as you approach that positive situation (Miller, 1944). However,
in the negative situation, the rate of apprehension increase is
markedly faster than is the rate of eagerness increase for the
positive situation. For instance, after having planned a vacation,
you become slowly, increasingly eager to go as time progresses
toward departure, but after a surgery has been scheduled, you
become very quickly, increasingly apprehensive as the operation
date draws closer.

How close is close, and why the differential impact of the
perceived closeness? Emma Bruehlman-Senecal and Ozlem
Ayduk (2015) wanted to know, and so they set out to study the
ways that "temporal distancing," or the time perspective that we
assign to upsetting future events, affects us emotionally.
Consistent with the 1940s results, Bruehlman-Senecal and

Ozlem's series of four studies indicated that when an individual expects a stressful situation to occur in the "distant-future" (in the coming year or years) he/she is less troubled than when expecting the same event in the "near-future" (in the coming days or weeks). The researchers explained the results as due to the fact that distant-future events are conceptualized more abstractly and schematically, whereas near-future events are conceptualized in a more concrete, more detailed manner. In essence, far-future stressors are regarded as less real and less significant than near-future ones and, therefore, are less troubling.

Temporal distancing has a cousin—temporal landmarks—that also can be critically important for your emotional well-being, decision making, and vulnerability to influence. Some of these temporal landmarks are common to most people, since they are pervasive in a culture. For instance, they include early or initial times, such as Monday or January, versus Friday or December. Those early markers represent culturally recognized starting points that could be used to plan the rest of the week or year. Other temporal markers are highly person-specific. The specific ones might be deeply and idiosyncratically ingrained in your psyche, such as your birthday or wedding anniversary. Other person-specific temporal markers could be more fleeting or arbitrary, as when you have established a habit of visiting a restaurant, or buying a new car at a particular time interval.

Regardless of whether the marker is culture-wide or highly personal, it can render you susceptible to an influencer who knows about the temporal marker's importance to you, and who delivers a pitch concordant with it. Of course, some of us are more time-vulnerable than others. Psychologists Białek and Sawicki (2018) found that cognitively unreflective persons tend toward time discounting, meaning that they are predisposed to seeking more immediate, smaller rewards over larger but more time-distant ones. Their decisions favor first alternatives that they have entertained. To compound the problem, the unreflective ones also are too quick to accept time reference points imposed on them by influencers. For instance, they might readily succumb to a salesperson who reminds them about the supposed relevance of a culture-wide or highly personal temporal marker to an issue being discussed. On the other hand, reflective individuals do less time discounting, consider later alternatives, and resist imposed reference points. Accordingly, they are less influencer-susceptible.

One final feature of time is more about you than about your influencer. It is your chronotype, your roughly 24 hour a day biorhythm. All people, and all animals, have their own chronotype. Some of us awaken early and go to bed late, a pattern colloquially called "larking." And some of us awaken late and go to bed early, called "owling," Of course, the lark-owl distinction falls along a continuum, with most people having only a moderate tendency toward either type. Some, such as the business journalist, Daniel Pink (2018) claim that extreme larks and owls have their own distinctive patterns of vigilance, the former with a morning peak, afternoon trough, and late day recovery, and the latter with the opposite pattern. However, the research on the implications for decision making is questionable, at best. One study worth mention, however, was that of María Juliana Leone and her colleagues (2017) who studied the decisions of chess players.

As expected, the Leone study discovered that larks played more chess games in the mornings and owls, more in the night. However, chronotype did not determine the quality of their decisions. Regardless of their chronotype, all persons made faster and less accurate decisions as the time passed. Play was more cautious earlier in their activities and riskier, later. That is, not chronotype, but the passage of clock time was the most important factor. For us then, if anything, the chronotype-chess study suggests that we should think about our own specific biorhythms when anticipating an influence situation. You quite likely will be more independent and circumspect earlier in an influence situation than you will be as time progresses whether you are more larkish or more owlish. The deterioration of decision quality probably occurs due to such factors as fatigue, impatience, or frustration. The long, drawn-out, extremely time-consuming, automobile sales ritual common in America certainly seems designed to promote customer fatigue, impatience, or frustration. When that does occur, the customer is likely to make suboptimal decisions that increase the final purchase price, and the salesperson's commission.

Time, then, truly is a subjective experience: a matter of what you tell yourself that affects your well-being. Try to conceptualize challenging decisions as near-future, so that you treat them as deliberately and concretely as possible. Conversely, you can afford to regard positive events more distantly, abstractly, and schematically. Know, too, your orientation toward temporal distancing and temporal landmarks. Consider your chronotype, the time and the time span during which you are exposed to an influencer. Use all this knowledge to become optimally reflective and to resist influencers who try to impose reference points. Do your best to seize control of the time element involved in every influence situation, from start to finish.

All this underscores that you can seize control of your own destiny. Refrain from bad faith rationalization—denial of personal responsibility and of existential freedom. In accord with Jean-Paul Sartre's principle of bad faith (1993), I believe that almost everyone almost always has enough potential freedom of thought and action to resist undue influence. You need to adopt a resistance warrior's stance toward external persuasion. First, maintain a justifiably paranoid frame of mind. Second, understand how your habits of thought, emotion, and behavior render you vulnerable. And third, counter your natural human proclivity to mindlessly and automatically respond by becoming mindful and deliberate relative to external influences. Use time to your advantage. Have proactive mindsets and strategies that enable you to take advantage of opportunities to use your internal locus of control adaptively.

CHAPTER 21: Time Bandits' Assaults on Health

In all cultures familiar to me, robbery has been considered a crime. Accordingly, those societies have imposed penalties upon thieves. That of course presumes that the robbery was detected, reported, and the perpetrator was convicted. On the other hand, failure to report or failure to apprehend robbers renders robbery both a lucrative and comfortable profession that requires no formal education or training.

History documents that the targets of robbers have varied from age to age. Since ancient Romans allegedly were paid in salt, salt presumably was stolen then. When coal was the home heating fuel of choice in the early 20th century, it, too, was stolen.

Having just discussed the importance of time perspective, we all should be alarmed to realize that in the 21st century, our precious time is stolen and manipulated by contemporary influence time bandits organized into a variety of cartels led by multi-millionaires and billionaires. Some of these thieving conglomerates are software and hardware manufacturers, Internet providers, and entertainment producers and directors. A regiment of marketers and other influence troopers assist those who traffic in time theft. Many of us are unaware of the extent of our victimization, and few report the thievery about which they become aware. Victims of time thieving influencers, nevertheless, frequently suffer profound negative physical- and mental-health consequences.

Let's now specifically address a few of the preferred electronic instruments of time crooks: personal devices, such as cell phones and computer tablets. These so-called mobile devices have an addictive allure, and permit unprecedented intrusive manipulation by persons seeking to exploit us. Virtually all technology hardware and software manufacturers, Internet providers, and entertainment producers and directors create and disseminate products, methods, and memes to keep us perennially focused on whatever they are promoting. The more they can do so, the more power and money they accumulate. When we become compulsively attached to their items, ideas, and agendas, we have little time for many personal activities that occupied us in previous centuries. To cite one well-publicized and obvious example: We rarely talk at length on the telephone anymore, and often prefer to keep our face-to-face meetings to a minimum. If circumstances require us to be physically present with another flesh and blood person, we do not hesitate to interpose an electronic device between them and us. Electronic hardware, software, and the Internet are specifically structured to continually present a never-ending array of enticing stimuli to capture and monopolize our attention and our time.

Monopolizing our attention and time, in fact, has become one of Influencers' primary preoccupations. And they no longer are content to monopolize via formal computer devices. Influence warriors now have weaponized everyday objects by embedding microchips within them. Those chip-embedded "smart' objects are designed to exert influence on us, and to gather strategic intelligence about us. The relentless smart object assault is designated by three synonyms: "pervasive computing," "ubiquitous computing," and "the Internet of things." Smart objects are being created day after day, and already range from smart windshield wipers that turn on, off, and adjust their speed according to the rain they "perceive" on your windshield, to smart pillboxes that determine whether medication was taken and that automatically reorders them. Some reading this book, perhaps most, will regard the smart wipers and pillboxes as very positive innovations, and that could be a defensible opinion.

My concern is not with helpful, smart objects per se, but with the ways in which they are programmed and promoted. People obviously are responsible for doing both, and people consciously or inadvertently can program and promote a smart device in ways that have negative consequences for the end user. Perhaps an auto parts giant encourages the windshield wiper company to make its product run faster or more often than needed, so that the wipers wear out quickly. Or a pharmaceutical company advises the pill box maker to reorder medication more often than necessary. You might argue that any item can be used negatively, but unlike other items, smart items lull us into passivity and complacency, so that we are less likely to monitor them and to be aware when they are being misused.

Another example is the fact that electronic hardware, software, and the Internet specifically are structured to continually present a never-pending array of enticing stimuli to capture and monopolize our attention. Pervasive computing poses a major challenge in large part because smart devices are omnipresent, functionally autonomous, and programmed and monitored by some company's electronic network.

Prior to the computer and Internet revolutions, our activities possessed explicit, or at least clearly implicit, start and stop boundaries. Our books had first and last pages. Movies began with the title and concluded with "The End." However, electronic media characteristically lack an obvious start and stop boundary. We can pick up anywhere and continue indefinitely. This is most apparent in the Internet surfing experience. Whenever you find a "page" of interest that page includes bold or subtle cues directing you to other pages. In fact, sometimes one page launches another page without cueing us of its "intention" to do so. The progression from page to page can be interminable.

Immobilized By Mobile Devices

Every minute of indiscriminate, continuous, compulsive electronic device use is a minute not spent on something else. Only you can determine the physical- and mental-health consequences of your personal, unique electronic device usage.

Do your devices keep you in your chair rather than moving about? Do the devices interpose a barrier between you and authentic, in vivo human experiences? On the other hand, do you use devices sparingly and prudently—think FitBit—in ways that can enhance your physical and/or health? The choice is yours to make.

As we have noted, of all available electronics, mobile devices—such as smartphones, tablets and smart watches—provide influencers virtually limitless access to us. Moreover, mobile devices can be so addictive that we sometimes unwittingly use them in ways that readily permit and even welcome unprecedented intrusive manipulation by persons seeking to exploit us.

If you believe that time robbing influencers are satisfied with their success, think again. Consider the research of Nicholas H. Lurie and his colleagues (2016). Their paper written for the Invitational Choice Symposium, Lake Louise, Canada, May, 2016 entitled, *Everywhere and at All Times: Mobility, Consumer Decision Making, and Choice* seeks to improve strategies to steal our time through mobile electronic mobile ecosystems, their contexts, and the interactions between the ecosystems, contexts, and the minds of the consumers. Because the Lurie group's issues encapsulate critical electronic influence questions that profoundly affect your well-being, I use their questions to structure the remainder of this chapter:

> "How does mobility affect cognitive capacity and the influence of incidental information?"
> "Are mobile decision-makers more myopic?"
> "How do mobile ecosystem capabilities and pervasivity affect socially undesirable and personal choices?"

In the event that the Lurie group succeeds in their quest, electronic hardware, software, and the Internet will be all the more effective in monopolizing your time. Please note that I am not condemning all electronic devices and the persons who make, distribute, or use them. The devices of course can and do save us time if used with discretion. My point is that the "system" promulgates indiscriminate, continuous, compulsive use.

The Lurie group (LG) researches and advises marketers about the following: The **mobile ecosystem**, meaning all the electronic communication devices that we can carry with us. LG is concerned to better understand and manipulate how we specifically **search** for information and about how the **capabilities** and **pervasivity** of the system affects the searches. They hope, for instance, to uncover how and when you do your searches, what you are able to access with your devices, and how widely you search. They also hope to learn what you regard as the **credibility** of information sources that you employ. Of course, by knowing that, influencers can try to increase your perception of their own credibility. Finally, they seek to learn about any of your **embarrassing** and **personal choices**. That's right! Why? They don't say, but presumably it is because they want to be able to address all types of your "intimate" concerns. Those are the concerns toward which you are most naturally, intensely, and emotionally motivated. If the influencers can know and exploit those concerns, they can inform you about their desire and ability to satisfy the concerns and profit tremendously from doing so.

The **mobile context** is LG's second focus. They are looking see how mobile **situations** relate to the **breadth** of your choice alternatives. Marketers might want to broaden your choices sometimes and narrow them other times. In addition, LG is considering the manner of **competition** between your mobile and non-mobile sources of information. This dimension, for instance, might involve comparing the information that your cell phone reveals about a product versus what your friend had told you previously. The final feature of mobile context is the ways in which it does or does not **constrain us cognitively**. LG might want to determine such factors as the extent that a mobile device frees working memory, thus enabling us to devote more mental energy to considering our purchase options. To return to our previous example, such information obviously would appeal to an influencer who hopes to broaden or narrow your attention from what you want to what he wants you to want.

The third and final LG category is **mobile mindset**. Foremost is LG's wish to determine whether an **action-orientation** prompts you to respond **heuristically**. If you are in an action frame of mind, are you inclined to rely on simple heuristics —mental rules of thumb—that we discussed earlier, rather than on slower, more deliberative thinking? Similarly, is a sense of **urgency** biasing you toward information that confirms or disconfirms your urgent desire? LG would expect that the urgency inclination would involve a **present focus** and/ or **myopic** focus rather than a non-present, broader one. LG also wonders how **anytime, unlimited** mobile device information impacts your **purchase confidence** and **post–purchase mental processes**. Given the common and natural human tendency toward social comparison, LG would love to understand whether you are more **self- vs. other-focused**. To employ the language that I introduced earlier, at the moment of influence, do you possess an internal or external locus of control (LOC). Marketers also would desire to know the answers to all the LG mobile mindset issues. Suppose they correctly know that right now you are in a mobile mindset that is action-oriented, heuristic, urgent, present-focused, myopic, purchase confident, with minimal deliberate mental processing, and a self-focus. In that case, you are ripe to make an impulsive decision with little concern about its implications, and that is dollar-ka-chinging music to an influencer's ears.

There is a broader issue here that goes beyond mobile mindsets: To make the best decisions that you can, it is not merely a matter of choosing, it is a matter of deciding. To choose is to restrict yourself to a limited number of candidate choices. The worst choices often are the ones presented to you by someone or, worse, some "bot" (software robot device). However, even your self-generated choice candidates too often are non-reflectively selected, based on heuristics rather than careful thought. Psychologists typically use the expression "fast and frugal" to emphasize the quick, effortless aspect of heuristics. And given the pervasiveness of heuristics, research is devoted to that subject.

As one example, consider the work of S. Bobadilla-Suarez and B. Love (2017). They questioned whether heuristics could be fast, frugal, and still effective. Their investigation compared a Tallying heuristic with a Take-the-Best heuristic. The former primarily involved culling a larger amount of information and then quickly choosing what seemed to lead to the best choice, and the latter, quickly searching a smaller amount of information only so long as needed to discover a reasonable answer.

Applied to shopping, a Tallying heuristic might involve superficially skimming a list of weight reduction products to choose the products with the most features shared among them. By contrast, a Take-the-Best heuristic might involve skimming the same list in a search for the one product that has the best consumer satisfaction rating.

Bobadilla-Suarez and Love found an effectiveness trade-off, such that either strategy could confer an advantage, sometimes favoring speed and other times, efficiency. In some contexts, Tallying was more effective while Take-the-Best was faster, or vice versa. Although either strategy might work in one given context, neither simultaneously included both a speed and efficiency advantage.

You may not be surprised that speed sacrifices efficiency and vice versa. But when you make your automatic, heuristic choices, you probably are not mindful of that trade-off as it occurs in real time.

It is unrealistic to think that you will or should abandon all heuristic thinking. After all, heuristics help reduce the effort required to make decisions. However, important decisions demand more than quick choices; you need to deliberate among your options, both to select the best ones and to overcome established unhelpful habits.

In short, you need to deliberate carefully before settling on heuristic choices. To do so, consider the sources of your candidate heuristics. Many heuristic preferences amount to instinctually imitating the behaviors and choices of your friends, acquaintances, or celebrities. Even if you have created your own personal relatively autonomous heuristic choices, you should evaluate them objectively. Some that you have created never worked properly, and some have worked properly in the past, but not now. The bottom line is this: critical decisions that you make should never be relegated to automatic heuristics. Take time to deliberate. That, at minimum, gives you a chance to affirm or revise your own personal heuristics to make them more compatible with your best interests.

Emphasis on Technology: Institutional True-Gooders?

From the outset, I acknowledged the reality that some people are influence true-gooders, such as many parents, teachers, and doctors, who know you intimately and who really have your best interests at heart. However, some persons and/or institutions either masquerade as true-gooders or have divided loyalties, sometimes for you and sometimes against. And when they ply their strategies, even authentic true-gooders inadvertently can cause you grief or harm. The ultimate results never are guaranteed when attempting to influence another person.

Much earlier, I mentioned that Stanford University, one of the most highly respected American institutions of higher learning, has a five star influence program called, the Stanford Persuasive Tech Lab, headed by B.J. Fogg. The Lab presents its mission statement as creating "insight into how computing products—from websites to mobile phone software—can be designed to change people's beliefs and behaviors." However, the Persuasive Tech Lab does not limit itself to using "computing products" per se, but also includes low tech everyday influence methods. For instance, the Fogg Behavior Grid is nothing more than a simple chart, illustrating a system to enable an individual to start, increase, decrease, or eliminate a behavior for a particular duration.

I have chosen to mention the Stanford Lab again here because of its renown, reputation of integrity, and apparent good intentions. For instance, their Peace Innovation Lab includes the Peace Innovation Project whose Peace Dot program is intended to "persuade any individual, organization or corporation with a website to create a peace subdomain that spotlights what they are doing to help promote peace in the world." How could anyone find fault with that?

I am all for peace and, harkening back to the World of Aquarius, love. But Fogg spends half his time working for industry. And industry generally is much more interested in money and power than peace and love. In fact, B.J. Fogg was the first person mentioned in the November, 2008 Fortune magazine article entitled, "10 new gurus you should know" and subtitled, "You've heard of Peter Drucker, Jim Collins, and C.K. Prahalad. Here we introduce the next generation of management experts who are changing the way business gets done." They wrote specifically that Fogg "researches how Web site or cell-phone design can impact consumers."

You might recall that the Fogg system now is called "captology" (which I associate with "captivity, but that's just me) whose primary focus is the "design, research, and analysis of interactive computing products (computers, mobile phones, websites, wireless technologies, mobile applications, video games, etc.) created for the purpose of changing people's attitudes or behaviors." Like Cialdini and many others, Fogg not only has created a personal influence marketing empire, but he also is an educator and for-hire lecturer who profoundly "influences" thousands of students and leaders of all types, most notably those in industry and government. Thanks to persons like Fogg, Cialdini, and marketers such as those referenced in Fortune magazine, persuasion forces have been increasing exponentially, growing toward the size and power of China's People's Liberation Army, but not intending to liberate anyone.

CHAPTER 22: The Future of Influence Has Arrived

High tech marketers, who combine mobile device exploitation with brain assault, dissection, and re-programming, are trying their best to control our minds and wallets. Not only are they extremely effective in what they do, they are refining their strategies relentlessly. In addition to all the usual methods to do so, the highest of high tech marketers profit from and contribute to the brave new world of applied artificial intelligence (A.I.) research and practice.

The Public Face of A.I.

Many in America and around the world have been introduced to nation-wide marketing spectacles promulgated through sensationalized media reports. Let's consider a couple of these: In 1962, it was the Battle of the Monsters between King Kong and Godzilla; in 1973, the Battle of the Sexes between 55-year-old Bobby Riggs and 29-year-old Billie Jean King; and in 1974, the Rumble in the Jungle between boxing ballerina, Muhammad Ali, and back street brawler, George Foreman. The purpose of each marketing event was to make money and to advance a product. However, A.I. did not appear on the media hyper-marketing scene until 1996 when IBM's computer, Deep Blue, squared off in a six-game chess match against Garry Kasparov, the Russian-Croatian who many believe was and is the greatest grandmaster ever.

You undoubtedly know that Deep Blue emerged victorious, dashing forever the belief of some people that human intellect could never be matched. However, a significant minority rationalized that since language-oriented cognition is the cornerstone of human exceptionality, humankind would win any purely verbal-oriented battle; thus, homo-sapiens became hopeful-sapiens.

Unfortunately, language-rooted hopefulness also evaporated when in 2011, IBM's Watson crushed Jeopardy quiz show superstars, Brad Rutter and Ken Jenning. Finally, in May 2017, Google's A.I. program "AlphaGo" took on China's Ke Jie, the planet's premier player of Go, considered the most intellectually challenging strategy game ever created. You guessed it: Ke Jie was obliterated, three to zero.

A.I. has been embraced enthusiastically by 21st century society. In medicine, for instance, medical administrators consider A.I. as a near perfect way to satisfy the federal government's demand for easily disseminated and tracked electronic medical records (EMRs). Viewed from a medical boardroom, the EMR mandate seems eminently sensible. One would expect A.I. to provide great efficiency and enhanced quality communication. However, many medical practitioners feel otherwise. Writing in the *Journal of the American Medical Association*, for instance, Abraham Verghese, M.D and his colleagues (Verghese, et al, 2017) complain:

> The redundancy of the notes, the burden of alerts, and the overflowing inbox has led to the "4000 keystroke a day" problem and has contributed to, and perhaps even accelerated, physician reports of symptoms of burnout. Even though the EMR may serve as an efficient administrative business and billing tool, and even as a powerful research warehouse for clinical data, most EMRs serve their front-line users quite poorly. The unanticipated consequences include the loss of important social rituals (between physicians and between physicians and nurses and other health care workers) around the chart rack and in the radiology suite, where all specialties converged to discuss patients.

Another medical A.I. application is predictive analytics in which big data informs clinical decision making. Although acknowledging its potential, Shah, et al. (2018) emphasize worrisome drawbacks. Most notably, they make the point that although a single physician error deleteriously can affect a particular patient, an algorithm miscalculation can harm scores, hundreds, or thousands. They write, too, that predictive analytics often are proprietary methods under the exclusive control of profit-oriented companies, and, as such, might not be sufficiently open to rigorous oversight. Moreover, those who use the analytics in a clinic or hospital would not have the backgrounds to recognize or evaluate some problems that do arise.

EMR and predictive analytics are merely two medical examples of how A.I. and its variants produce unintended, deleterious side effects. They also illustrate, more generally, that all A.I.-related innovations are created, distributed, and controlled by elite influencers, not by everyday concerned end-users. A.I.-enabled influencers often have an unspoken agenda that may or may not be consonant with those of vulnerable, unsuspecting citizens. Consider a recent scandal involving Apple's iPhone batteries. It took a blog post by John Poole of Geekbench for Apple to admit that in 2016 they started programming older iPhones to slow down, allegedly to compensate for battery degradation that naturally occurs over time. However, Apple did not reveal that practice to their consumers beforehand. The average iPhone user probably was left thinking that the slowdown signaled their device's impending death. Kyle Wiens, iFixit CEO, charged, in fact, that Apple deliberately failed to publicize the availability of an $80 replacement battery in order to sell more new $700 or $800 iPhones (McMahon, 2017).

The Scientific Face of A.I.

What of artificial intelligence as a science? It makes sense to begin with a definition. And since almost no one of prominence has what I believe is a truly objective view of A.I., let's start with Merriam-Webster who defines it as "a branch of computer science dealing with the simulation of intelligent behavior in computers" and "the capability of a machine to imitate intelligent human behavior." Those are as objective statements as we are likely to find. The Cold Fusion website helps add to our understanding by providing a very comprehensive, thoughtful account of A.I., and is the foundation for much of what I am about to write next.

How about a succinct introduction? That starts by acknowledging John McCarthy, a computer scientist pioneer, who at the 1956 Dartmouth Conference proposed that A.I. should aspire to the following goals that I paraphrase:

1 Automatic Computation—Any job that a machine can do should be approximated by an "automatic calculator," provided that adequate programs can be written.
2. Program a Computer to Use a Language—Since human thought often requires language, a computer must be able to manipulate words to approximate rules of reasoning and of conjecture.
 3. Neuron Nets—Mimicking the human brain will demand that a computer can form concepts by applying a set of hypothetical neurons.
4. Theory of the Size of a Calculation—We must find a way to limit the number of calculations required to answer a problem. To do so, there must be an objective measure of calculation efficiency toward which we strive.
5. Self-improvement—An intelligent computer should be one that can develop its own intelligence and, therefore, its functionality and efficiency.
 6. Abstractions—Before computers can be designed to perform abstractions, we need to define the relevant types of abstraction and learn to create a machine capable of using sensory data to effect the abstractions.

7. Randomness and Creativity—Since creativity by definition is unscripted, the ideal computer is one that engages in sufficient, controlled randomness to produce novel, or at least non-obvious, solutions.

Some Applications of A.I. That Evolved After Dartmouth

The Dartmouth Conference ignited an A.I. rocket that continues to accelerate, upward and onward. The topic is far too broad to treat here in detail, but some aspects are critically important if we are to understand 21st century influencers. Think, for instance, about everyday examples of A.I. in action. To name a few, we have contemporary robots of many kinds. Some are fixed in place, capable only of riveting an automobile metal connection or two. Some are mobile, designed to sweep our floors. Taking an intellectual step-up, we encounter smart machines who can park our cars, or who can telephone, and, speaking in a very human voice, remind us to have our car inspected. At the pinnacle of A.I. competence are such services as provided by Modernizing Medicine, Inc. who claim: "Every day we help physicians increase efficiencies in their medical practices while improving both treatment and business outcomes…Our solution, EMA™, the Electronic Medical Assistant®, holds a distinctive position in healthcare technology that blends smoothly into your practice." Consider also the SpaceX Falcon 9 rocket whose "intellect" is so respected that the United States Air Force on February 19, 2017 permitted the rocket to "decide" whether to self-destruct the launch. That is, for the first time in the history of our world, there was no human seated at the mission flight control console to ensure rocket safety

.

Why You Should Care

To elaborate, SpaceX, or the Space Exploration Technologies Corporation, is a company founded by Elon Musk in 2002 to "revolutionize space technology, with the ultimate goal of enabling people to live on other planets" —the highest of high tech A.I. endeavors. Therefore, we must take notice when we read Maureen Dowd's March 31, 2017 Vanity Fair article entitled, "Elon Musk's Billion-dollar Crusade to Stop the A.I. Apocalypse."

Dowd details Musk's uncompromising campaign against A.I., including his opposition to the intelligentsia forces that support it. In short, he believes that A.I. is a grave danger to humanity because it incrementally is developing capabilities that are rivaling and threatening to surpass those of the brainiest people. Referring at times to A.I. efforts as moving toward "summoning the demon," he elaborates the nightmare scenario of a thinking machine that someday may be able to pursue and actualize personal goals counter to our species' well-being. The title of Fortune magazine's August 12, 2017 article penned by Lisa Marie Segarra also underscores the purported severity of threat: "Elon Musk: A.I. Poses 'Vastly More Risk than North Korea'."

Maureen Dowd reminds us, too, that Elon Musk's alarm is shared by such eminent intellectuals as Stephen Hawking and Bill Gates. And Joel Achenbach (2015) of the Washington Post adds to the list Max Tegmark, a Massachusetts Institute of Technology physics professor and Musk collaborator. Achenbach writes that "In April 2014, 33 people gathered in Tegmark's home to discuss existential threats from technology. They decided to form the Future of Life Institute … Tegmark put together an op-ed about the potential dangers of machine intelligence, lining up three illustrious co-authors: Nobel laureate physicist Frank Wilczek, artificial intelligence researcher Stuart Russell, and the biggest name in science, Stephen Hawking."

To be fair, there are many high-profile intellects who scoff at the A.I. "scare mongering," among them, Facebook's Mark Zuckerberg and Andrew Ng—highest high tech scientist for China's version of Google, Baidu. In fact, Ng goes so far as to raise the possibility that the Musk campaign might be little more than a brilliant marketing ploy.

Influencers Looking Out for Us

I certainly do not know who is right or wrong regarding a future A.I.-created Apocalypse that rids the planet of homo-sapiens. After all, everyday situations often, more or less, successfully apply A.I., such as the fact that according to a survey of Boeing 777 pilots, they spend only about seven minutes manually controlling their planes, the rest being A.I. automated (Markoff, 2015).

Despite what has been written thus far, a few influence professionals are on our side. Scott Galloway, New York University Professor of Marketing, is one par excellence who has taken on the four biggest of big corporations—Google, Facebook, Amazon, and Apple. In an entertaining, animated, and informative manner, he (Galloway, 2017) describes the behemoths in terms of body organs and bodily functions germane to them. Google is the brain, since we no longer need to remember or problem solve; we merely google the desired information. Facebook is the heart. Our Facebook page contains everyone who means anything to us and more; on it, we compare our worth vis-a-vis others, indicate what we like, and determine who "likes" and doesn't like what we post. Amazon is our gut, capable of providing virtually any material good we desire from an apricot to a zipper. And Apple is our groin, the locus of our sexual prowess. Apple products broadcast our potency, indicating our success and sophistication. Only one of the proverbial FAANG companies escapes Galloway's presentation—Netflix, the media mammoth that dominates the entertainment airways. Netflix enables us to binge into television-induced oblivion whenever that suits our purposes.

Steve Kroft, a journalist and correspondent for the television program Sixty Minutes ranks as a first class posfluencer from the ranks of the media. Like Galloway, he had the temerity to publically criticize Google, and did so during prime time when it had the most impact. His 2018 expose enabled credible spokespersons to make their cases. Gary Rebeck, a renowned antitrust lawyer, asserted that Google maintains monopolies over internet search and on-line advertising. Jonathan Taplin, director emeritus at the University of Southern California's Annenberg Innovation Lab, claimed that Google's business is primarily advertising, rather than technology. Jeremy Stoppelman, co-founder of Yelp, admitted that he was fortunate to have begun his business as early as he did, because Google now would "snuff out" new start-ups similar to his. Of all the commentators interviewed for Kroft's show, none was more courageous or blunt than the European Union's competition commissioner, Margrethe Vestage, who accused Google of illegal business practices. Among other things, she said she can prove that Google regularly uses its search algorithms to promote its own services by preferentially placing them at the earliest position of a search result. More specifically, she stated, "It's very difficult to find the rivals. Because on average, you'd find them only on page four in your search results" and I don't know anyone who goes to page four in their search result."

Probably due in large part to negative publicity, Google has become slightly more transparent and more willing to allow users a modicum of choice in what they see on their search pages. For instance, as of the present time, Google is permitting patrons some ability to customize advertisements. Google explains that "Ads are based on personal info you've added to your Google Account, data from advertisers that partner with Google, and Google's estimation of your interests. Choose any factor to learn more or update your preferences;" relevant choice menus then are presented. However, patrons who persevere throughout the new policy announcement eventually arrive at a section entitled,

"What doesn't change." The announcement then explains that ad personalization does **not**:

> "Stop all ads: If you turn off personalization,
> Google ads will use info like your general location
> or the content of the website you're visiting.
> Change other networks' ads: Your Google ad
> settings don't change other ad networks.
> Update your settings on signed-out devices: Learn
> how to get your ad preferences on all your
> devices.
> Keep your signed-out preferences without
> cookies: If you delete your cookies or use a
> browser that blocks cookies, your ad settings
> won't apply."

The ad personalization change does represent progress in limiting Google's influence over the pages that you see. But, it does not address most of the criticisms asserted by Kroft, Galloway, Rebeck, Taplin, Stoppelman, and Vestage. Moreover, cyber manipulation certainly is not confined to the giant, Google; the behemoth, Facebook, has been accused of social manipulation. Noel King (2018), for instance, reported an interview with Tim Wu, a former Federal Trade Commission senior advisor, who claimed that after "settling" a privacy dispute with the agency in 2011, Facebook never fully implemented the agreed-to terms.

Maya Kosoff (2018) also took Facebook to task. She reminded her readers how Mark Zuckerberg had vigorously attempted damage repair after the Facebook Cambridge Analytica privacy debacle: In March, 2018, he apologized to the nation in print by paying for full page newspaper advertisements. And in April, he apologized to Congress during a televised congressional hearing. However, by December, another privacy-centered fiasco was raging concerning Facebook's profiting from their users' information. To quote Kosoff, "Technically, neither Facebook nor any of its partners are guilty of selling user data—Facebook simply slots its users into categories based on their data, and sells the right to advertise against them, while companies like Netflix, Spotify, and Microsoft trade their own data for access to Facebook's unparalleled store. But taken together, there's no doubt that vast swaths of the tech sector benefit from a business model wherein user data is commoditized."

Although state attorneys general quickly reacted to the allegations against Facebook, the efforts of critics and governmental agencies are insufficient to control corporate influence intrusions. You must make it your business to know who is attempting to manipulate you, and implement your own resistance defenses.

In summary, I firmly do believe that our minds and wallets already are under withering, unremitting assault from contemporary weak forms of A.I. that have and will continue to advance the efforts of influence-hungry companies such as Google, Facebook, Amazon, and IBM, as well as similar businesses yet to emerge. Others who have not endorsed the A.I. Apocalypse nevertheless share concerns similar to mine.

Chamath Palihapitiya, a past Facebook vice president for user growth, expressed "tremendous guilt" about the part that he played in the company. For instance, in 2016 he told a Stanford Graduate School of Business audience that "I think we have created tools that are ripping apart the social fabric of how society works" by enabling "bad actors" to manipulate groups (Vincent, 2017). The sad fact is that even an apparently innocuous social strategy can be perverted. For instance, Dao Nguyen of Buzz, an Internet entertainment and social media company, recommends that advertisers simultaneously appeal to an individual's personal desire along with their wish for group affiliation, a strategy subsumed under the term "cultural cartography." She cites how her company produced a video bonding together people's love of chocolate, baking, and their desire to accept a challenge. That "Fudgiest Brownies Ever" posting competition was viewed 70 million times. You readily can imagine how bad actors might use bonding to create a video combining hatred of an out-group with a contest to create demeaning jokes about them.

Cathy O'Neil, a former University of California, Berkeley undergraduate, Harvard mathematics Ph.D., and Barnard College/Massachusetts Institute of Technology mathematics professor specifically addressed A.I. and its elements without limiting her attention to any single factor. She particularly worried about the influences of "big data" derived from computer algorithms that the public and private sectors use to make decisions that affect our confidence and general wellbeing. In her words, (O'Neil, 2017)

> Algorithms are opinions embedded in code. It's really different from what you think most people think of algorithms. They think algorithms are objective and true and scientific. That's a marketing trick. It's also a marketing trick to intimidate you with algorithms, to make you trust and fear algorithms because you trust and fear mathematics. A lot can go wrong when we put blind faith in big data.

O'Neil's concerns echo what I have written previously: An influencer sometimes presents what seems to be an impressive array of data from an impressive source to disarm your resistance to their goals. Although we all can be intimidated by such data, those who value objective and/or scientific information are especially at risk. You realize that you do not know everything; you want to remain "open-minded," and that's understandable. But you cannot blithely accept anyone's data because you never know how accurate, relevant, unbiased, or contextualized to your situation that "objective information" is. To O'Neil's concerns, I must reiterate another critical one: it's not just people using A.I. that should alarm us. We also must be very concerned about A.I.'s relentless, incremental, and inexorable march toward the day when A.I. will be using us more than we use it. The Swedish philosopher, Nick Bostrom (2015), is most concerned. He sounds the alarm on A.I.'s existential threat to humanity, suggesting that "Making superintelligent A.I. is a really hard challenge. Making superintelligent A.I. that is safe involves some additional challenge on top of that. The risk is that if somebody figures out how to crack the first challenge without also having cracked the additional challenge of ensuring perfect safety."

CHAPTER 23: Brain Dissection & Re-programming

The latest and most hyped influence approach is "neuromarketing." Since most would-be money makers and persuasion peddlers of all sorts want to be as effective as possible, they have seized upon exalted neuroscience as their Holy Grail, imagining how wonderful it could be actually to crack open your brain to understand and manipulate your thoughts, feelings, and behaviors— pushing, pulling, and prodding them in whatever direction that they choose. Neuromarketers are the special forces of marketing, equipped with all the latest training, high tech weaponry, and always plotting their attack strategies. They of course are marketing themselves, as well as their methods. Some have been described as "buyologists" (Satel & Lilenfeld, 2013) who grossly exaggerate their capabilities in order to "sell themselves" to companies eager to jump on the neuroscience bandwagon.

The brain invasion beachhead has been well-established, and there is no absence of eager combatants. Roger Dooley provides an introduction on his website, neurosciencemarketing.com, where he has posted the following companies as primarily engaged in neuromarketing of various types:

> Affectiva, Brain Intelligence, Buyology, Emotion Explorer Lab, FKF Applied Research, Forbes Consulting, Forebrain, Gallup & Robinson, HCD Research, Innerscope Research, Institute of Sensory Analysis, Keystone Network, Labiometrics, Merchant Mechanics, Mindlab International, Mindmetic, MindSign, MSW Research (MSW/LAB), Neurensics, Neuro-Insight, NeuroFocus, Neurosense, NeuroSpire, Olson Zaltman Associates, One To One Insight, Realeyes, SalesBrain, Sands Research, Sensory Logic, and True Impact Marketing

Dooley specifically noted that "more firms are being added to this list," and invited readers to provide updates to him. So, brace yourself.

Surprisingly absent from Dooley's list are two very heavy hitter neuromarketers—Nielsen, the famous media raters, and Emotive Analytics who claim to "specialize in consumer research that reveals the emotional dynamics of consumer behavior." Given their scope and reach, we will consider neuromarketing through the lens of both companies. Please know that I am not suggesting that either group has nefarious intentions. Given their reputations and accomplishments, I assume that they truly believe in the value and profitability of what they are doing. However, that does not mean that you should!

Battle-Hardened Troops

Founded in 1923 to sell engineering performance surveys, the AC Nielsen Company pioneered market research. Having been at the top of the game from the outset, it is natural that Nielsen has parachuted into neuromarketing with both feet.

Nielsen's consumer neuroscience webpage boasts that their approach is able to "capture a more comprehensive view of the non-conscious aspects of consumer decision-making with the most complete set of neuroscience tools at a global scale." More specifically, they claim that they can assess non-conscious responses, create brand value via emotion, deliver granular diagnosis, and guarantee efficient and timely decision making. Nielsen, of course, is marketing to the marketers, and, understandably, speaks in trade parlance. Since virtually any competent marketer can determine a consumer's conscious response, Nielsen does the unconscious. Since virtually any can promote brand value via intellectual argument, Nielsen does emotion. Since virtually any can execute a gross diagnosis,

Nielsen's is granular. And since virtually any can promise efficient, timely decision, Nielsen guarantees it.

Let's look at the armament Nielsen has amassed to empower their campaigns by briefly describing a couple relevant psychological studies. It is important for you to be aware that science and Nielsen frequently combine two or more information extraction modalities, and that the information from different modalities sometimes is at least partially redundant.

Biometrics

Biometrics is a rather general, even vague, term used to refer to physiological measures of many types, such as visual tracking, brain activity, blood pressure and heart rate. These measures allegedly indicate whether an individual is turned on, turned off, or indifferent to the stimuli presented.

Imagining sweet advertising benefits, the Mars Company, of candy-bar fame, funded research by Steven Bellman and his associates (2017) to investigate biometric factors that determine the effectiveness of television advertising. The Bellman group looked at 20 Mars brands promoted in over 100 advertisements. In this case, biometrics included assessing the frequency of smile-like expressions, interval between heartbeats (a measure of stress), and galvanic skin response (a skin reactivity measure) from over 1000 subjects. The results purportedly indicated that biometrics correctly predicted product sales 78 percent of the time, whereas survey-based tests managed only 58 percent.

EEG

The idea here is to determine by EEG the extent of engagement with a given influence method, and the subject's emotional response to it, if any. Evidence is accumulating that the EEG does produce worthwhile data. For instance, Rafal Ohme and his colleagues (2009) combined EEG, EMG (a muscle tension measure), and galvanic skin response (the aforementioned skin reactivity measure) to assess a skin care product ad. They found that the measures were able to differentiate consumer reaction to two versions of the ad, despite the fact that the experimental subjects were not conscious of the difference. Bhattacharya, et al. (2017) explored the electrical brain activity of subjects during TV and radio advertisements that included strategic, tactical, or no background music. For the study, strategic music was defined as music that previously had been used during consecutive ad campaigns. And tactical music was music that had been varied during consecutive ad campaigns. The investigators concluded that electrical brain activity reliably differed during the three conditions (strategic, tactical, or no background music), and provided specific recommended "indications for an optimum use of background music to promote advert effectiveness."

A more recent study, conducted by Garczarek-Bąk and Disterheft (2018), also supported the value of EEG for marketing. In that case, purchasing decisions were found to be correlated with activity in the brain's frontal lobes. Moreover, asymmetry of frontal lobe activity also predicted whether preferences were for buying a name brand product, or a private label one.

Facial Coding

As mentioned, the Mars study assessed frequency of smiling, an obvious index of facial expression. However, since smiling is the prototypic positive affect expression, it is not surprising that smiling is a frequent facial coding component. Alicia Kulczynski, Jasmina Ilicic, and Stacey M. Baxter (2016) wanted to know whether smiling could transfer from an agent of selling to consumers. To do so, the researchers conducted three studies. Significant findings resulted. A smiling agent induced a feeling of consumer pleasure, but only when the agent was familiar and appeared to match the product being endorsed. For instance, a smiling buff person depicted in an ad for a fitness product would be likely to cause the effect, whereas an obese one would not. Accordingly, source-product consistency was required to cause the positive emotion associated with the agent to be favorably associated with the brand and to increase the consumer's intention to buy.

Eye Tracking

Since eyes are windows to the soul, soul-searching marketers look to the eyes. However, eyes are integrated with the entire body, so researchers regularly combine eye tracking with other consumer senses and behaviors to determine their maximal usefulness.

Klemens M. Knoeferle et al. (2016) chose to explore how the meanings of sounds cue consumers' eye tracking. In five experiments, they presented sounds associated with using products, or jingles appropriate to the products, and observed product-related eye movements. The research group found that even during the early stages of product consideration, the relevant sounds did increase visual search and selection. Reaction times decreased, especially when the visual display was complex rather than simple. It was noteworthy that the enhanced visual processing occurred not only for familiar brands, but also for unfamiliar ones. This implied that the sound enhancement helped new visual associations to form beyond that which normally would have been expected.

Self-report

Self-report is a most traditional way to determine what is on the minds of those whom you want to influence. Like virtually every other marketer or marketer-to-marketers, Nielsen does assess what people say about areas of interest.

You undoubtedly are familiar with self-report and probably have participated in some fashion, at least when your medical provider presents a questionnaire. Therefore, rather than citing psychological research, I merely will mention how Nielsen instructs respondents about the way to complete their famous television surveys.

To their candidate survey completers, Nielsen explains the ground rules, such as how to answer survey questions, list local TV channels, tell who in the home is watching, specify which programs are watched and how to return the survey. The instructions emphasize the survey's importance, and explains that the money contained in the Nielsen survey envelope is a token of the company's appreciation.

All of this effort of course is merely to capture what presumably are the honest, conscious behaviors of the survey participants.

Implicit Testing

Whereas self-report is an individual's conscious belief, an implicit belief is non-conscious, at least at the moment that the opinion is delivered. You can appreciate, then, that marketers want to know implicit as well as self-report beliefs. To explore that dichotomy, Walla, Koller, Brenner, and Bosshard (2017) employed an evaluative conditioning strategy. That is, they sought to change subjects' attitudes toward those subjects' ten most disliked and ten most liked brand names.

Consistent with previous studies, Walla and associates concluded that evaluative conditioning did change attitudes, even for established brands. They specifically addressed the facts that attitudes have three components—knowledge, emotions, and behaviors—and two aspects—explicit and implicit. Most important for our purpose was that the researchers concluded that evaluative conditioning primarily affected the emotional and implicit components rather than the cognitive and explicit ones. Therefore, the evaluative conditioning influence was essentially unconscious, and beyond the affected individuals' awareness and control.

Functional Magnetic Resonance Imaging

One could argue that functional magnetic resonance imaging (FMRI) is the most "neuro' of the neuromarketing dimensions mentioned on Nielsen's website. FMRI peers deep within the brain to measure its activity through observing changes in its blood flow, and is critically important since neuronal activation and cerebral blood flow are tightly related.

The example chosen for our FMRI discussion is one describing the work of Amanda S. Bruce, et al. (2014) who targeted attitudes toward food. More precisely, it assessed consumers' neurological reactions to food prices, and to ethics and safety related to the technology employed to produce the food.

The researchers measured subjects' openness to food and their neophobia. As you might guess, the former term related to a willingness to try new things and the latter, to fear of the same. When subjects viewed food images and attributes of both food price and technology, the dorsolateral prefrontal cortex (under and side portion of the front-most cerebrum) revealed changed activation. That meant that working memory (the memory needed to perform such real-time routine tasks as remembering a new phone number long enough to make a call) and uncertainty both were engaged. Based on their findings, Bruce and colleagues advised that food labels should not contain ambiguous information, as that stresses consumers' cognitive abilities and exacerbates their sense of uncertainty.

The Nielsen's website boasts about the company's attention to biometrics, EEG, facial coding, eye tracking, self-report, implicit testing, and FMRI. FMRI is noteworthy mostly because it checks off all the proverbial boxes of significance for neuromarketing. It is not that Nielsen alone is aware of the dimensions; any truly comprehensive neuromarketing company would want to cover as many of the dimensions as possible. The advantage of their comprehensive approach is that Nielsen legitimately can claim and advertise their extensive coverage, and their ability to determine which neurometrics are most valid for what.

Raw Recruits

Despite the fact that Paul Conner, company founder and CEO, has been a consumer researcher for over thirty years, his Emotive Analytics, started in 2004, is a newbie when compared with Nielsen. That said, since it boasts an impressive list of credential, seasoned troops, Emotive Analytics is well worth mentioning.

As the company name suggests, Emotive Analytics wants us to believe that emotions are their special province. Apropos of its Latin root (emovere "move out"), emotion moves us; it takes control. Marketers of course seek to move us toward that which they promote. And there is a wealth of psychological science that supports the beliefs that emotion is a prime mover of human thought and action. Typical is Gerald Zaltman, professor at Harvard Business School, who has been quoted as saying that "95 percent of our purchase decision making takes place in the subconscious mind." (Schlesinger, 2003). Although the subconscious mind includes thoughts as well as emotions, emotions figure most prominently. The website Emotive Analytics' mission statement is "We specialize in consumer research that reveals the emotional dynamics of consumer behavior—including subconscious, implicit, System 1 emotional dynamics. This inspires emotional marketing for increased revenue," with System 1 describing thought that is instinctive, quick, and emotion-dominated. Thus, Emotive Analytics is cultivating a rock-solid brand identity that would appeal to anyone impressed with neuromarketing.

Emotive Analytics explains that they use the term "emotional dynamics" to include cognition and experience, along with affect (emotion), and the combination explains "why people do what they do." To support their claims, they enumerate the range of professionals whom they involve, including Social and Cognitive Psychologists, Clinical Psychologists (also "Psychodramatists") Psychophysiologists (also "Neuroscientitsts"), Anthropologists, and Behavioral Economists. Having listed that cadre of professionals, Emotive Analytics specifies that their approach employs: Implicit Association Measurement, Relaxed-Mind-State (Hypnosis) Interviewing, Psychodrama, Metaphor Elicitation and Text Analytics, Anthropological Ethnography, Psychophysiology, and Traditional Explicit Data Collection. If you are not impressed by that comprehensive neurological-psychological armamentarium, you are beyond being impressed by any marketer!

All this emphasis on emotion and System 1 requires us to take a step back to understand some rationales that govern neuromarketing. Although I do not believe that he is involved directly with Emotive Analytics and his ideas are not linked specifically to them, Patrick Renvoise (2007) explains some common beliefs about the emotional bases of marketing.

Renvoise approaches neuromarketing by referring to the triune brain, attributed to Paul D. MacLean (1990), which suggests that our brains are divided into reptilian, paleomammalian, and neomammalian regions. To grossly simplify: we share the reptilian with lizards, the paleomammalian with dogs and cats, and the neomammalian with great apes. Since MacLean's reptilian division is most primitive, instinctual, non-rational, and stimulus-response, it is used by Renvoise as a metaphor to describe neuromarketing strategies that he believes are most automatic and effective.

Because Renvoise purports that the reptilian brain only responds to six stimulus situations, he advises aspiring influencers to approach their targets accordingly. First, appeal to *self-centeredness*. Make sure that everything is all about them. Second, exploit *stimulus contrast*. Juxtapose your idea, object, or whatever alongside something that makes it pop. Third, what you present must be *tangible*. Find some concrete object to represent your message. Fourth, since the lizard in us attends mostly to *beginnings and endings*, start and finish strong. Don't worry too much about the middle. Fifth, consistent with the one picture is worth a thousand words meme, emphasize *visual communication over auditory*. And last but certainly not least, make *emotion* work for you whenever and wherever possible.

Renvoise even outlines a step-by-step plan for marketers to follow. That advice is particularly emotion-based. He asserts that the persuader must "diagnose the pain of your customers." Next, "differentiate your claims," meaning that the claim must be made unmistakably clear, distinctive, and consistent. Once that is achieved, the persuader has to "demonstrate the gains" to reveal obvious benefits that derive from the claim. And, of course, the steps must be "delivered to the reptilian brain," meaning that you have packaged your delivery to correctly address the six stimulus situations to which lizards respond.

Take Away

I have read and heard neuromarketers so often assert that "customers don't know what they want" that I just had to google that sentence, resulting in 83,600,000 hits. A moment's reflection suggests the reason for the neuromarketing mantra: if customers knew what they wanted, there would be no advantage to neuro-based techniques. Neuromarketers must "persuade" their clients that only electronic brain wizardry is sufficient to determine customers' real desires, and that the more neuron-probing the instrumentation, the more effective the method.

The neuromarketing mantra hides an implicit assumption that no marketer ever would utter aloud: customers are so out of touch with themselves that they readily can be manipulated, if you know how to push their reptilian buttons. The mantra also offers a marketer-soothing rationalization for their manipulations which is that the persuasion is merely educating targets about what is **best** for them, since ethical marketers (and almost all convince themselves that they are ethical) only would promote the best.

We never should trust that influencers with our neuro-information will be ethical and/or will proceed in ways that serve our best interests. The bioethicist, lawyer, philosopher, and Duke professor, Nita Farahany certainly does not trust them. In fact, Nita is so concerned about the dangers of neuro-surveillance and neuro-influence, she (Farahany, 2018) advocates "special protection for our mental privacy." Dr. Farahany wants every person to have the legal right and the legal redress to safeguard their personal information. The professor goes as far as to recommend that those rights be included in and protected by the Universal Declaration of Human Rights, applicable to all people, everywhere.

CHAPTER 24: You Ultimately Determine Your Influences

Justifiably Paranoid began with a circumscribed sniper metaphor and proceeded with a more inclusive war metaphor. Central among the ideas cited was President Dwight D. Eisenhower's Military-Industrial Complex Speech. Repeatedly, we have seen that professional influence efforts truly amount to a variant of mental warfare. With only a few word changes, mental influencer assaults are consistent with the guidelines regarding military psychological warfare operations as defined in the January 7, 2010 United States Department of Defense Joint Publication 3-13.2 :

> The specific purpose of psychological operations (PSYOP) is to influence foreign audience perceptions and subsequent behavior as part of approved programs in support of USG policy and military objectives. PSYOP professionals follow a deliberate process that aligns commander's objectives with an analysis of the environment; select relevant target audiences (TAs); develop focused, culturally, and environmentally attuned messages and actions; employ sophisticated media delivery means and produce observable, measurable behavioral responses.

My point has been to sensitize you to the fact that 21st century marketing campaigns assault us from America's public and private sectors. In war, the military hierarchy: plan a general strategy, train the troops, surveil the enemy to learn its strengths and weaknesses, infiltrate with spies, and adjust to changing battle field conditions. Since marketers do that, you must behave similarly to avoid being overrun. *Justifiably Paranoid* is a manual that you mindfully can employ to be able to do so.

The last two chapters have illustrated that elite influencers know what they want, and increasingly are exploiting science to get it.

They believe they can invade your neural networks and manipulate your thoughts and feelings through cyberwarfare. The influencers know that the battle is in progress, and hope to catch you unawares in a September 11, 2001 or December 7, 1941 sneak attack fashion.

Fortunately, the elite special force influencers do not know that you now understand their tactics. That is your ultimate secret weapon. Hopefully, you will remain justifiably paranoid and, at minimum, conduct a guerilla campaign of resistance.

Being forewarned and forearmed against direct elite influencer assaults is essential. However, as we have seen, harmful influencers do not always operate directly on you. They infiltrate your life in myriad non-obvious or subtle ways. Let's conclude by again addressing their two most important entry portals.

Homophily and Heterophily

You almost certainly will not be subjected directly to an elite marketer's fMRI scan or to his other A.I.-enabled neuro-physiological machines. Rather, you are much more likely to be affected by everyday marketers using their "scientific" knowledge to infiltrate your social networks, and to booby trap your personal predilections.

As the words suggest, social networks are assemblages of people who have some connection(s) to each other. You will recall that one of Cialdini's seven marketing principles is "social consensus," meaning that you often look to your interpersonal reference groups to make decisions concordant with theirs. Psychology has confirmed this tendency toward "homophily"— love of the same—in studies investigating the adoption of innovations. The undisputed expert in the field, Everett M. Rogers, popularized the concept in his 1962 book, *Diffusion of Innovations*, whose last edition was released in 2003.

According to Rogers, four factors determine the extent to which ideas spread. They are: the particular innovation offered, the time period during which it is extant, the channel by which it is communicated; and, to my major point, the social context in which it is embedded. As is common sense, some people are the innovators, and others vary in the speed with which they adopt the innovation that they eventually do adopt, if they adopt it at all. For our discussion of influence, consider that many of your most important decisions were at some point a reaction to something that, in the broad sense, was an innovation to you. Your social network probably played a significant or major role in your innovation-oriented decision and in your decisions in general.

Most people intuitively perceive the power of social networks. In fact, the 75-year-plus Harvard Study of Adult Development—that combines current longitudinal data with longitudinal data first obtained in 1939—has indicated that good relationships keep us happier and healthier, and that bad ones do the opposite. But, when decisions are involved, some members of our network tend to be more influential than others. Hikaru Yamamoto and Naohiro Matusmura (2009) found that word-of-mouth innovation influence is determined not by your network member's opinion leadership alone, but also by "optimal heterophily," meaning that you probably would be more open to an acquaintance who is different in that she is "slightly more knowledgeable" than you, but not a "distant expert." Professional persuaders understand, and that is why they always try to recruit more adventuresome social network standouts. Think home parties that have moderately knowledgeable, but high profile persons marketing to their compadres.

You might not resent your neighbor-marketer making a few dollars in commission when you buy some make-up or auto parts. Perhaps you will be the next to sponsor a sales party and your friend can reciprocate. But widen the scope of your scrutiny to include the company that provides the products to the parties, and you might be less sympathetic to home-parties as a financial system. Economists have a concept called "concentrated benefits and dispersed costs," meaning that a large number of persons at the bottom of a social pyramid each pay a little in order that a few persons at the top reap high returns. For instance, in 2017, the cosmetics and beauty company Avon Products Incorporated reported a net income of $21.7 million, due in large part to its home-party orientation. By contrast, the party-givers earned a pittance.

Although this book has focused on professional influencers, I often have emphasized that your relatives, friends, and acquaintances (rfa) sometimes can exert the most posfluence or negfluence. We have discussed hub persons who often are rfas, and who, therefore, have regular access to you. Be aware, that professional influencers increasingly attempt to recruit rfas into their marketing army to serve as "micro-influencers."

Since people always have influenced those around them, one might dismiss any fuss about micro-influencers. However, again, it is a matter of the manner and extent of the current practice. Today, professional influencers easily and quickly can assemble squads, platoons, or battalions of everyday people to fight their battles—it is a matter of scale. With enough money, deep-pocketed pros can create and fund so extensive an army that each soldier's victory produces results that far exceed the cost of maintaining him. Think Avon representatives created via a rapid cloning procedure. Each representative brings in a few hundred dollars, but their combined successes aggregate company income into millions.

Consider the Soviet Cold War strategy implemented in East Germany from about 1950 to 1989. Having lost about fifteen percent of the empire's population during World War II, the

Soviets were determined to keep their feet on the German throat. To facilitate that goal, they created the Ministry for State Security (Stasi), a secret police army. That army however, derived its real power from everyday East German citizens that they "recruited" to spy for them. According to Britannica.com, "By 1989 the Stasi relied on 500,000 to 2,000,000 collaborators as well as 100,000 regular employees, and it maintained files on approximately 6,000,000 East German citizens—more than one-third of the population."

The Soviets rationalized that informants were critical for the motherland's survival, and they did all they could to convince German collaborators that spying was in their best interests, as well. Similarly, today's professional influencers believe that they need rfa and other people to be their hub micro-influencers so as to stave off invasion from competing influence armies. That is true for pros of any type, including but not limited to politicians, other government officials, media controllers, celebrities, salespersons and advertisers, educators, and scientists that we have considered within this book. Hopefully, persons subjected to them and their professional micro-influence propaganda war machines will be able to resist far better than the East Germans did.

Because powerful individuals and institutions will be incrementally more effective in influencing you if they appeal to and align with your social networks, you need to be wary of following your relationship herd. Try your best to make decisions that you customize for yourself, and not ones that you embrace mostly because they enhance acceptance by your group.

You and Your Predilections

We often are advised to take control. So, the question naturally arises: take control of what? Where do we look to promote our well-being? Since I discussed this issue at length in my

Conversation: Striving, Surviving, and Thriving book, I will address it only briefly here.

As implied earlier, there are four critical sources of tension that we target for improvement, and that determine our physical and mental well-being: body, environment, thoughts, and feelings (BETF). These four elements are always interacting, and always affecting us to some extent. A change in any single element of the BETF system can produce a change in any of the others, although not necessarily at the same order of magnitude. Most often when we seek health, we desire to change BETF to a more optimal level. Imagine the four as housed within a vehicle that is the self and that has four functional steering wheels. Any individual BETF element or combination of elements can steer the self while the remaining one or ones go along for the ride.

Each BETF element also exists both as trait and state tension. To simplify our discussion, let's illustrate by talking only in terms of the body. Trait body tension refers to our modal level of physiologic tension—our usual resting level. Trait body tension differs from person to person, much as blood pressure does. For instance, a person who always seems "uptight" is high in trait body tension while a "laid back" person is low in trait body tension. Like blood pressure, however, body tension is not completely static for any single person. State body tension describes an individual's tension fluctuations within his trait-circumscribed range, temporary peaks or valleys soon replaced by his modal, resting level.

A resting level of trait tension represents a readiness that permits us to quickly respond to everyday circumstances of life. An individual's resting level of trait tension can be subjectively comfortable or uncomfortable. In the latter case, the uncomfortable condition could be due to such factors as physical pain, noxious environment, disturbing thought, or dysfunctional mood.

Regardless of the comfort or discomfort of the trait condition, our physical and mental selves periodically are roused from the complacency of this relatively stable, resting trait level and moved into a changed state. Physical change is perceived by us when it exceeds a given biological threshold. The change can be caused by alterations in the internal milieu, such as when blood sugar or hormonal levels drop precipitously. Or it could be caused by an external source as when a cold blast of air chills our skin. Mental change is perceived by us when thoughts or feelings occur that are qualitatively or quantitatively different from the extant baseline. When any one of the BETF constants deviates from its trait baseline significantly, the foregrounding of that factor amounts to increased "press" (pressure to seize our attention and/or to influence our behavior) prompting us to seek satisfaction of the foregrounded constant.

The changed tone of the constant sometimes evolves slowly over time, as when people become less aggressive with age. Or the changed tone sometimes erupts into our consciousness, as when we are jolted by a leg cramp, surprised to see a sky that abruptly turns black and foreboding, alarmed precipitously to realize that we forgot to turn off the oven, or overwhelmed by an unanticipated emotion. Moreover, the constants interactively influence each other. Sometimes there is conflict among them, as when, through our thoughts, we "talk ourselves" into engaging in overly strenuous physical exercise, pitting thought against body. But more often the constants achieve a harmonious amalgamation appropriate to an individual in her milieu. For instance, happy thoughts typically occur in a context of relatively happy feelings, happy bodily conditions, and a happy environmental setting,

When a changed state occurs from our current trait baseline, we habituate to it and establish a new trait-circumscribed baseline. We then perceive subsequent changes as deviations from this, habituate to the new condition, establish a new trait-circumscribed baseline, and so the dynamic process continues.

How about a concrete example to simplify the admittedly abstract ideas above? For instance, as I walk along the beach, I may be totally absorbed in and conscious of vacation-related ideas, and oblivious to my reddening skin, the roar of the surf, and my serene mood. At this point my conscious physical and mental life is steered by my thoughts. However, in the next second, I could slash my toe on a sharp seashell, instantly foreground my bodily self, background the heretofore engrossing vacation-related thoughts, and direct myself to restoring my body-oriented GBH [recall that this abbreviation means good, better, and homeostatic] integrity. My previous thoughts can be lost forever. Instead, I function at a reactive level of state arousal, become attentive to my bodily self, and direct my activities toward my injury, comfort, and safety. Subsequently, I habituate to the "shock" of my injury, establish a new trait-circumscribed resting level of bodily tension, background the concern about my toe, and foreground some other BETF element. In short, mental life can effortlessly move back and forth among BETF elements. The more you can control each of your BETF elements, then, the more you can take control of your overall physical and mental health, and the more you can control external influences.

The aforementioned walk along a beach, even along a secluded beach, does not insulate us from unsolicited external influence. Since I enjoy walking or running surfside, I often listen with my smartphone to available Internet lectures. Because I usually am in bright sun and my phone keys are small, I don't mind that the talks often launch one after another with no intervention on my part. However, I recently was surprised when I first noticed that the Ted.com site not only was launching the next lecture (autoplay), but also was interjecting marketing commercials between talks, such as one by an insurer boasting of an alliance with an investment company. Curious, I later watched the same

Ted talk on television. There, I discovered not only that the commercial self-launched, but that I could not fast forward through the ad, as was possible with the Ted talk itself.

Even though I realize that the automatic launching process is commonly employed by many influence assault troops to keep us locked onto their sites, I accept that I am responsible for either attending to or disconnecting from any information that assails me. So, I usually choose to ignore the fact that I am being influenced by whoever wrote the algorithm that determines the automatic launch, and either listen or cancel the proffered message based on my extant interests.

All this means that I can be as vulnerable as anyone else to predilection-oriented influences. And that is what influencers count on. We can refer again to some of Cialdini's seven, this time to "commitment," "consistency," "liking," and "identity." Any savvy person who has access to my Internet or other choices over time easily will deduce my commitments, consistencies, likings, and identity-orientations. With those in mind and a little imagination, he then can exploit my predilections, strategically and subtly sprinkling into his presentation, messages central to his agendas. By doing that, he will be tapping into my so-called "reptilian brain" and perhaps into my higher-level cortical regions as well.

Predilections almost always reside within the proverbial reptilian unconscious, and evidence the automaticity about which I have written. Therefore, you must develop and maintain a strong habit of justifiable paranoia. That supra-skeptical orientation needs to be as near unconscious as it can be. The more reptilian your skepticism, the better off you will be. That means that you will be able to control your decision making process to the extent humanly possible.

Making Decisions

Most accounts of decision making look much like the one listed on the University of Massachusetts, Dartmouth website that presents decisions in a coldly rational manner. According to their paradigm, the decider should follow common sense steps: identify the decision issue, collect appropriate information, consider alternatives, evaluate the alternatives, select the best alternative, act accordingly, determine whether the decision has produced the result that you sought, and recycle through the steps, if necessary. Steven Novella (2012) adopts a similarly rational approach to decisions. He advises you to examine your logic and to think through the implications of your beliefs. Novella encourages humility in accepting what you do not know, and in being comfortable with uncertainty. He suggests that you check with others and seriously consider ideas different from yours, especially those for which there is a large consensus of opinion.

The Dartmouth and Novella schemes are higher cortical, ignoring virtually everything that has been said thus far about the unconscious features of decisions. You will remember, however, that Harvard Business School professor, Gerald Zaltman, asserted that 95 percent of purchasing decisions occur subconsciously, and Emotive Analytics said that they specialize in System 1 emotional dynamics. Many marketers are quick to cite "System 1," since Daniel Kahneman, earned a Noble Prize mostly because of his work around that idea. In brief, he advised that System 1 executes unconsciously-based decisions that are intuitive—rather than reflective—fast, and frequently emotional. Zaltman and Kahneman would have little faith in the value of the Dartmouth formula for most significant everyday decisions.

Antonio R. Damasio (1999), Professor of Neuroscience, Psychology and Philosophy, is even more emphatic about the centrality of emotion and the unconscious. He asserts that virtually all practical decisions literally are gut-level decisions. In fact, he believes that consciousness only occurs when we perceive a bodily change in response to our internal and/or external environment. If you accept Damasio's thesis, that means that when you make a meaningful decision, you first have experienced a physiological change with a significant emotional component, typically with no awareness of the process whatsoever. A meaningful decision, by definition, is one associated with emotion, whether or not you realize that at the time during which you choose. The emotion need not be monumental, but it is significant if you ultimately act in accordance with the decision. If you do not act, then no substantial decision actually occurred anyway.

System 1, unconscious, gut-level decisions certainly are most likely to occur when an influencer exploits our homophily, social networks, and predilections. We all find it so much easier to decide when we consciously or unconsciously expect that our decision will be the same as that of our reference group and/or what we have done in the past. And, obviously, the stronger our history of making such group- and/or self-consonant decisions, the less inclined we will be to question them, or even think twice about them.

Although I just have emphasized homophily, social networks, and predilections, I do not mean to minimize the other primary vehicles of influence. We have seen that influence can be exerted not only by people per se, but also by their institutions. And we may be less alert when institutions push our emotional buttons. Similarly, not only predilections but certain objects, ideas, processes, and situations can give us an emotional rush. Each primary influence vehicle singly and in combination has the potential to be manipulated by influencers to sway our decisions. It is just that homophily, social networks, and predilections often tend to be prepotent, because they usually are associated with all the other influence vehicles. You can be sure that professional persuaders will not limit themselves to any single influence vehicle; they will use all the strategies and perspectives advocated by Fogg, Cialdini, and other influence gurus to channel you toward their own goals. And the more they can move you emotionally, the more likely their success.

You, however, can reduce your emotional vulnerability to persuasion. Decades of psychological studies have shown that you are more receptive to influence when you are in a positive mood (Forgas, (2003). When you are feeling well, for instance, you don't usually want to bicker or otherwise cause trouble. During positive states then, when someone is attempting to sway you, you must rein-in that susceptibility through conscious effort. But susceptibility is not limited exclusively to your positive states. In some circumstances you also can be swayed easily during negative states. If you and a persuader have been talking about an injustice that you recently experienced, the persuader might be able to induce you to inflict retaliatory harm that you ordinarily would never consider. Seunghee Han and her colleagues (2007) showed that decisions frequently vary relative to specific dimensions of positive or negative emotion. They posited six dimensions—pleasantness, responsibility, attentional activity, personal control, anticipated effort, and certainty. To simplify, you are more likely to be influenced when the persuader can craft a message that aligns well with each emotion-specific dimension. Suppose that you are discouraged and have the following six dimension profile: Pleasantness-low, Responsibility-high, Attentional Activity-low, Personal Control-low, Anticipated Effort-high, and Certainty-low. That emotion profile might make you more susceptible to a person who could help you in one or more of the following ways—feel more pleasant, alleviate your responsibility burden, reduce your need to be actively attentive, increase your perceived self-control, reduce your effort expenditure, and enhance your certainty. If the influencer is a true professional, he/she will manipulate one or more of those dimensions merely be enacting the persuasion strategies that they have been taught and have cultivated over the years.

So, the more you control your emotions, the more resistant you are to unwanted influences. Of course, emotional control is much easier said than done. The essential point of *Justifiably Paranoid* is that you must develop a strong, enduring habit that enables you to maintain skepticism robust enough to resist the power of System 1. That is, you want to deliberate internally and/or externally before you succumb to someone's influence. That certainly does not guarantee that all decisions will be the best ones, but it at least should allow you to accept responsibility for the decisions that you do make.

Action Tendencies

Decision making depends not only on cognitive processing and emotional response, but also on behavioral action. After being subjected to an influence—sought or unsought—you have a chance to respond motorically. According to Dean Keith Simonton (2016), whenever you have an opportunity to respond overtly, three factors come into play. First, there is a particular statistical likelihood that you personally will respond at all. Some influence options will evoke a strong response tendency, some a moderate one, and some of low probability. Second, some of your potential responses will be adaptive; some will not. And, finally, even before you respond, you usually will have a general sense of whether your response will produce a successful or an unsuccessful outcome. There are eight general classes of responses:

Routine or Habitual Responses
Lucky Guesses or Other Impulsive Actions.
Recurrent Irrational Maladaptive Responses
Problem Finding That Defies Conventional Expectations
Irrationally Failing To Do What You Know Is Good For You

Responding Creatively
Suppressing Your Usual Response
Exploring Various Behavioral Options

Let's apply Simonton's notions to you, presuming that you are sleeping poorly and looking for a solution. And since a detailed explanation of his ideas would extend beyond what it appropriate to this book, I merely will present schematic examples. That way, all readers will derive a basic sense of his concepts, and the most interested ones can process and pursue further information on their own.

Imagine that you have been exposed to one or more influences regarding your sleep, ranging from professional guidance to that which you received from a colleague, book, or other source. How do the eight response tendencies apply to the way you might react to the influence? Knowing how the eight classes of options affect you will help increase your ability to become more introspective about your response tendencies in general. Let's add that you are very stressed, and in desperate need of more sleep. To make the point, I provide examples of extreme responses, both positive and negative as follows:

Routine or Habitual Responses - Positive = You listen to your doctor who prescribes a sleeping pill, because you always follow her advice. Negative = You do not fill the prescription because you always ignore your doctor's advice.
Take Away = If it's not broken don't fix it, but if it is, do something different.

Lucky Guesses or Other Impulsive Actions - Positive = Although you do not need one, you buy a new bed and sleep much better. Negative = You waste your money by buying an unneeded new bed. It doesn't help, and you make no other effort to address your sleep problem.
Take Away = It's usually better to look before you leap.

Recurrent Irrational Maladaptive Responses - Positive = By definition, there are no positive outcomes. Negative = You continue with your typical maladaptive reaction to problems which is to rationalize; in this case you recall that many famous people, such as Benjamin Franklin, Thomas Edison, and Winston Churchill, slept far worse than you do.
Take Away = You are not Benjamin Franklin, Thomas Edison, or Winston Churchill.

Problem Finding That Defies Conventional Expectations - Positive = You decide to follow the advice of the 19th Century Bavarian priest, Sebastian Kneipp, who advised sleeping in wet socks to combat insomnia, and it works for you ! Negative = You decide to follow the advice of the priest and it does not work for you.
Take Away = Most people prefer not to "wet the bed."

Irrationally Failing To Do What You Know Is Good For You - Positive = Once again, by definition, there are no positive outcomes. In this case, however, you know what works for you and merely choose not to make the effort to do it. Negative = You continue sleep deprived and in so doing reinforce your irrationality.
Take Away = Unwarranted defiance is self-defeating and masochistic.

Responding Creatively - Positive = You believe that your insomnia is due to reduced blood flow to your brain. You decide, therefore, to sleep upside down with your feet resting upon three stacked pillows and it works! Negative =You believe that your insomnia is due to reduced blood flow to your brain. You decide, therefore, to sleep upside down with your feet resting upon three stacked pillows and awaken with a migraine headache.
Take Away = Creativity is wonderful, but only when it works.

Suppressing Your Usual Response - Positive = You usually ignore your doctor's advice, but this time you do fill the sleeping medication prescription that she wrote and it works. Negative = You usually ignore your doctor's advice, but this time do fill the sleeping medication prescription that she wrote and you have an allergic reaction, reinforcing your belief that doctors are incompetent.
Take Away = Trying something new is good, as you do so after some deliberation.

Exploring Various Behavioral Options - Positive = You research and try an series of somewhat trial and error options, and one works for you. Negative = You try a series of haphazard, un-researched trial and error options and none work for you.
Take Away = Exploring various behaviors also can be useful, if you know how to proceed.

So, if Simonton is correct, when in a decision situation, if you are inclined to respond at all, you also are likely to have at least a general sense of whether your response will be successful or unsuccessful. Moreover, you almost certainly will tend toward one or more of the aforementioned eight responses that have developed in accordance with your temperament, personality, and usual environments. Most of your responses probably occur automatically—outside your consciousness. Therefore, whenever a response opportunity presents itself, you first must recognize it as an opportunity to respond mindfully, not automatically. You then can make a rational choice to behave in your characteristic manner if that is adaptive, or to behave uncharacteristically if that is more adaptive.

To change your customary response tendencies, when confronted with any sought or unsought influence, first think about the eight options, and then consciously choose the one that facilitates the best decision. Needless to say, no one response tendency is inevitable, and tendencies depend on context. For instance, you might habitually respond to your doctor's advice in the most positive way possible, but react most impulsively and maladaptively to a jeweler's sales pitch.

From Decision to Action to Habit

Having mindfully read this book, what next? Knowing what to do is only step one. You need to start acting in ways consistent with your knowledge. Since early change tends to be very context-specific, you can begin by targeting a particular context applicable to a carefully chosen primary vehicle of influence that is important to you. For some, that could be choosing to cope with a particular person; for others, a particular situation. Since everyone finds her- or him-self in influence situations, let's use that as our example, and let's make the situation one that involves having lunch with your business associates where the irrational boss always tries to dictate who should eat what and how much of it. Let's further presume that you regularly submit to his unsolicited controlling advice. So, you need begin taking action in order to resist. Once you have acted, you can modify your strategy and work toward developing the needed habit.

Since the only way eventually to develop an unconscious influence-resisting habit is first to repeatedly practice conscious influence-resisting behaviors, you need to be attentive to and take advantage of relevant initial opportunities. Let's suppose that next week your work team will have its routine luncheon meeting. You establish the goal of pleasantly declining the irrational boss's culinary suggestions; rehearse the language you will use to decline his advice; imagine what he might say to pressure you; prepare a rebuttal for each pressuring comment; and have a plan to exit the discussion when it is advantageous to you. The language that you use could be language co-opted from the boss. For instance, if he cites the health benefits of the food that he is recommending, you might counter with the healthfulness of the meal that you plan to choose. And if he becomes overbearing, you might say, "I just remembered something I have to tell Julie," turn toward to her and away from him.

The example above is a short-term approach to a discrete, circumscribed influencer. For those who want to develop a strong, long-term habit of resistance, or any sort of habit, there is a detailed, tried and true protocol that is highly effective. That protocol (McCusker, 2016) involves the following steps.

1. Choose a Concrete Attainable Influence-Resisting Goal—identify the influence that you are ready and willing to resist. Ideally it should be something toward which you are intrinsically motivated.

2. Quantify the Goal—determine a measureable outcome of success. If you can't measure it in some way, you will never know whether you are progressing, regressing, or remaining stationary in your pursuit of self-determination.

3. Imagine the Process—be detailed, specific, and creative in the plan to achieve your outcome. Research strongly suggests that actively imagining a plan is preliminary to its successful implementation.

4. Determine a Starting Point—find the place to begin that offers the best chance for achieving your goal. Better to start slowly than to try to do too much too soon.

5. Maintain Goal Preoccupation—be obsessed in your determination to follow-through. Preoccupation will enable you to persevere long enough for your conscious effort to become an unconscious habit.

6. Establish a Regular Schedule—have times to enact the resistance strategies that you have selected. By scheduling

opportunities, you continue to exercise your resistance, and to develop your resistance muscle.

7. Structure the Environment—locate yourself in the space conducive to your resistance. Everything is more likely to happen in some places than in others. Find the environments that most facilitate your resistance.

8. Procure Any Material Resources That Facilitate Success—obtain any resistance-supportive material that you can. For instance, resistance-related educational material and objects can be found on-line.

9. Include a Human Facilitator—partner with a like-minded person who will support your resistance. United you stand; divided you fall.

10. Slowly Increment the Goal—having started with a simple obtainable goal, gradually ratchet it up until you reach the level that you seek. If you remain stagnant, your resistance skills will atrophy.

11. Find Substitute Gratification—realize some satisfying result from your resistance. Your resistant behavior probably will cause you to lose something that you need to replace. For instance, if you cease slavishly following the group mentality, you may need to find another group more in-line with your current self.

12. Provide for Continuous, Multidimensional Reinforcement—ensure that resistance satisfaction is maintained over the long run. In addition to substitute gratifications, you need to vary resistance-supportive reinforcement over time so that you do not become satiated with the initial gratifications.

13. Plan a Recovery Strategy—in case you falter in your resistance and permit yourself to be manipulated, have a way to restart your resistance efforts. Just knowing that you have a reasonable recovery plan will enable you to get back on track should that become necessary.

POST SCRIPT

In 1975, most of the roughly 9 million women married that year had wanted "a rock," meaning a diamond. And by their wedding days, about 60 percent had gotten one. For one-half carat, the price averaged about $3400, a considerable sum back then. That meant that approximately 600,000 got their rocks by year's end. By contrast, in only a few months, 1.5 million more popular rocks were sold across America—pet rocks. The "pets," almost literally, were garden variety, smooth egg-shaped beach stones imported from Mexico (Fox, 2015). Each stone cost Gary Dahl, their promoter, about one cent, and he sold them for $3.95. Margalit Fox suggested, correctly I believe, that Dahl managed his marketing coup by packaging—setting the rocks on a pillow of thin, fine wood slivers, called "wood wool," and providing detailed instructions about proper ways to tend to, and to train the little darlings.

How quaint, the silly seventies. Earlier decades, however, seemed even worse. You, no doubt, have heard of Charles Ponzi—predecessor of Bernie Madoff—whose investment scheme defrauded thousands of 1920s Bostonians, netting the scammer over $15 million in eight months by persuading tens of thousands of investors that he had unlocked the secret to easy wealth. You probably also know about other people in the 1920s, like George C. Parker, who several times sold the Brooklyn Bridge to naïve "customers." Certainly, no 21st century American would be duped by inane marketing schemes. We understand value. We can google to determine what is being sold, its price, and determine its worth. And when it comes to value, nothing is more precious to us in this anti-smoking, safe-sex culture than is our health. Contemporary citizens, for example, prize organic foods and resveratrol-rich, red wine. We search relentlessly for new, exotic healthful foodstuffs, whether from Asia, Africa, or Australia. Sometimes, too, we are surprised to discover research suggesting that an everyday local item, like blueberries, confers special health benefits.

One amazing new finding surfaced at Vancouver, Canada's annual Car Free Day festival. There, a small, non-descript booth advertised "unfiltered hot dog water"—one water-immersed dog packaged in a small glass bottle. The item was said to improve the consumer's brain function and energy, as well as to help them lose weight. Thirty-eight dollars seemed reasonable for this research-based, scientifically-certified drink, so reasonable that over 16 gallons soon were purchased on opening day by health-hungry festival visitors. Few consumers had read the bottom of the display sign at the booth's entrance that prominently stated: "Hot Dog Water in its absurdity hopes to encourage critical thinking related to product marketing and the significant role it can play in our purchasing choices."

The pet rock could be construed as an up-front farce that everyone readily should have recognized and accepted as such. And the unfiltered hot dog water qualified as an effective, well-intentioned gimmick that delivered a valuable lesson. Many, many other marketing schemes, on the other hand, have been accused of being nefarious and, even, cruel. The schemes of Ponzi and Parker surely inflicted pain on their victims. However, if true, one of the most damnable advertising campaigns of all time would be that conducted by the food industry to discourage breast feeding in lieu of bottle feeding. To quote Mike Muller's 1974 booklet, *The Baby Killer*:

> Third World babies are dying because their
> mothers bottle feed them with western style infant
> milk. Many that do not die are drawn into a
> vicious cycle of malnutrition and disease that will
> leave them physically and intellectually stunted
> for life.

The aforementioned brief historical recap provides a final, succinct perspective on professional influencers. You know as well as I that influence can result in any number of consequences. Some are humorous, educational, harmful, or dire. Although the possibilities are endless, the more you know about the possibilities, the better prepared you will be for any influence combatants who threaten to assault you.

Maintain an Anti-Influence War Footing

Know What You Want

Every day you are besieged by people who think they know better than you. That conviction is especially strong among marketers, and others intent on selling you an item or service. Three leaders of the most powerful companies on earth have subscribed to the "We know them better than they know themselves attitude." One was the late Steve Jobs of Apple who in a 1998 *Business Week* interview said, "A lot of times, people don't know what they want until you show it to them." The others are Eric Schmidt and Jonathan Rosenberg of Google who, in their 2014 book, *How Google Works*, wrote, "Giving the customer what he wants is less important than is giving him what he doesn't yet know he wants."

Obviously, all three of the aforementioned technology titans are correct to a point: one certainly cannot want something until she/he becomes aware of it. Marketers, and others who sell, must presume that they correctly know what you will want, otherwise they never would invest the time, money, and other resources to develop products and innovations.

This book, however, has not been as much about marketers, and others intent on selling you an item or service, but rather, about you, and self-determination. More specifically, it is about what you must do, if you wish to assume more deliberate, autonomous control of your decisions. Consider for the moment a sector involving one of your most critical health decisions—your diet. If Jobs, Schmidt, and Rosenberg are right that you truly do not know what you want diet-wise, you are especially vulnerable to whatever food marketers are out to promote. They firmly believe that they know what you want, and that is foods replete with excess calories, sugars, and salts. Armed with that knowledge, they conduct relentless advertising campaigns to maximize sale of those products. You buy them and you are the loser.

So, you need to strive to know as precisely as possible what you personally have to do to be in control of your diet and of all other critical lifestyle sectors. With that secure self-understanding, you can establish your values, and be more discriminating in your decisions. Accordingly, when marketers, and others intent on selling you an item or service, try to exert their influence on you, you will know whether what they offer will contribute to your well-being or will undermine it. Some people possess personality traits that enable them to be more naturally resistant to certain influence methods. The investigation of such traits is in its infancy. For instance, you recall that influencers often try to invoke our social need to reciprocate by giving us something small in the hope of receiving something big later—You get a page of return address envelope stickers, along with a request for a donation to one cause or another. However, research does suggest that some people have a relatively high tendency toward "reciprocity anxiety." People of that type are alert to reciprocity manipulation. And the greater the influencer's "gift" is, the more resistant the reciprocity anxious person becomes (Xiong, et al., 2018). Reciprocity resistance should be one trait that you, too, should attempt to cultivate. You can do so, if you adopt a predisposition toward vigilance.

Force Yourself to Remain Vigilant

We often lower our guards—willingly delegating at least a portion of our decision making to sources that we presume are most capable. For instance, like so many Americans, I gradually ceded a good part of my casual television viewing choices to whatever Netflix designated as 5, or at least 4, star. Accordingly, when I saw that their television series called "The Assets" had received only 1.5 stars, I was unimpressed. Only when I read that the show concerned the Aldrich Ames incident, an authentic spy case that I had remembered, did I decide to watch the first episode. That viewing piqued my interest, and I liked it so much that I continued through all the entire series. By episode 6, I realized that the Ames program was the first engrossing one that I had seen in many months that contained no gratuitous sex, violence, pyrotechnics, car chases, or computer simulations. For instance, one episode clearly indicated that the Soviets shot one of their traitors in the head, but the scene did not show a geyser of blood. Prior to finding The Assets, my wife and I had complained that virtually every 5 or 4 star series that we watched—such as, Breaking Bad and Peaky Blinders—were replete with gore. I can't help but believe that entertainment influencers, who dole out stars for shows, place a premium on gratuitous sex and violence.

Cultivation theory (Hawkins & Pingree, 1983) proposes that television programs profoundly influence our conceptions of social reality. And there is research to support that contention. Krongard and Tsay-Vogel (2018), for instance, assessed several popular online original TV series for violence, finding nearly six violent events per hour that they rated as serious, and/or explicit, and/or intentional, and/or graphic. The violence typically could not be justified. Most important, show binge watchers later evaluated the real world as more often being "mean" than did show non-watchers.

The point is this: every time we mindlessly accept influence, we pay a price. Binge watching violent television likely will result in negfluence. But even in instances of mindless posfluence, we pay a price. Sometimes the price is "only" that of not having exercised our autonomy, and sometimes it is not having had the chance to learn first-hand from our own mistaken decisions.

Ideas presented by Nassim Nicholas Taleb (2012)) are relevant here. Taleb encourages us to become "antifragile," meaning able not only to endure stress, but also to profit from it. He believes that we can cultivate antifragility by being able to make the best of volatility, disorder, and randomness. Although no one deliberately seeks any of those negative conditions, all are inevitable features of daily life. For our purposes here, let's think specifically about influence. You become more antifragile in a number of ways. First, accept ultimate responsibility for every decision. Second, recognize the reality of any given issue's volatility, disorder, and randomness so that you do not expect to make a perfect decision. Third, educate yourself beforehand about what reasonably could be the worst and best possible outcomes. Fourth, find the most helpful, relevant resources to reduce the volatility, disorder, and randomness to the extent possible. If, after step four, you remain unable to decide autonomously, look for the best professional influencers that you can; select at least two who disagree with each other. Meet with each separately. Only after each one independently and thoroughly explains their advice, ask her/him to respond to the information that you already had found on your own. Next, independently confront each disagreeing influencer with the other's contradictory recommendation. In the end, collaborate fully with the best of the influencers, and try to get her/him to have "skin in the game" regarding what they advocate. For instance, if you are talking about the stock market—a system rife with volatility, disorder, and randomness—negotiate such that the advisor's fee is at least partly contingent on the final outcome that you experience should you do what they say.

The single most important message of this book is that, in order to become influence anti-fragile in the broadest possible sense, you must **LEARN** to know yourself better than the influencers do, and better than their machines know you. That is true because so much of their influence is informed by the skill and programs that they have developed that tap into your unconscious tendencies and unattended-to habits. Another most important message is that you must be perennially vigilant and skeptical whenever you enter an influence situation. You are likely to be alert to large influences, but don't make the mistake of lowering your guard in influence situations that seem unimportant. Know that influencers strive to get their foot in your door, which often means getting you to make some small decision in their favor that becomes a prelude to more substantial negfluential future ones. More often than not, it is the accumulation of small negfluences over time that is most likely to impact you deleteriously. Most negfluences are like minor skirmishes that accrete incrementally. You lose a small skirmish one day, and a small skirmish another day. Your metaphorical, or veritable, anti-influence battles can become a long-term campaign of attrition. It is not until you are completely out of ammunition, and completely encircled by hostiles that you finally realize you have lost the war.

REFERENCES

Amanpour, C. (2017). Interview with Jane Fonda about sexual abuse. October 13. CNN Media

Bailey, T. & Staples, J. (2014). Interactive Intelligence. Customer Service Experience Study (Wave II)

Basu, T. (2015). New Google Parent Company Drops 'Don't Be Evil' Motto. October 4 http://time.com/4060575/alphabet-google-dont-be-evil/

Baumeister, R. F. (1994). The crystallization of discontent in the process of major life change. In T. F. Heatherton & J. L. Weinberger (Eds.), Can personality change? (pp. 281-297). Washington, DC, US: American Psychological Association. http://dx.doi.org/10.1037/10143-012

Berger, J. (2013). Contagious: Why Things Catch On. New York: Simon and Schuster.

Bhattacharya, J., Zioga, I., & Lewis, R. (2017). Novel or consistent music? An electrophysiological study investigating music use in advertising. Journal of Neuroscience, Psychology, and Economics, 10(4), 137-152. http://dx.doi.org/10.1037/npe0000080

Białek, M., & Sawicki, P. (2018). Cognitive reflection effects on time discounting. Journal of Individual Differences, 39(2), 99-106. http://dx.doi.org/10.1027/1614-0001/a000254

Big Bucks, Big Pharma: Marketing Disease and Pushing Drugs http://www.mediaed.org/transcripts/Big-Bucks-BIg-Pharma-Transcript.pdf

Bobadilla-Suarez, S., & Love, B. C. (2018). Fast or frugal, but not both: Decision heuristics under time pressure. Journal of Experimental Psychology: Learning, Memory, and Cognition, 44(1), 24-33. http://dx.doi.org/10.1037/xlm0000419

Bostrom, N. (2015). What happens when computers become smarter than us? TED, March. https://www.ted.com/talks/nick_bostrom_what_happens_when_our_computers_get_smarter_than_we_are?language=en

Burns, P., McCormack, T., Jaroslawska, A., Fitzpatrick, Á., McGourty, J., & Caruso, E. M. (2018). The development of asymmetries in past and future thinking. Journal of Experimental Psychology: General. Advance online publication. http://dx.doi.org/10.1037/xge0000464

Cameron, J. (2019). Stasi. Encyclopædia Britannica. In East German Government https://www.britannica.com/topic/Stasi

Christian C. (2014) A Poor Imitation of Alan Turing. The New York Review of Books. http://www.nybooks.com/daily/2014/12/19/poor-imitation-alan-turing/

Cleckley, H. (1982). The mask of sanity. Revised Edition. Mosby Medical Library.

Clifford, C. (2017). Mark Zuckerberg and wife Priscilla Chan reveal their top tips for working together—and how they will spend their billions. CNBC.com, December 14.

Colvin, G. (2016). Why great presidents are often psychopaths. August 18. http://fortune.com/2016/08/18/great-presidents-psychopaths/

CXO today (2018) Speech Analytics Can Boost Customer Experience. Newsx Desk. February 14. http://www.cxotoday.com/story/speech-analytics-can-boost-customer-experience/

Davies, J. (2014) Getting Value From Speech Analytics in the Contact Center. Gartner, Inc. (ARCHIVED Published: 06 January 2014 ID: G0025948. https://www.gartner.com/doc/2644915/getting-value-speech-analytics-contact

De Fruyt, F.; Van De Wiele, L.; Van Heeringen, C. (2000). Cloninger's psychobiological model of temperament and character and the Five-Factor Model of personality. Personality and Individual Differences. 29, 3, 441–452 doi:10.1016/S0191-8869(99)00204-4

Dutton, K. (2012). The wisdom of psychopaths : What saints, spies, and serial killers can teach us about success. New York : Straus and Giroux

Eisenhower, D. (1961) Military-Industrial Complex Speech, January. http://avalon.law.yale.edu/20th_century/eisenhower001.asp

Farahany, N. (2018). When technology can read minds, how will we protect our privacy? TED Salon: Zebra Technologies, November https://www.ted.com/talks/nita_farahany_when_technology_can_read_minds_ how_will_we_protect_our_privacy?language=en

Federal Trade Commission (2018). FTC Consumer Guide for Loud TV Commercials. https://www.fcc.gov/consumers/guides/loud-commercials-tv

Forbes Series (2017). The Business of Influence. April 10, 2017 @ 09:59 am. https://www.forbes.com/video/5392564088001/#11854aa6640

Forgas, J. (2003). Affective influences on attitudes and judgments. In R. J. Davidson, K. R. Scherer, & H. H. Goldsmith (Eds.), Handbook of affective sciences (pp. 596–618). New York: Oxford University Press.

Frank, T. (2017) What Harvey Weinstein tells us about the liberal world. The Guardian. https://www.theguardian.com/commentisfree/2017/oct/21/harvey-weinstein-liberal-world

Frei, F. (2018). How to Build (and Rebuild) Trust. TED April, 2018. https://www.ted.com/talks/frances_frei_how_to_build_and_rebuild_trust?utm _source=newsletter_weekly_2018-05-06&utm_campaign=newsletter_weekly&utm_medium=email&utm_content=t alk_of_the_week_button

Garczarek-Bąk, U. & Disterheft, A. (2018). EEG frontal asymmetry predicts product purchase differently for national brands and private labels. Journal of Neuroscience, Psychology, and Economics. doi: 10.1037/npe0000094

Gleason, T.R., Theran, S.A., & Newberg, E. M. (2017). Parasocial interactions and relationships in early adolescence. Frontiers in Psychology, 8, 255. Published online, February23. doi: 10.3389/fpsyg.2017.00255.

Greene, R. & Elffers, J. 48 Laws of Power https://www.tke.org/files/file/The_48_Laws_of_Power.pdf

Grice, H. P. (1989). Studies in the way of words. Cambridge MA: Harvard University Press

Hall, M. & Raimi, K. (2018). Is belief superiority justified by superior knowledge? Journal of Experimental Social Psychology, 76, 290-306. https://doi.org/10.1016/j.jesp.2018.03.001

Hamby, A., Brinberg, D., & Jaccard, J. (2018). A conceptual framework of narrative persuasion. Journal of Media Psychology: Theories, Methods, and Applications, 30(3), 113-124.

Hamilton R. (2018). How You Decide: The Science of Human Decision Making. The Great Courses.

Han, S. & Lerner, J. (2007). Feelings and consumer decision making: The appraisal-tendency framework feelings and consumer decision making. Journal Of Consumer Psychology, 17, 3, 158–168

Hare, R. D. (1996). Psychopathy: A clinical construct whose time has come. Criminal Justice and Behavior, 23, 1, 25-54

Harvard Health Publishing (2018). "Harvard Medical School offers special reports on over 60 health topics. www.health.harvard.edu (healthbeat@mail.health.harvard.edu)

Hawkins R.P & Pingree, S. (1983). Televisions influence on social reality. In: Wartella, E., Whitney, D., Windahl, S., (eds) Mass Communication Review Yearbook, vol. 5, Beverly Hills, CA, Sage

Health, A. (2017). Mark Zuckerberg clashed with Facebook execs over letting employees work on his philanthropy. Sep. 29 http://www.businessinsider.com/facebook-execs-opposed-mark-zuckerberg-wanting-employees-work-on-philanthropy-2017-9

Helfinstein, S. M., Mumford, J. A., & Poldrack, R. A. (2015). If all your friends jumped off a bridge: The effect of others' actions on engagement in and recommendation of risky behaviors. Journal of Experimental Psychology: General, 144(1), 12-17.

Hertwig, R. & Grüne-Yanoff, T. (2017) Nudging and Boosting: Steering or Empowering Good Decisions First Published August 9. Perspectives on Psychological Science. https://doi.org/10.1177/1745691617702496

Holtzman, N. (2012). "People With Dark Personalities Tend to Create a Physically Attractive Veneer". Social Psychological and Personality Science. 4: 461–467. doi:10.1177/194855061

Hu, M., Cotton, G., Zhang, B., & Jia, N. (2018). The influence of apology on audiences' reactions toward a media figure's transgression. Psychology of Popular Media Culture. Advance online publication. DOI: 10.1037/ppm0000195.

Jackson, J., et al. (2015). Your friends know how long you will live: A 75-year study of peer-rated personality traits. Psychological Science, January 12. Retrieved from doi 10.1177/09567976614561800.

Jamieson, K. (2017). Jamieson offers new name for fake news: 'Viral Deception' or VD. Retrieved from http://www.annenbergpublicpolicycenter.org/on-cnn-jamieson-offers-new-name-for-fake-news-viral-deception-or-v-d

Jobs, S. (1998). "It's really hard to design products by focus groups. A lot of times, people don't know what they want until you show it to them." Business Week, May 25, interview

Jonason, P., Lyons, M., Baughman, H., &.Vernonc, P. (2014). What a tangled web we weave: The Dark-triad traits and deception. Personality and Individual Differences, 70, November, 117-119

Jones, D. N., & Paulhus, D. L. (2017). Duplicity among the dark-triad: Three faces of deceit. Journal of Personality and Social Psychology, 113(2), 329-342. http://dx.doi.org/10.1037/pspp00001392461284

Jones, P (2017). Fake news is nothing new — it was de rigueur in ancient Greece. The Spectator, November, 18.

Kelly, G. A. (1955). The Psychology of Personal Constructs. New York: Norton

King, N. (2018). Facebook Previously Failed To Keep Privacy Promises, Ex-FTC Adviser Says. Morning Edition, March 27. https://www.npr.org/2018/03/27/597221954/facebook-previously-failed-to-keep-privacy-promises-ex-ftc-adviser-says

Kooij, D., Kanfer, R., Betts, M., & Rudolph, C. W. (2018). Future time perspective: A systematic review and meta-analysis. Journal of Applied Psychology, 103(8), 867-893. http://dx.doi.org/10.1037/apl0000306

Kosoff, M. (2018). Another Facebook scandal confirms you can't trust Zuck: Time and again, the Facebook C.E.O. has broken user trust, apologized, and promised to do better. Can Mark Zuckerberg ever change his ways? Vanity Fair, December 19 https://www.vanityfair.com/news/2018/12/another-facebook-scandal-confirms-you-cant-trust-zuck

Krongard, S., & Tsay-Vogel, M. (2018). Online original TV series: Examining portrayals of violence in popular binge-watched programs and social reality perceptions. Psychology of Popular Media Culture. Advance online publication. http://dx.doi.org/10.1037/ppm0000224

Lachmann, B., Duke, É., Sariyska, R., & Montag, C. (2017). Who's addicted to the smartphone and/or the Internet? Psychology of Popular Media Culture http://dx.doi.org/10.1037/ppm0000172

Leone, M.J., Slezak, D.F., Golombek, D., Sigman, M. (2017). Time to Decide: Diurnal Variations on the Speed and Quality of Human Decisions. Cognition. doi: 10.1016/j.cognition.2016.10.007

Leong, Y. C., & Zaki, J. (2018). Unrealistic optimism in advice taking: A computational account. Journal of Experimental Psychology: General, 147(2), 170-189. http://dx.doi.org/10.1037/xge0000382

Leslie, I (2016). The scientists who make apps addictive. The Economist, October/November 2016. https://www.1843magazine.com/features/the-scientists-who-make-apps-addictive

Loman, J., Müller, B., Oude Groote Beverborg, A., van Baaren, R. & Buijzen, M. (2018). Self-persuasion in media messages: Reducing alcohol consumption among students with open-ended questions. Journal of Experimental Psychology: Applied, 24, 1, 81-91

MacLean, Paul D. (1990). The triune brain in evolution: role in paleocerebral functions. New York: Plenum Press. ISBN 0-306-43168-8. OCLC 20295730

McCornack, S, & Morrison, K. (2012). Information manipulation theory 2 (IMT2): A preliminary explication of the production architecture underlying deceptive discourse. Paper presented at the Annual Meeting of the National Communication Association, Orlando, FL.

McCornack, S., et. Al. (2014). A Propositional Theory of Deceptive Discourse Production. Journal of Language and Social Psychology 33, 4, 348-377.

McCornack, S.., Morrison, K., Paik, J., Wisner, A. & Zhu, X. (2014). Information Manipulation Theory 2

McDermot, R. et al. (2013). Breaking up is hard to do, unless everyone else is doing it too: Social network effects on divorce in a longitudinal sample. Social Forces, Volume 92, Issue 2, 1, 491–519

McMahon, J. (2017). Apple had way better options than slowing down your IPhone. Gear, December.https://www.wired.com/story/apple-iphone-battery-slow-down/

Miller, D. (2017). Building a StoryBrand: Clarify your message so customers will listen. New York: Harper Collins

Moray, N. (1959). Attention in dichotic listening: Affective cues and the influence of instructions. Quarterly Journal of Experimental Psychology, 11, 56-60.

Morgan, N. (2013). How You Can Dominate the Conversation and Extend Your Influence. April 25. https://www.forbes.com/sites/nickmorgan/2013/04/25/how-you-can-dominate-the-conversation-and-extend-your-influence/#1cbecd057ba0

Morrison, T. (2011). The selfish gene. All-TIME 100 Nonfiction Books. August 17. TIME.com entertainment.time.com/2011/08/30/all-time.../the-selfish-gene-by-richard-dawkins/

Muller, M. (1974). The baby killer: A war on want investigation into the promotion and sale of powdered baby milks in the Third World. (March) London: War on Want

Nedelman, M. (2018). Should you take statins? Guidelines offer different answers. CNN. Updated 5:02 PM ET, January 1, 2018https://www.cnn.com/2017/04/18/health/statins-guidelines-conflict-study/index.html

New York Times, Special (1973) Jane Fonda grants some POW torture. Special to the New York Times, April 7

Nguyen, D. What makes something go viral? October 2017 at TEDNYC

Novella , S. (2012). Your Deceptive Mind: A Scientific Guide to Critical Thinking Skills THE GREAT COURSES. The Teaching Company

Nowacki, J., Heekeren, H. R., Deuter, C. E., Joerißen, J. D., Schröder, A., Otte, C., & Wingenfeld, K. (2018). Decision making in response to physiological and combined physiological and psychosocial stress. Behavioral Neuroscience. Advance online publication. http://dx.doi.org/10.1037/bne0000288

O'Hara, C. (2014) How to tell a great story. Harvard Business Review. July 30 https://hbr.org/2014/07/how-to-tell-a-great-story

Ornstein, C. & Thomas, K. (2018). What These Medical Journals Don't Reveal: Top Doctors' Ties to Industry. The New York Times, December 8. https://www.nytimes.com/2018/12/08/health/medical-journals-conflicts-of-interest.html?utm_source=STAT+Newsletters&utm_campaign=9e15130ef8-MR_COPY_12&utm_medium=email&utm_term=0_8cab1d7961-9e15130ef8-150620977

Paulhus, D. & Williams, K. (2001) Shedding Light on the Dark-triad of Personality: Narcissism, Machiavellianism, and Psychopathy." Presented at 2001 SPSP Convention in San Antonio Society for Personality and Social Psychology of the University of British Columbia

Penn, M. (2018). Microtrends Squared: The New Small Forces Driving the Big Disruptions Today. New York: Simon and Shuster

Pieters, R. & Wede, M. (2004) Attention Capture and Transfer in Advertising: Brand, Pictorial, and Text-Size Effects. Journal of Marketing, 68, 2, 36-50.

https://pdfs.semanticscholar.org/024a/badb72c44848321c7148728a248c385c1
503.pdf

Piltdown Man. The Natural History Museum. Cromwell Road London SW7
5BD. http://www.nhm.ac.uk/our-science/departments-and-staff/library-and-
archives/collections/piltdown-man.html

Pink, D. (2018). When: The scientific secrets of perfect timing. New York:
Riverhead Books

Plous, S. (1993). The psychology of judgment and decision making. New
York: McGraw-Hill

Postman, N. (1986). Amusing ourselves to death: Public discourse in the age
of show business. New York: Penguin Books

Prnewswire (2018) Fleishman Hillard Launches Tech Trends 2019 Report:
Provides brands tech insights for the New Year, December 18
https://www.prnewswire.com/news-releases/fleishmanhillard-launches-tech-
trends-2019-report-300767945.html

Pulford, B. D., Colman, A. M., Buabang, E. K., & Krockow, E. M. (2018).
The persuasive power of knowledge: Testing the confidence heuristic. Journal
of Experimental Psychology: General. Advance online publication.
http://dx.doi.org/10.1037/xge0000471

Quote investigator (2018). You're Not the Customer; You're the Product.
https://quoteinvestigator.com/2017/07/16/product/

Reich, T (1948) Listening with the third ear: The inner experience of a
psychoanalyst. New York: Grove Press.

 Renvoise, P. (2007). Neuromarketing: Understanding the "buy button" in your
customer's brain. International Edition, Nashville, TN: Thomas Nelson.

Renvoise, P. (2007). Neuromarketing: Understanding the "buy button" in your
customer's brain. Nashville, TN: Thomas Nelson.

Rosenberg, E. (2018). Coffee must carry cancer warning, California judge
rules. March 29. 2018 at 10:25 PM.

https://www.washingtonpost.com/news/to-your-health/wp/2018/03/29/coffee-must-carry-cancer-warning-california-judge-rules/?utm_term=.02270ff10e9d

Rovelli, C. (2017). The order of time. London: Allen Lane.

Schmidt, E., Rosenberg, J., & Eage, A. (2014) Google: How Google Works. First edition. New York: Grand Central Publishing

Sellen, A., Louie, G., Harris, J., & Wilkins, A.. (1997). What brings intentions to mind? An in situ study of prospective memory. Memory, 4, 483-507

Shah, N. et al. (2018). Big Data and predictive analytics recalibrating expectations. JAMA. Published online May 29. doi:10.1001/jama.2018.5602

Sigman, M. & Ariely, D. How Can Groups Make Good Decisions? April 2017 at TED Studio

Simonton, D. (2016). Creativity, Automaticity, Irrationality, Fortuity, Fantasy, and Other Contingencies: An Eightfold Response Typology. Review of General Psychology, May 5, No Pagination Specified

Sixty Minutes, Season number: 50, Episode number: 36, Air date: May 20, 2018. The Real Power of Google, The Theranos deception, The Spotted Pig

Spitz, R., & Cobliner, W. G. (1965). The First Year of Life: A Psychoanalytic Study of Normal and Deviant Object Relations. New York: International Universities Press.

Sullivan, H. S. (1953). The Interpersonal Theory of Psychiatry. New York: NortonSanborn, M. (2018). 9 differences between transactional and relational: How to tell the difference. https://marksanborn.com/9-differences-between-transactional-and-relational-how-to-tell-the-difference/

Swire, B., Ecker, U., & Lewandowsky, S. (2017). The role of familiarity in correcting inaccurate information. Journal of Experimental Psychology: Learning, Memory, and Cognition, 43(12), 1948-1961. http://dx.doi.org/10.1037/xlm0000422

Taleb, N. (2012). Antifragile: Things that gain from disorder. New York: Random House.

Taleb, N. (2017). Skin in the game: Hidden asymmetries in daily life. New York: Random House.

Thaler (2016). Misbehaving: The making of behavioral economics. New York: Norton

Thaler, R (2015B) Economist Richard Thaler visited Google's office in Cambridge, MA to discuss the topic "The behaviorializing of economics: Why did it take so long? Talks at Google. Published on Dec 9 https://www.youtube.com/watch?v=D9Uk-YsjQsI

Thaler, R. "The Behaviorializing of Economics: Why Did It Take So Long? Talks at Google. Published on Dec 9, 2015.(A) https://www.youtube.com/watch?v=D9Uk-YsjQsI

Thaler, R. (2015). The power of nudges, for good and bad. New York Times, Oct. 31 https://www.nytimes.com/2015/11/01/upshot/the-power-of-nudges-for-good-and-bad.html

Thompson, D. (2015). Lotteries: America's $70 billion shame. The Atlantic https://www.theatlantic.com/business/archive/2015/05/lotteries-americas-70-billion-shame/392870/

To, C. et al., (2018). We take more risks when we compete against rivals. Harvard Business Review, July. https://hbr.org/2018/07/research-we-take-more-risks-when-we-compete-against-rivals

Toplak ,M. West, R. & Stanovich, K. (2011). The Cognitive Reflection Test as a predictor of performance on heuristics-and-biases tasks. Memory & Cognition, 39, 7, 1275-1289. https://link.springer.com/article/10.3758/s13421-011-0104-1

Verghese, A, et al, (2017). What this computer needs is a physician humanism and artificial intelligence. JAMA. Published online December 20. doi:10.1001/jama.2017.19198

Victor, E. (2015). Creating memes that help your online marketing efforts. April 13. https://www.socialmediatoday.com/social-business/2015-04-13/creating-memes-help-your-online-marketing-efforts

Vincent, J. (2017). Former Facebook exec says social media is ripping apart society. The Verge, Dec 11 .
https://www.theverge.com/2017/12/11/16761016/former-facebook-exec-ripping-apart-society

Vize, C., Lyam, D., Collison, K., & Miller, J. (2016). Differences among dark-triad components: A meta-analytic investigation. Personality Disorders: Theory, Research, and Treatment, Oct 13. No Pagination Specified.
http://dx.doi.org/10.1037/per0000222

Walton, A. (2011). Steve Jobs' cancer treatment regrets. Forbes Oct 24.
https://www.forbes.com/sites/alicegwalton/2011/10/24/steve-jobs-cancer-treatment-regrets/#56cbe2be7d2e

Washington Post (2018) Eugene Scott, E. Identity reporter.
https://www.washingtonpost.com/people/eugene-scott/?noredirect=on&utm_term=.a3fab0acbfb4

Wikipedia (2018). In 2016, Variety endorsed Hillary Clinton for President of the United States, marking the first time the publication endorsed a candidate for elected office in its 111-year history.
https://en.wikipedia.org/wiki/Variety_(magazine)

Wilson, M.(2004). Michael Moore Hates America. Premiered September 12, 2004, in Dallas, Texas, at the American Film Renaissance film festival.
https://en.wikipedia.org/wiki/Michael_Moore_Hates_America

Wissman, B. (2018). Micro-Influencers: The Marketing Force Of The Future? Mar 2, 2018, 09:52am.
https://www.forbes.com/sites/oracle/2018/12/27/at-kubecon-2018-kubernetes-lifts-cloud-native-coders-to-new-heights/#4f4c393b17e8

Xiong, X., Guo, S., Gu, L., Huang, R., & Zhoua, X. (2018). Reciprocity anxiety: Individual differences in feeling discomfort in reciprocity situations. Journal of Economic Psychology, 67, August, 149-161
https://doi.org/10.1016/j.joep.2018.05.007